The Philosopher's World Model

ARCHIE J. BAHM

CONTRIBUTIONS IN PHILOSOPHY, NUMBER 12

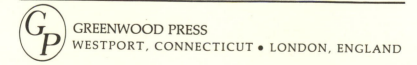

GREENWOOD PRESS
WESTPORT, CONNECTICUT • LONDON, ENGLAND

Library of Congress Cataloging in Publication Data

Bahm, Archie J
    The philosopher's world model.

    (Contributions in philosophy; no. 12 ISSN 0084-926X)
    Includes bibliographical references and index.
    1. Civilization—Philosophy. 2. Civilization,
Modern—1950-   3. Philosophy. I. Title.
CB19.B272   901   78-67569
ISBN 0-313-21198-1

Library of Congress Catalog Card Number: 78-67569
ISBN: 0-313-21198-1
ISSN: 0084-926X

First published in 1979

Greenwood Press, Inc.
51 Riverside Avenue, Westport, Connecticut 06880

Printed in the United States of America

10 9 8 7 6 5 4 3 2 1

To RAYMOND,
My Son

CONTENTS

FIGURES

ACKNOWLEDGMENTS

The author acknowledges with appreciation the following permissions:

Permission by the Macmillan Publishing Company, New York, to quote from the following publications: Rajni Kothari, *Footsteps into the Future: A Diagnosis of the Present World and a Design for an Alternative* (1974), Saul H. Mendlovitz, editor, *On the Creation of a Just World Order: Preferred Worlds for the 1990's* (1975), Richard A. Falk, *A Study of Future Worlds: Preferred Worlds of the 1990's* (1975), Ali A. Mazrui, *A Federation of Cultures: An African Perspective* (1976), all published by the Free Press, New York, a division of the Macmillan Publishing Company, and copyrighted by the Institute for World Order.

Permission by the Institute for World Order to quote from W. Warren Wager, *Building the City of Man: Outlines of a World Civilization* (1971), published by Grossman Publishers, New York, and copyright by the World Law Fund.

The
Philosopher's
World
Model_____

1

THE HUMAN PREDICAMENT. CAN MANKIND SURVIVE?

ACCELERATING CRISES

Crises! Crises! Crises! Earlier crises came one at a time. Now they seem to come tumbling upon us at accelerating rates. Formerly crises developed in one cultural sector. Now all sectors at all levels seem to be caught up in them. Mankind is being overwhelmed by "a storm of crisis problems."[1]

We have come to expect rapid changes, but "the onrush of change has become so drastic that people are utterly confused."[2] Our problems multiply so rapidly that we cannot solve all of them. We are living in a "world out of control."[3] Have problems now exceeded human capacity for solution?

History is replete with cries of dismay about the human predicament. But when complexes of crises baffle us, we face a new level of problems. Prospects of unsolvability challenge faith in progress; worse, they promise the extinction of mankind.

It is time to be frank about human folly. But while there is life, there is hope that mankind may possess enough intelligence to delay extinction. Human nature is tough. Unless we succumb to despair, resort to nuclear warfare, or submit to irrational impulses, let us hope that we are still masters of our fate. Pessimism can only aggravate our predicament. But are we ready to change our ways of thinking and acting enough to tackle crises problems with intelligence?

The purpose of this book is to help us understand our predicament and to offer suggestions that may help mankind survive. The first part exposes our predicament from my own viewpoint. Chapter 1 reviews some doomsday predictions and evaluates plans, mostly unsatisfactory, for surviving. Chapter 2 summarizes recent efforts to diagnose our predicament and to propose solutions, now called *world models*. Each has merit, yet all are deficient. Chapter 3 explains why a Philosopher's World Model is needed.

The second part of the book explores philosophy, ethics, religion, economy, and government, offering suggestions about each. The facts of increasing complexity, interdependence, and dynamism characterizing megalopolitan and global living call for quantum-leap conceptions. Crisis problems appear unsolvable partly because we try to remedy them with obsolete, deficient philosophies. What we need urgently is a philosophy enabling us to comprehend the complex, interdependent, dynamic causes of our crises. In contemporary language, these suggestions are called a *world model*.

Current efforts to understand our predicament have focused on many issues pertaining to population, resource consumption, maldistribution, overkill armaments, and pollution. But with rare exceptions, popular pronouncements have failed to penetrate the depths of faulty philosophical presuppositions. Critics of earlier efforts have forced concern for values, but values continue to be misunderstood. Diagnosing crises as value crises is not enough. The absence of a willingness to use scientific methods in understanding the nature of values and obligations is itself a major cause of our crises and of our inability to propose intelligent solutions.

I shall charge that growing inadequacies in popular and professional philosophies and religions contribute more to our crises and to our incapacities than most of us realize. The influence of these deficiencies has become especially vicious because attention to them has been neglected. In some places, doctrinal freedom and, in other places, established authoritarianism have discouraged controversy. In the United States, courses in religion, ethics, and logic have been dropped from school curricula, and rightly so, because traditional explanations of their ultimate bases became increasingly inadequate. But a respect for the ideals of freedom of thought had the unfortunate effect of failing to replace obsolete explanations with something more adequate. The result is a chaos of sectarian doctrines, private opinions, skepticism, and fantastic speculations. Cultural relativism encourages public irresponsibility regarding truth seeking, except in sciences pretending to be isolated from value doctrines.

Ordinary people, as well as politicians and research scientists, have put philosophy out of their minds as something of vital significance. Not only has the conscientious reexamination of philosophical assumptions been neglected, but tendencies of issues about presuppositions to demand attention seem to be habitually suppressed. Decades ago while I was still a student, an editorial cartoon depicted a filing cabinet filled with folders marked as containing pressing problems. A man, responsible for grappling with urgent issues, was filing a folder marked "philosophical problems" in the back of the drawer. So far as the American public is concerned, our most basic philosophical problems are still filed in the back of the drawer.

Unfortunately failure to keep these problems solved has contributed to a condition in which the gap between earlier solutions and the philosophy needed to solve crisis problems now seems too great to close. A failure to revitalize philosophy constantly has created an incompetence to meet the present crises. Our neglect to face each philosophical difficulty as it arose has left us without the ability to meet and solve the accumulated complex of difficulties inherent in the now-accumulating crises. It would not be unreasonable to claim that the greatest crisis today in America and in the world is a philosophical one. Those who isolate philosophy from life and those committed to dogmatic philosophies will not agree. But since our political, economic, social, religious, and educational practices depend on and interdepend with the reasons we give ourselves for acting the way we do, our inability to solve our political and economic problems intertwines with our inability to explain to ourselves why we cannot give adequate reasons for our failures.

If I can alert many to an awareness of our philosophical deficiencies and of their significance for world crises, my effort here should be worthwhile, even if the constructive suggestions offered are ignored. But prolonged and dedicated concern for solving basic philosophical problems and fortunate opportunity for studying Asian as well as Western philosophies, historical and contemporary, in all fields of philosophy and keeping updated somewhat in the major sciences have enabled me to observe the growing need for some fundamental revisions. My suggestions result from my personal struggles to understand self, society, and the universe. They have been conditioned by the necessity of facing questions asked by college students for forty years and by my philosophical colleagues, both Western and Asian. I have always lived in booming cities, taught in growing universities, and occupied my mind with increasingly complex systems. My apparent partial success in comprehending some of our difficulties and some of the quantum-leap explanations of them has given me confidence that my insights may prove useful in giving some direction, even if not an adequate or final solution.

The philosophy we need, I suggest, is one with principles discovered operating in intricate megalopolitan interdependencies rather than in nomadic, agricultural, city-state, medieval, or early modern societies. A philosophy that accepts the challenge of formulating principles accounting for existence in terms of dynamic energy rather than of permanent substances or eternal forms is needed. We require a philosophy recognizing both creative and destructive tendencies in human nature, and personal capacities for more complex kinds of responsibility needed for megalopolitan and world welfare. The cumulation of crises calls for a philosophy making clear how individual welfare depends increasingly on world welfare and how world welfare depends increasingly on the welfare of more and more individuals.

The philosophy we need is humanitarian, humanistic, scientific, comprehensive, adequate, and quantum leaping. The cumulation of problem complexities is so great that conceptions adequate to comprehending them will require a system with its own principles of organic unity complex enough to incorporate multileveled, multidimensional dynamic factors, as well as what remains true from our many historical stages of discovery and many divergent cultures.

Just as the Hegelian synthesis incorporated a much richer set of conceptual polarities than the important Augustinian synthesis had, so the needed synthesis will embody greater varieties of conceptual polarities and more variably dynamic kinds of processes. Whereas both Augustinian and Hegelian systems were monohierarchical, the needed system is not so much antihierarchical as multihierarchical. Dialectic, still misunderstood and excluded from most Asian and Western systems, will, I suggest, be discovered to exist omnipresently. Discovery that self, society, and the universe evolve through varieties of multidialectical interdependent processes can help explain emerging kinds of interexistence that appear worthwhile because they enable persons to identify themselves with many kinds, levels, and rates of self-development properly called *luxuriant*.

The teamwork of many interdisciplinary research institutes, with programs comprehensively conceived and affluently funded, will be required for the full development of the needed system gestalt. I have confidence that at least some of the proposals incorporated in the Philosopher's World Model point in the right direction.

DOOMSDAY PREDICTIONS

Doomsday threats are not new. The Druids, the Teutons, the Hindus, and the Hebrews, to name just a few ancient examples, all heard warnings. Hebrew prophets proclaimed the wrath of Jahweh, pointing to the example of the universal flood from which Noah was saved. Recent astronomical writers (including science fiction authors) have explored our prospects for planetary collision. Immanuel Velikovsky writes about "cosmic catastrophism"[4] and cataclysmic geologists have prophesied that "not a single surviver was left."[5]

Fears of human extinction from biological warfare have not disappeared. Dangers of death to mankind in a nuclear holocaust do not diminish while overkill military budgets continue to increase and nuclear bomb construction capacities spread from nation to nation. These follies are prime examples of our failure to use intelligence.

Our concern here focuses on issues that have become more alarming during the past five years. The issues are not new. What is new is the rapidity with which their mutual agitation appears approaching a critical mass, and the increasing frequency of cries of alarm about a possible early end of mankind: "Mankind is galloping in the direction of assured and possibly total disaster."[6] What is new is the number of well-informed professionals speaking out boldly on the subject. Economist Robert L. Heilbroner, for example, has asked:

"Is there hope for man?" Interpreting the question as whether crisis challenges can be met without fearful costs, he replies: "No, there is no such hope."[7]

Twelve mutually interpenetrating tendencies (and others not mentioned here)[8] contribute to the festering sore emerging as world civilization. Contemporary peoples, cultures, and persons participate unevenly in sensing the seriousness of louder warnings. But spreading awareness of the severity of present crises may have to arouse willingness to try to save ourselves before it is too late.

In addition to mounting military budgets, persisting proverty, widening maldistribution gaps, and increasing varieties of social injustice—problems that have been with us for a long time—there are eight more recently obvious degenerative trends contributing to American and global crises: accelerating cultural lag, overpopulation, exhaustion of resources, environmental pollution, stagflation, deficit spending, growing political incompetence, and spreading demoralization.

Accelerating Cultural Lag

Alvin Toffler's *Future Shock*[9] made us realize that changes have become so rapid that increasing numbers of persons lack the capacity to adjust to them. The result—more and more persons are becoming disoriented, ill adapted, and decapacitated—has a significant bearing on the effectiveness, or ineffectiveness, with which they encounter the following problems. The shock has also penetrated institutions, which often resist change more stubbornly than do individuals with personal habits. The full story of institutional rupture is still to be told. I shall claim that lack of institutional flexibility is part of our incapacity to cope with crisis issues.

Warren Wager condemns change as inimical: "The enemy of modern civilization . . . is change, the geometrically accelerating pace of change in the growth of all the powers of mankind."[10] But he is correct only if mankind succumbs. I argue that crises result also from the fact that we have not changed enough. We have not yet overcome those stagnant portions of our civilization, sectarian religions, ancient philosophies, and rigid ideologies that resist change. When changes accelerate faster than we can adjust to them, they will destroy us unless we can accelerate changes in our conceptions fast enough to make the needed adjustments.

Overpopulation

Rumblings about overpopulation, sparked by Malthus's *Essay on Population* (1789), have surfaced many times. But Paul Ehrlich's *The Population Bomb*[11] and especially the Club of Rome's *The Limits to Growth*[12] have aroused widespread attention to how soon unrestricted population growth will outstrip available resources. Although critics quickly objected to details,[13] Aurelio Peccei and his colleagues have won respect for their willingness to take responsibility for alerting mankind to serious collective thinking about extinction prospects.

Charting the mathematics of exponential growth and considering additional variables regarding fertilizer production, urbanization, industrial production, food requirements, energy consumption, pollution increase, and use of numerous irreplaceable resources, Dennis Meadows and his colleagues predict that, unless we change our ways, "sometime within the next hundred years" mankind will reach the end of growth.[14] Despite obvious doomsday implications of extrapolated pictures, they believe that it is still possible to influence trends, and they urge us to try—the sooner the better. Since they use the language of models fashionable with computer programmers, I shall examine their proposals more fully in chapter 2.

Exhaustion of Resources

Resources are of two sorts: those that are irreplaceable, such as minerals, oil, and gas, and those that can be replaced, such as wheat, cotton, and milk. Irreplaceable resources used up by one generation or in one century will not be available for those in later generations. The more rapidly these resources are used, the sooner they will be used up entirely. If any are essential to human existence, their exhaustion means human extinction.[15] Enough variation and uncertainty exist about predictions so that many are willing to ignore their doomsday significance. But if present trends continue, many such resources will come close to exhaustion by the end of this century and most by the end of the next. If developing countries join the race for industrialization, as they have a right to do, the end will come more quickly.

Replaceable resources, such as cereals, vegetables, fruit, meat, and fish, depend on conditions having their own inherent limitations. The amount of arable land, the availability of fertility and water, and the maintenance of ecological balance required for plants, domesticated animals, and marine life all have limits. Overfishing, overfarming, and deforestation may cause some now-replaceable resources to become irreplaceable. Overpopulation and pollution hasten the exhaustion of both irreplaceable and replaceable resources. The hope that science will supply us with substitutes soon enough again lulls many into a state of indifference. Such indifference has its own way of contributing causally to augmenting crises.

Pollution

There are many kinds of environmental pollution. Each seems to be growing exponentially, and the processes have advanced long before we became alarmed about them. The eutrophication of Lake Erie seems to have aroused more anxieties than New York or San Francisco smog. 16 Rigorous countermeasures promise at least a partial restoration of fishing possibilities. But now attention is shifting to larger bodies of water, such as the Mediterranean Sea and the oceans, where sewage from cities poisons more and more fishing waters. The cumulating effects of chemical fertilizers and pesticides on runoff water feeding rivers and lakes now cause much concern. The necessity for obtaining drinkable water for growing cities has caused many local crises quite apart from mounting pollution as a global crisis.

Air fouled by motor exhausts and factory smokestacks has become so serious a problem that federal legislation has become necessary to control this pollution. But the costs of such controls are so high that business fights to postpone their effectiveness. Some smaller businesses have been forced to close because they could not afford the costs. The fight against cancer-causing cigarette smoke has been only partially successful.

Soil pollution from pesticides, acid rain, and nuclear bomb explosions, added to the usual quotas of drought, frosts, floods, and insect pestilence, makes farming tasks more hazardous and assurance of safe food supplies more difficult. Garbage and trash disposal and open-pit mining reduce usable land. Initial efforts have been made to increase recycling and to restore mine pits to previous utility, but soil pollution continues to be a serious source of resource destruction.

One estimate of our environmental crises paints a black picture: "The present system of production is self-destructive; the present course of civilization is suicidal." "The World is being carried to the brink of ecological disaster."[17]

Stagflation

Having survived the Depression of the 1930s, people in the United States and in the rest of the world regained confidence about managing the economy. Recovery from smaller recessions has bolstered that confidence. But the arrival of stagflation by 1975, combining the symptoms of both depression and inflation at the same time, presented a new challenge to our confidence. Economists, puzzled by unpredictable trends, disagree both about the causes and solutions. Growing awareness that we may have reached the peak of a rapid-growth economy has led to cautious efforts to refrain from drastic movements in either direction. Economic disturbances in the United States have caused disturbances in other countries, which in turn are having reverse repercussions.

Stagflation is not only an economic crises; it is a crisis in understanding. As Alvin Toffler interprets it, "Our economy is running out of control. . . . What is happening is the breakdown of industrial civilization."[18] Our failure to understand the complexities of current economic processes, which intricately interdepend with political and other unpredictable changes and decisions, may doom us permanently. World War II made new demands on production and employment. This fact begot a saying, only partly facetious: "You

can always cure a depression with a war." But if we avoid World
War III because it promises to consume us in a holocaust, with what
do we cure stagflation?

Deficit Spending

Those unaware of the fragility of the American (and world) economy, because they neglect to face up to the foundational significance
of deficit spending, received a shock late in 1975 when New York
City threatened to be unable to meet interest payments on its indebtedness. The seriousness of the problem for national and world
economy should not be underestimated. Not only private bankers
and the state government but also the United States government had
to pledge that the payments would be made after repeated budget
cutting and service reduction by the city of New York. The drastic
retrenchment measures were dramatized by the closing of the University of the City of New York, which enrolled more than 227,000
students. Managers around the world breathed easier when the city
passed its crisis date. Further crises are in prospect, but a willingness
to act responsibly in meeting the first one gives hope that the city will
cope in the future.

What is significant about the New York City drama is that it sym-
bolizes deficit spending by state and municipal governments, as well
as by the United States government. Although the government
makes a show of self-discipline by establishing a legal limit beyond
which the federal deficit cannot go, this limit is legally extended
whenever Congress so decides. On August 31, 1976, for example,
the total United States government debt was $633,329,000,000, and
the statutory debt limit was $636 billion.[19]

How much deficits can continue to increase without loss of confidence both at home and abroad is something of a mystery. Recently
when the amount of bank deposits federally guaranteed was raised
from $20,000 to $40,000, some persons seemed relieved. But this
guarantee will depend on drawing more out of the miraculous deficit. Abroad we participate in an international monetary system of
floating national currencies that fluctuate through both repeated de-
valuations of fixed exchange rates and blackmarket operations.
When payment imbalances are large enough, they inflate or deflate

national currencies. United States gifts and loans (some unrepayable) of money, food, technical equipment, and armaments to foreign nations deepen our deficit. Surely confidence in United States monetary reliability would have vanished except for the fact that most other countries have their own deficit-spending (or money-printing) problems and their own production, balance-of-payments, and inflation difficulties to cope with.

Clear thinking about prospects of ever repaying, whether to ourselves or others, the huge amounts of present deficits, both those in the United States and those in other countries, will cause most of us to fear, with Alvin Toffler, that our economy is "careening on the brink of disaster."[20]

Growing Political Incompetence

The problem of political incompetence is not new. The rise and fall of civilizations, empires, nations, political parties, and particular political leaders is a continuing story. But now that we live in an increasingly intricate global interdependence, the cumulative incompetencies at all levels of government and in all nations and alliances hardly provide the talent needed to cope with global crises. In addition to those more or less common causes conducive to incompetence in governments at all levels, the increasing magnitude and complexity of problems facing us at the world level promises to surpass the capacity of all of us, even if we mobilize our best minds cooperatively.

Despite many increases in capacity through better training, larger libraries, more rapid communication and travel, quicker computer calculations, and larger budgets for institute research, the existing conditions have become more complex more rapidly than our capacity for understanding has increased. The current normality of unmanageable complexities is expressed in a not-so-humorous story. Shopping for an educational toy, a mother was puzzled: "Isn't it too complicated for a little boy?" A clerk replied: "It was made to help children adjust to today's world. No matter how carefully the child tries to put it together, it won't work."[21] If mastery of the world is beyond the competence of research institute managers, national congresses, and United Nations secretaries-general should not children be taught to recognize and become accustomed to problem-solving incompetence?

Intelligent solution to complex problems involves more comprehensiveness of perspective and understanding of interrelations between multidisciplinary explanations, and much more international, intercultural, and intercorporational (both national and multinational corporations) cooperation than exists at present. The late United Nations secretary-general, U Thant, warned that if we do not cooperate effectively within the next decade, our problems "will be beyond our capacity to control." Now we should be warned that possibly they are already beyond our capacity to understand fully. We will not know whether we have the capacity to understand and control our future until we do organize our efforts cooperatively. Our present indisposition to do so seems to doom us to extinction.

An absence of confidence in a common cause, national or global, decreases our morale and leads to narrower self-interests. A lack of effective world government promotes excessive nationalism. A lack of vitality and virtuous service by national governments leads to emphases on state and local benefits in preference to willing support for the nation. An absence of higher loyalties contributes to more selfish expressions by individuals and special interest groups, whether they be professional, occupational, religious, cultural, racial, age, or ideological. When lack of national or world loyalty persists, morale is more easily supplied by sectarian groups, such as racial, religious, cultural, and linguistic minorities, which then function divisively relative to the larger groups. When growing incompetence is compounded by increasingly narrow self-interestedness, prospects for global cooperation seem dim.

The spread of nuclear bomb production capacity, plus probabilities that terrorists will obtain and use such bombs, make growing political incompetence all the more dangerous.

Spreading Demoralization

One trend entirely neglected by earlier doomsday alarmists and still underemphasized by most writers is an increasingly pervasive decline in morale. The trend seems most striking in the United States, but its appearance in other countries also seems to accompany the multiculturating effects of growing cities, increasing impersonality of associations in large populations, rising expectations, increasing costs of more complex required social and political services, disappearance of the frontier and genuine opportunities for small businesses, persisting poverty, maldistribution and social injustices, growth of both private and political corruption as the cost of effective law-enforcement exceeds present police, judicial, and penal capacities, growth in large-scale corruption as corporations increase in size, exposures by independent media of multiplying deficiencies, and denial of freedoms by dictatorial governments.

Growing demoralization is symbolized by rising crime rates. Occasional reversals in local situations seem not to retard the national, and perhaps world, trends.

Newspaper headlines highlight these trends. "National Crime Rate Is Reported Up 18%."[22] "Study Finds Most Crime Not Reported."[23] "Women in Crime: Why Are There More?"[24] "Organized Crime Growing."[25] "Police Corruption Termed Disease."[26] "Combatting Crime in the Schools."[27] Jane Kessler, director of the Mental Development Center at Case Western Reserve University, has stated that "parents and teachers are reluctant to even talk about moral education. This is partly because many parents see morals as relative and prefer to raise their children in a moral vacuum."[28]

The statistics confirm our fears. In 1975 the U.S. government presented the numbers from 1960 through 1975 (figure 1). The total crime index combines violent crimes and property crimes as reported by police. The chart depicts a steadily upward trend.[29]

One expert, commenting on trends, writes: "The probability that the criminal justice system will suffer a complete breakdown before the year 2000 should not be discounted. If law and social control systems are to accommodate change in their environment at the necessary rate, a new philosophy, as well as quite different operating procedures must be worked out. The present strategy of law enforcement agencies to develop more-of-the-same can only ensure breakdown."[30]

The six-volume report of the National Advisory Commission on Criminal Justice Standards and Goals to the Law Enforcement Assistance Administration of the U.S. Department of Justice makes many minor suggestions for improving police, courts, corrections, com-

FIGURE 1.
TOTAL CRIME INDEX, 1960–1975

Year	Total
1960	3,384,200
1961	3,488,000
1962	3,752,200
1963	4,109,500
1964	4,564,600
1965	4,739,400
1966	5,223,500
1967	5,903,400
1968	6,720,200
1969	7,401,900
1970	8,098,000
1971	8,588,200
1972	8,248,800
1973	8,718,100
1974	10,253,400
1975	11,256,600

Percent of Increase, 1960–1975: 232.6%

CHART OF CRIME INCREASES

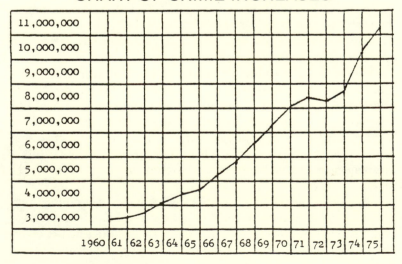

munity crime prevention, and the criminal justice system. But, from a broader viewpoint, the net effect of these suggestions seems to be continuation of past policies and practices. The sixth report, *A National Strategy to Reduce Crime*, concluded with a chapter, "A National Commitment to Change."[31] A National Governor's Conference in 1973 endorsed a goal of a 50 percent crime reduction in ten years, but prospects are not bright.

My chief criticism of this $1,750,000 study is that I discovered no evidence that any of the task forces looking for causes mentioned degeneration of philosophical, including ethical, foundations of their problems. And in looking for solutions, no one mentioned the need for reexamining and reconstructing the foundational presuppositions necessary for regaining moral understanding and confidence. Thus it appears that our law enforcement system, and the National Advisory Commission appointed to propose a strategy for reducing crime, are part of the problem.

Adding criminal trends in all other countries, and increasing international crimes, to the United States prospects, and the lack of a world law enforcement administration, what are our prospects for world crime? I do not trust predictions based on extrapolations. In a dynamic world too many changes can occur. But until they do, extrapolations of crime increase trends should be taken as warnings. I believe that growing demoralization is at least as serious a threat to human survival as any of the others now more loudly proclaimed. Part of the reason is that in an increasingly interdependent society increases in population, pollution, resource consumption, and so forth interdepend with increases in crime rates and demoralization: these and other trends contribute to demoralization, and demoralization contributes to these other trends. Our failure to become aware of our increasing interdependence is thus itself a cause of our present predicament. This failure is related to our growing incapacity to be competently philosophical relative to understanding how the insights achieved through specialized research contribute to a changed total picture.[32]

Many other trends leading to doomsday might be added. Each specialist and each special-interest-group loyalist I meet seems to have his own complaint about what the world is coming to. But to extend this discussion would unnecessarily belabor a point becoming increasingly obvious: we must respond both individually and collectively with greater intelligence if we are to survive. What course of action will be most intelligent is not something that I can predict. But since I am especially aware of our philosophical deficiencies, the Philosopher's World Model proposed here is one in which an attempt has been made to remove these deficiencies.

PLANS FOR SURVIVING

Responses to doomsday evidence and predictions have been various. A brief survey of six types of plans for surviving may throw some light on our predicament, for the options we perceive do themselves condition our prospects and may serve as a basis for evaluating any hopes we may have.

Reassert Present Methods

Is it not still hard to teach old dogs new tricks? Is not the natural reaction of any person already having a solution or a philosophy sustaining his present practices to defend his ways? Habits are hard to change. They were acquired with too much effort to discard easily. Each person nurtured by his culture has vested interests in the old, established methods. Any person at home in his community feels a loyalty to its traditional policies. If they are failing to work now, then we must try harder to make them work.

How often have you heard, when a critic condemns Christianity, "But it's never been given a fair trial!"? The critic cries: "It's been tried for two thousand years. Look where it has gotten us." The defender repeats: "If you love your neighbor as yourself, and your enemies, all our crises will disappear. *You* haven't tried it!" The same may be asked about Hindu *ahimsa*, which Gandhi practiced with remarkable success. Islam, the religion of peace, makes its own claims to utility: when wars to end all infidelity succeed completely, world peace can be assured. Marxists, promising a utopian withering away of the state, regret that the ignorant bourgeoisie refuse to try their proven methods. Every traditional religion, every prominent ideology, and every political party makes the same claim. In American political campaigns, Republicans blame Democrats for failing to try their methods, and Democrats blame the Republicans for not following the Democratic way. Each assures us that his own version of the established way is best.

But the fact remains that present crises have resulted from the past and present practices of these old ways. Even if each worked under ideal circumstances, none is working well enough in present circumstances. So unless each can transform circumstances into something closer to his ideal, must he not confess his way incompetent to meet our present needs?

Reaffirm Democratic Ideals

Democracy still works, at least in the United States, even if ever more imperfectly. Such reaffirmation may seem like merely another example of the previous plan. Perhaps it is, except that democracy is different. Instead of advocating just one old way, democracy is open to all ways, old and new. It had a philosophical basis in British empiricism, which advocated that each person receives his own share of ideas with which to judge the world. The doctrine of religious toleration, which has come to be accompanied by philosophical toleration, moral toleration, economic toleration, and even political toleration up to certain points, opens the way to many different methods.

But in practice, laws, including those regarding property, taxes, military service, and personal and corporate liability, have restricted such openness. The possibility that, since anyone may suggest, and any Representative may introduce, another method, enables the system to maintain the hope that, when compromise of struggling contenders is reached, a better way will emerge.

Democratic methods do still work better, apparently, in small groups. But growth in numbers of people, as well as in numbers of kinds of problems and in increasing complexities of problems, has diminished the quality, and perhaps quantity, of democratic practices. In a presidential election, for example, each vote is one among sixty million. It thus counts at most as only one-sixty-millionth of the total.[33] Such a vote, only once every four years, merely delegates one's power to a person or party to make decisions on all forthcoming issues.

In practice, the power of special-interest pressure groups (such as labor unions, minorities, consumers' unions, and associations of physicians, teachers, and manufacturers), overshadows individual influence so much that participatory democracy in national affairs has practically disappeared, except through indirect means. The high costs of government, the relative ease of corruption, and the purchasing power of large corporations all militate against effective personal participation. If democratic practices increasingly fail to solve crucial problems in the most democratic countries, how can we expect them to work at the world level?

Continue to Muddle Through

Governmental practices at all levels (community to nation and world) and in all branches (legislative, administrative, judicial) consist mainly of meeting crises as they arise. This practice implies an endorsement of the policy of solving only short-range problems. Long-range problems are neglected too long, so that they then generate more numerous immediate crises.

The muddling-through policy also has origins in our British political and philosophical heritage. Ideals of individual freedom encourage putting off problems and solutions that seem to interfere with that freedom. These ideals beget the slogan: "That government governs best which governs least." Both the most conservative Republicans and the most radical anarchists support this slogan. Recently Existentialists and Libertarians have been added to its list of supporters.

But neglect of government begets government by neglect. Those few able to isolate themselves may succeed in shirking political responsibilities for a short period. But how can crises growing out of increasingly intricate interdependencies of peoples around the world, swarming in metropolitan areas, affecting all of us economically, politically, ecologically and militarily, be remedied by neglect? Our most crucial problems are too complex, too widespread, and too long range to be dealt with effectively by short-range solutions, much less by neglect. Short-range solutions deal with only parts of our problems. Neglect of long-range solutions tends to aggravate them.

Our muddling-through policy is itself a major contributor to the magnitude of present crises. Long-range problems have been neglected for so long that they have grown beyond our capacity to deal with them. If we become victims of economic, political, military, or ecological catastrophe, we may be reaping the harvest of our own neglect. Is not doomsday the deserved reward of neglectful muddlers? Is not muddling through a kind of plan to have no plan for survival?

Drop Out

Dropping out of social responsibilities has become increasingly popular, especially among the young, because it has come to seem increasingly reasonable to them. Social (political, economic, ecological, military, educational) problems have become so complex, and the knowledge, the money, the political power, and the time and effort required to work through to solutions are so great that many have come to seem unsolvable. If they are unsolvable by national or state senators, how can citizens whose capacities, knowledge, money, power, and time are very limited hope to solve them? Personal efforts to participate in solving such problems usually end in frustration. Is it not foolish to try? Is it not wise to drop out?

Dropping out is not a new method. Orthodox Christianity, focusing on sin and repentance, discouraged persons from engaging in activities tempting sinfulness. Roman Catholicism provided monasteries and nunneries as sanctuaries enabling members to drop out of worldly life. Calvinistic predestinarians idealized a theocratic system in which all is predetermined. Those believing they could change the course of history from that determined by God, no matter how critical the issues may seem, revealed ignorance of God's power and plan. Hindus, like some Greeks, believe in a cyclical interpretation of history, known as the Days and Nights of Brahman, divided in *Yugas* (long periods) devoted to the rise and fall of civilization. If the pattern of one's life in one's society is repeated exactly every round of the circle, any seeming influence one may have on social affairs is already determined. Why believe one can have any influence on any plan to survive?

Mechanistic materialists, who hold that every effect is a predictable result of its causes, not only plead in court as psychiatrists claiming that the murderer was not free to do otherwise but imply that the course of history is also completely determined. Freedom of will is an illusion, so one will devote efforts to helping mankind to survive only if he happens to be caused to do so. If something in his environment causes him to drop out of society, so be it. The tychists, believers in a world of chance, also regard our predicament, and any consequences of it, as resulting from chance. Marxist dialectical materialism, although not totally deterministic, holds that the succession of stages in the dialectic of history (such as communism succeeding capitalism) is inevitable. Thus a person who drops out of social responsibilities is carried along as inevitably as one who fights and dies for its progression.

Whether one is just lazy or uses liquor or psychedelic drugs, electric guitars and strobe lights, brothels, opium, transcendental meditation or yoga, or hides away in a mountain cabin or a rural commune, immunity from feelings of social responsibility is regarded by some as great freedom. They are trusting to fate, or good luck, or chance, to grace them with the best that they deserve. They, too, plan not to plan to try to solve the world's crucial problems.

Hope for a World Dictator

Perhaps least desirable, and yet most probable, are prospects for human survival aided by a world dictator. Can we not say that we are planning for such a dictator? Military budgets of nations already equipped with multiple overkill capacities continue to grow. The doctrine of balance of power (or balance of fear) is admittedly a temporary measure. If one nation, or block of nations, cannot conquer its enemies, then the best it can hope to do is to prevent itself from being conquered. But if its enemies become weakened or it can acquire allies to strengthen its power, of what further use is the doctrine? Having invested so much in military preparedness, would it not be foolish not to take advantage of an opportunity for world dictatorship?

Once a dictator is in control of the whole world, the enormous expenses of military budgets would decline and then practically disappear. There must be enough arms already in existence to police the whole world until its planetary end. Just as a family, community, state, or nation seeks to end internal disharmony, perhaps a world dictator would seek to care for all of his own.

American political ideals are staunchly antipathetic to dictatorship of any sort. Ideals of personal freedom, freedom from bureaucracy, and freedom from government controls are barren soil for dictatorial ideas. Yet the spreading awareness of growing demoralization is causing uncertainty about our future. Rising crime rates make us fearful that we have too much freedom.

Fearing for their lives and their property, and losing confidence in democratically elected officials to protect them, will not increasing numbers call for a United States leader with a strong hand? There are limits to demoralization before a society collapses. As we approach, or pass, those limits, the desirability of a dictator capable of restoring our confidence that rights will be respected because others will be forced to do their duties in respecting those rights will increase.

Today we suffer not only increasing corruption but also increasing corruptibility. Crime does pay, and pays more and more, if you can get away with it. Victims of unemployment may feel forced to steal. Many university students, instead of dropping out, now exploit opportunities for finding out how to benefit from illegal actions. One has to be a specialist to succeed these days, whether as a producer of specialized goods or as a thief of such goods. How long will it take before the corruption of the increasingly corruptible becomes intolerable? How long will it take before we cry for a dictator who can eliminate corruption?

Emergence of a dictator in the United States will not solve the world's critical problems. In fact, it may aggravate them. Unless he can understand the complexities of world interdependence, see the need for cooperation, and willingly cooperate, the dictator would become a stumbling block to their solution. Furthermore would not the temptation of a United States dictator to become a world dictator be too much to resist? He could ignore the many special-interest groups that now fare better with perpetual peace. He could ruthlessly provoke quarrels among his enemies so as to weaken them. He could infiltrate their technologies and cripple their economic and military systems. He could even use terrorist tactics and at least threaten weaker enemies by asking them to choose between capitulation and atomic warfare. Are those hoping (or possibly planning) for an American dictator also hoping for a world dictator? If the growing demoralization observable in America is symptomatic of demoralization throughout the world, will not the people of other nations also welcome a world dictator who promises to restore morale?

Unfortunately many populous movements exist that are themselves not only willing, but anxious, to promote world dictatorship, provided they can have it on their own terms. Marxist leaders in the U.S.S.R. spell out explicitly their plans for elimination of bourgeois capitalism. They do not hesitate to express desires for such world domination. The same has been true of Maoist China. Islam, stalled in its conquest of much of the world from Morocco to the Philippines, remains ready to regain momentum to fulfill its aims. Failing to conquer India, Moslems created Pakistan and Bangladesh as Moslem states, in addition to Morocco, Tunisia, Libya, Algeria, Egypt, Saudi Arabia, Syria, Turkey, Iraq, and Iran. Large Moslem populations occupy India, China, Russia, Indonesia, and the Philippines. The military capacity of Arab states confronted by American-backed Israeli aggression is strong enough to cause a stand-off. The growing military power of the shah of Iran and the expanding wealth of Moslem OPEC nations provide hopes to some that the goal of Islamic domination of the world may yet be realized.

Christian plans for dominating the world, which seemed to succeed as the Holy Roman Empire dominated Europe and as European adventurers colonized much of the world, have received much setback. The Vatican, a tiny political state, nevertheless still exercises powerful influences in political and economic affairs through its continuing control over its millions of members. Spain and South America seem unlikely candidates for world domination just now. But if the United States, the U.S.S.R. and the People's Republic of China should knock themselves out in mutual combat, as they are obviously preparing to do, what is to prevent a United States of South America from accomplishing what others did not?

My point is that world dictatorship is being planned elsewhere in the world, even if not very effectively. If growing prospects of dictatorship in the United States are added to these, the climate of world opinion may become more favorable than it is now. The more that people everywhere become convinced that we have permitted the development of crises beyond the capacity of present governments to handle, the more likely willing acquiescence, if not active support, of a world dictatorship will become.

I deplore the prospects. The arrival of such a dictator will cost much in lives and resources, and many of the precious freedoms that some people do enjoy will be eliminated. It seems unlikely that whoever has the qualities to achieve dictatorship of the world will also have a philosophical perspective enabling him to be fair to all. If he is a Marxist, a Moslem, or a Christian, will he not impose one set of views upon all of us? Will he not, out of necessity in regimenting a government capable of controlling all of the different peoples, cultures, languages, and established interests in the world, adopt a single philosophy, a particular religion, a definite code of ethics, and a description of the ideal life for our inspiration? Mankind might be lucky in such an event and person, but the chances seem against it.

Furthermore what evidence do we have that a world dictator would have the wisdom or capacity to cope with our crises? Does our feeling of incompetence to grapple with these crises generate wishful thinking that a sufficiently powerful dictator could automatically handle them? Power is not always accompanied by wisdom. What makes anyone believe that a person who happens to become world dictator could do better than dozens of well-financed research institutes?

And with the proliferation of nuclear terrorist techniques, what makes us believe that we might not have a series of coups, and a series of dictators, each costing more in lives, resources, ecological livability? Crises facing us now may pale in viciousness when compared to the disasters likely when terrorist power cliques vie for world control. Let us avoid dictatorship if we can.

Extend the Use of Scientific Methods

Our accepted way to reliable knowledge is through scientific methods. We have used them with remarkable success in the physical and biological sciences. Automobiles, airplanes, submarines, skyscrapers, tunnels, wells, electricity, hydrogen bombs, nuclear power plants, moon rockets, electronic computers, mechanical hearts, immunization against disease, increased food supply, and longevity—all result from science.

We are using these methods, at least somewhat, in dealing with our crises. Departments in the social sciences of anthropology, sociology, economics, political science, and business and administrative sciences have been established in universities, and many social scientists have been drafted as consultants by congressional committees. Many have been employed in public and private research institutes, as well as in some administrative positions. The knowledge and insights of expert social scientists constitute valuable resources that are being used increasingly. Support for social science research is growing both at home and abroad, even if slowly.[34]

Five-year plans that nations, such as the U.S.S.R. and India, prepare officially require the services of more social scientists. Corporations, including banks, facing a dynamic world with variable complexities need sound advice about future prospects if they are to risk millions in investments. Thus private corporations increasingly depend on social science research services, and some support their own private research laboratories. Some of these, because asked to try to predict the future, have come to be called *futurologists*. The World Future Society, which publishes a monthly journal, *The Futurist*, specializes in concerns about the human predicament and proposals, both models and techniques, for improving it.

The most obvious locus of futures research is in the host of interdisciplinary research institutes, especially those contracting to provide assistance to persons responsible for making policy decisions. Since this sixth plan for surviving—extended use of scientific methods and interdisciplinary research institutes—will be incorporated into the Philosopher's World Model and treated more fully in chapter 8, further details will be delayed until then. But since we have failed to extend the use of scientific mehtods and failed to develop sufficiently competent, comprehensive, interdisciplinary research institutes, these failures have contributed to our present predicament and will continue to do so until we replace failure with ample success.

OTHER WORLD MODELS. WHY THEY FAIL

The world models depicted in the major religions—Judaism, Christianity, Islam, Hinduism, Jainism, Buddhism, Confucianism, and Shintoism—have failed to solve our contemporary problems. Indeed they are contributing more to these problems than to their solution. The continued existence and persisting influence of these religions are obstacles to present efforts.

Intelligent solutions to our world problems doubtless will include truths extracted from each of these religions. But when such truth is overlaid and inextricably interwoven with doctrinal details now regarded as essentially mythical and with claims to knowledge that have been demonstrated as false, active efforts to terminate such influences should be initiated. The suggestions made here will be examined further in chapter 6, but the point in mentioning them is that world models, and their failures, are not new. Some of them have lasted for centuries and even millennia.

I cannot take time to review utopian literature, such as Edward Bellamy's *Looking Backward, 1887-2000*, George Orwell's *Nineteen Eighty-four*, or the interstellar visions of science fiction writers. Nor can I explore political ideologies ranging from anarchism to totalitarian fascism, including the ideals of republican, democratic, socialist, and communist parties, and subvarieties, such as national socialism, Christian socialism, and the Christian democrats, prohibitionists, and libertarians. Perhaps we should pause to consider

Marxism and Maoism as world models because their numbers of followers and current political and military power continue to influence many.

Marx's ideas were derived from conditions in early modern industrial cities—Berlin, Paris, and London. They were pre-Darwinian and thus preevolutionary. Marx's conceptions of historical development were primarily dialectical rather than biological. He achieved insights enlightening our interpretation of the evils of early factory conditions and of class struggles. But if we now are desperately trying to grasp some complex system gestalt that will provide at least temporary guidance through the dynamic, intricate, multileveled, multidimensional, and multinational maze of crises in what some call a postindustrial society, Marx's vision is much too simple and too static to serve as the model needed for today and tomorrow.[1]

Mao's modifications of Marxism adapted it to agrarian China. Although fraught with both theoretical and practical difficulties, it has been useful in bringing the Chinese people from familialism and feudalism to more modern modes of thinking and living. But despite some physiological, psychological, sociological, economic, and political benefits of forcing intellectual workers to devote some of their time to physical labor, technological progress making possible massive farm food production efficiencies has made such practices impractical and thus obsolete so far as pointing the way to a better future for mankind. In the near future, life promises to become more megalopolitan, and such life can find little to guide it from a world model idealizing agrarian practices.

Just as with traditional religions, so with traditional ideologies and practiced political ideals. There is some truth in all of them. Maoist ideals may yet prove a useful antidote to the evils of too much megalopolitanization. But in their current form, Marxism and Maoism do not shed much light on the complexities of our predicament or show much promise of rescuing us from it. It is the military power rather than the Marxism and Maoism of the U.S.S.R. and the People's Republic of China that threaten world peace. The ignorance of the complexities of the causes and kinds of our crises embedded in Marxist and Maoist doctrines contribute to those crises. And all the more so when their political, economic, and military power enable them to perpetuate that ignorance.

World models proposed during the past ten years are now being put forth as serious contenders for dealing with world problems. Some see these as significant because they are efforts arising in response to spreading awareness of the seriousness of our crises and of doomsday probabilities if we fail to organize ourselves with sufficient intelligence to cope with them. Profiting by advances in computer technology and enabling us to store and recall amazing quantities of data in ways that may be useful in dealing with complexities, these models may be viewed as representing the latest achievements of mankind in grappling with world crises today.

CLUB OF ROME MODELS

The most successful efforts to arouse popular and professional attention to dangers threatening human survival are those of the Club of Rome.[2] Aurelio Peccei and colleagues deserve congratulation for their concern, responsibility, and exertion and for their success in alerting more of us to developing dangers. They are not alone in these endeavors. But their intercontinental cooperation embodies in their actions a significance beyond their individual achievements.

Research projects commissioned by the club have appeared in three stages thus far. Each is indicated by the name of a book: *The Limits to Growth, Mankind at the Turning Point,* and *Goals for Mankind.* The proposals presented in each have come to be called first-, second-, and third-generation models, A progression has been intended and has been achieved.[3]

The Limits to Growth

During a 1968 meeting called to examine the predicament of mankind, both at present and especially in the future, the Club of Rome decided to sponsor research projects needed to understand festering global problems. The first project focused on dangers to human survival from too rapid use of irreplaceable resources if technological, industrial, and population growths continue their present trends. The team, directed by Dennis L. Meadows at the Massachusetts Institute of Technology,[4] studied five major trends pertaining to increases in population, use of natural resources, agricultural production, industrial production, and pollution. Their report was *The Limits to Growth*.[5]

The Meadows team profited by the previous work of J. W. Forrester whose *World Dynamics*[6] included many statistical tables. They worked in an atmosphere already stirring with alarms by many thinkers. Paul R. Ehrlich's popular *The Population Bomb*[7] was supplemented by his more scholarly *Population, Resources, Environment*.[8] John McHale's *The Ecological Context* urged that "we need to reconceptualize our global, man-made environ facilities within more comprehensive and coherent systems" and to redesign our technological systems "so that they may be more compatible with the overall ecological system."[9] Barry Commoner's *The Closing Circle: Nature, Man and Technology* warned that the real significance of environmental crises is that the world is being brought to "the brink of disaster" by a complex of forces.[10] Numerous criticisms of *The Limits to Growth*, exemplified by *Models of Doom*,[11] resulted in further refinements: *Dynamics of Growth in a Finite World*[12] and *Toward Global Equilibrium*.[13]

In addition to warnings about catastrophe in prospect from continuing present trends, *The Limits to Growth* aimed to advance world modeling as a planning technique. Claiming to be a formal or mathematical model, it asserted that implications from present data for future functioning of the world as a system can be "traced without error by computer."[14] Growth of computer technology and its use in gathering global data have been partly responsible for the flourishing concern for world modeling. Critics have chastened those who claim that computer technology results in reliable predictions. Now more and more emphasis is being placed on models as alternative guesses that may be used experimentally for testing assumptions.

Conclusions typical of *The Limits to Growth* are that such limits will be reached within the coming century, if present trends continue, that trends can be changed so that a global equilibrium, the primary goal envisioned by this first-generation project, can be achieved, and that the sooner we act the better.

The Limits to Growth did succeed in its aims. It aroused fears about global dangers. It presented sufficient evidence to provoke serious reflection. It stimulated world modeling efforts. It did propose an ideal of global equilibrium as a desirable goal if mankind can arouse itself to do what is needed to achieve it. But it also failed to consider all of the trends and all of the needs to be considered for ensuring human survival. Some of these failures have been pointed out, and partly overcome, by those working at second- and third-generation projects. But still others have not even been touched on by previous world modelers. These failures are the reason why the Philosopher's World Model is needed.

Mankind at the Turning Point

Mihailo Mesarovic of the Systems Research Center of Case Western University in Cleveland and Eduard Pestel of the Technical University in Hanover, Germany were commissioned to cooperate in producing *Mankind at the Turning Point: The Second Report to the Club of Rome*.[15]

They agreed with *The Limits to Growth* that passive drift coupled with present tendencies will result in disaster and that human survival problems must be grappled with in a global context. But they criticized its perspective as too simplistic.

First, it took into account only five kinds of factors (population, resources, agricultural and industrial production, and pollution). It neglected human resources and many trends related to quality-of-living concerns that will influence future developments. It overlooked the significance of cultural, ideological, political, and many economic influences in determining the future course of events. It underestimated the probabilities that properly organized scientific research will discover new resources as well as methods for utilizing currently known resources.

Second, although some interdependence of factors was recognized, its five factors tended to be treated more as independent variables than as dynamically interdependent processes. It conceived both the problem and its solution through an equilibrium of forces too much in terms of aggregates and not sufficiently in terms of organic growth.

Third, it charted tendencies for the world as a whole in ways that gave insufficient understanding to regional and national differences.

The average curves depicted in *The Limits to Growth* offered little help for making policy decisions in particular regions and nations. Resources, population, technology, pollution, and industry vary greatly in different parts of the globe. Thus practical efforts to grapple with the problem, which must be done by the political agencies available, need both more detailed understanding of regional differences and a more complex insight into how interdependencies among regions can be harmoniously interrelated with interdependencies within regions and nations and cities.

Mankind at the Turning Point has positive contributions to understanding and dealing with the human predicament. First, it puts forth a more complex conception. Not only are more kinds of factors believed necessary for understanding, but also the interdependencies of factors are conceived in terms of organic growth. Only if we see mankind as an organic entity will we be able to devise plans needed for the kinds of organic growth that will enable mankind to survive. In contrast to those views satisfied with interpreting mankind's nature and future in terms of aggregates of factors and an equilibrium of their production and consumption, *Mankind at the Turning Point* predicts that successful solution in terms of organic growth "will lead to the creation of a new mankind."[16] What is needed is an holistic approach—sometimes termed *the systems approach*—to the human predicament.

The term *holistic* refers to recognizing the whole-part relations not only among the factors such as population, resources, production, and pollution but also between the differentiated regions of the world. Furthermore regions function as wholes with nations as parts; and nations are organized with provinces, counties, cities, and districts as parts. Whole-part relations need to be hierarchically conceived.[17] But hierarchy is not something static; it consists of multileveled organic processes growing interactively. Differential regional, cultural, and political growths influence both the nature of people and communities in one direction and the global whole in the other. Only by understanding the intricacies of multileveled organic growth can we hope to guide mankind on a path more conducive to survival. "Barring suicide, mankind will face the most awesome test in its history: the necessity of a change in the man-nature relationship and the emergence of a new perception of mankind as a living global system."[18]

The book also indicates urgency of global planning. Organic growth, especially its new levels of complexity emerging from increasingly megalopolitan and global interdependencies, has reached a point where holistic planning is needed if mankind as a whole is to survive. The time has come when it is necessary to begin to draw up an organic growth master plan for the world system. This view recognizes the incapacity of nations working independently to cope with the task: "Global issues can be solved only by global concerted action." An international framework capable of organizing the kinds of cooperation needed must be developed. Long-range developments resulting in present crises can be met only by long-range planning and commitment to action. In fact, short-range planning, the kind now occupying national efforts, has become not merely inadequate but counterproductive. [19]

Mankind at the Turning Point makes some specific proposals. One is regional organization. It proposes to divide the world into ten regions, conceived as having "political, economic and environmental coherence" and as "interdependent and mutually interacting." [20] Suggestions of this sort are not new. In 1952, F.S.C. Northrop's *The Taming of the Nations* depicted "seven major cultural political units" constituting the world. [21]

Another proposal considers world consciousness. Increased sensitivity of persons to human problems (such as poverty, famine, epidemics, and earthquakes) elsewhere in the world can be expected only if more feel identified with mankind as a whole. Properly guided organic growth would both promote and profit from greater world consciousness. It would include feelings of identification with future generations also.

A new ethic is required. Recognition of the limited amounts of irreplaceable resources requires more conscientious usage of such resources. Willingness to save and conserve instead of wasting and destroying are central to such an ethic.

The last proposal concerns harmony with nature. Man is integral to nature. Among the limits needing recognition are limits of human disharmony with nature. Awareness of the interdependence of man and nature begets an attitude that prolonged human survival can be expected only if persons are willing to live in harmony with nature rather than trying to exploit its limited riches for selfish and temporary desires.

Mankind at the Turning Point, however, does not go far enough. In spite of its call for "a new perception of mankind as a living global system," it still provides no hint (except as implicit in its mentioning greater complexity, multihierarchy, and organic growth) that the philosophical presuppositions must be reexamined and that quantum leap conceptions organized into a new system gestalt are needed. It neglects to recognize that obsolete philosophies making positive contributions to our crises need to be eliminated or reduced in their effectiveness.

Although clearly recognizing that values must be considered in understanding our predicament and that changes in values will be involved in the new perception, it fails to recognize that capacity for the intelligent reevaluation of values needed will require recognizing axiology and ethics as basic sciences requiring support by research funds to provide the reliable knowledge required.

Although it calls for "a new ethic in the use of resources," it fails to recognize the need for a new ethic in most fields and decisive efforts to meet and reverse trends toward progressive demoralization.

The role of philosophy in its comprehensive functioning as the chief interdisciplinary science is entirely ignored.[22] The need for a new metaphysics and a new logic is only partly recognized. Organic growth implies an organic metaphysics, an organic logic, and an organic mathematics. Mesarovic's insightful mathematical systems theory does not go far enough. Several other projects designed to advance research beyond the results presented in *The Limits to Growth* were commissioned and sponsored. Two additional books have become available as I write: *Catastrophe or New Society?* and *Reshaping the International Order.*[23]

Catastrophe or New Society? A Latin American World Model intentionally expresses a perspective of persons in underdeveloped countries. It claims that "the major problems facing society are not physical [resources are "practically inexhaustible," "pollution can be controlled"] but sociopolitical. These problems are based on the uneven distribution of power, both between nations and within nations." They can be solved only by radical changes, with a "shift toward a society that is essentially socialist, based on equality and full participation of all its members in the decisions affecting them." "The only truly adequate way of controlling population growth is by improving basic living conditions."[24]

They would eliminate both private and state ownership of land and the means of production and substitute "more universal concepts of the use and management of the means of production." "Management would be the responsibility of production units, ad hoc committees, and/or communes of the state." Although "the ultimate objective would be . . . some form of organization on a world scale, the model concentrates on developing regions: Latin America, Africa, and Asia." These regions would rely mainly on their own resources, but "regional complementarity plays an essential role in autonomous development." "The privileged sections of mankind . . . should reduce their rate of economic growth," and "part of the economic surplus of these countries should be channeled into helping the countries of the Third World."[25]

Although optimization of personal participation in social self-control at many levels is an ideal I share, proposing "full participation of all its members in the decisions affecting them" overlooks important facts of the increasingly complicated nature of many megalopolitan and global problems that puts understanding them beyond the reach of most members. All persons in developing countries may understand what they lack; but intricacies in processes for producing goods and political order in developed countries are far beyond the understanding of most (some would say all) persons. It is unrealistic to propose that every person participate fully in making decisions where the requisite understanding is possessed only by specialists who have become experts. I suggest that this model would be improved by replacing "full" by "optimum" participation and by recognizing that some persons well fitted for deciding some policy issues are completely unfitted for deciding others. In addition, some persons prefer to be freed from responsibilities for some kinds of decisions while devoting themselves more fully to other kinds or to other responsibilities.

The model fails to recognize the urgency of the need for a world government sufficient to rescue mankind from current crises. (It prefers not to see population, pollution, and holocaustic war as critical.) It fails to recognize the significance of growing demoralization—it attributes alienation to exploitation, and does not recognize that currently demoralization rates are more rapid in affluent than in poor countries—and the need for definite efforts to restore needed morality. It advocates a spirit of "solidarity," "international solidarity," and assumes that if "all humanity could attain an adequate standard of living" demoralization would somehow disappear automatically. It fails to recognize the evils of obsolete and false religious beliefs and practices. It claims, "In no way is it acceptable to have birth control imposed compulsorily, either directly or indirectly."[26] Whether intentionally or not, it minimizes the importance of overpopulation by rationalizations consistent with Roman Catholic doctrine. It seems unaware of the growing gap between human problem-solving capacities, guided by present philosophies, and the rapidly multiplying complexities of world crisis problems. The model contains no hint of a need for quantum leap conceptions in understanding our intricate and dynamic predicaments.

Reshaping the International Order resulted from an ambitious team research project (21 specialists consulting 350 persons and institutions all over the world) financed by the Netherlands Minister for Development Cooperation, coordinated by Jan Tinbergen and directed by Jan van Ettinger.[27]

This thoroughly researched review of the international order states its recommendations cautiously, intends its conclusions to be tentative, and expects follow-up activities. Although recognizing that the current system of nation-states fails to serve mankind as a whole, that there is a need for "reinterpretation of national sovereignty," and a gradual "conscious transfer of power" from nations to a world organization, it refuses to recommend a world government. Although it proposes "a system for global planning and management of resources" and "progressive internationalization and socialization of all world resources," it aims at a "decentralized planetary sovereignty" with a "network of strong international institutions." Although it aims at "an equitable social order," a "humanistic socialism," and "a world organization working on a truly democratic basis," it recognizes that each Third World nation must "strive for its own intellectual liberation" and that "each nation must, within the foreseeable future, be responsible for its own well-being."[28]

The means for achieving its aims, including "changes in the existing distribution of power," is the United Nations, which is "the only real machinery with the potential for constructing a fairer world." It realizes the United Nations needs restructuring but includes no proposals for restructuring that organization. It recommends changes in financial and monetary institutions, reduction in defense spending, a world disarmament agency, a stronger United Nations peace force, a world treasury, international taxation of international productive resources, international division of labor, control of technological development, reduction of social tensions, and "research institutes all over the world." It claims that the "world is ruled by ideas—rational and ethical—and not by vested interests" and emphasizes the "responsibilities of specialists."[29]

I am very sympathetic to the cautious and concerned explorations and tentative proposals presented in this report. But its refusal to recognize a need for an effective world government, even in the distant future, seems unrealistic. Governments are not ready to surrender national sovereignty today, but the progressive aggravation of crises, which cripple nations even without war, seems likely to force those that become desperate to call for effective collective action of some sort. Since the structure of a world government forced on the world by disastrous circumstances, whether of war, blackmail, or economic supremacy of some nation, seems less likely to be fair to all than one designed by the intelligent efforts of "scientists, moralists and concerned citizens," I do not see why the report does not propose the needed world government.[30]

Also in spite of its recommendations regarding research institutes, it fails completely to recognize the need for the use of scientific methods in developing the foundational principles of axiology and ethics as ultimate bases for moral appeals. It neglects the need for some minimal world philosophy, world ethics, and world religion to sustain the needed voluntary, wisely self-interested cooperation of persons in all nations in bringing about the redistribution of power required for democratic survival.

Goals for Mankind

Ervin Laszlo, a Hungarian musician turned philosopher and professor of philosophy in the State University of New York College at Geneseo, was commissioned to conduct a study on goals for global society, emphasizing values neglected in previous studies. His team (consisting of a core group, including Radh Achuthan, Alexander Bocast, Anthony J. Fedanzo, Joseph M. Firestone, Thomas E. Jones,

Hwa Yol Jung, Petee Jung, John H. Reinfrank, George Riggan, Steven Rosell, Charlotte Waterlow, Jong Y Yoo, and at least twenty-three consultants and collaborators) gathered material enabling him to write *Goals for Mankind: A Report to the Club of Rome on the New Horizons of the Global Community*.[31]

Laszlo reviews problems relating especially to the gap between developed and developing countries and believes that both kinds of countries should develop further, but not in the same ways. He approves satisfying legitimate demands for housing, food, clothing, jobs, and medical and social services. He warns against side-effects of efforts to improve the quality of life, such as urban congestion, alienation, invasion of privacy, unemployment, and inflation. He advocates reducing energy wastes, increasing conservation measures, improving education, the selective development of new technologies, and teaching the poor masses in developing countries to appreciate their own cultures as well as to make use of industrial achievements.

Laszlo does not advocate a world government but believes that an international agency to coordinate energy research and development is needed, and that global security may be sought through a balanced reduction of military strength. His major contribution to the Club of Rome modeling efforts is his emphasis on a "level of solidarity" that is necessary for the kind of collaboration needed to achieve mankind's goals. He holds that contemporary religions have vital roles to play, and he surveys in some detail their possible effects on world solidarity. After examining Judaism, Christianity, Islam, Hinduism, and Buddhism, he concludes that they have observable potential for promoting unity but that their performance falls short of achievement. He deplores prevailing divisiveness, exclusiveness, and intolerance but notes that some religions are beginning to evolve new forms of humanism.

Being highly sympathetic with Laszlo's project, I limit my criticisms to some differences in emphases: I believe that we cannot achieve global security without some minimal world government. I believe that, despite their potentiality, existing major religions are trapped in too much cultural lag to contribute much effectively, that their current influences are actually more harmful and disunifying than beneficial and unifying, and that efforts to design a new religion based on present needs and present knowledge should receive high priority. I believe that a sound foundation in axiology, the science of values, is necessary before we can construct a demonstrably reliable science of ethics that is needed as a basis for other value sciences—economics, sociology, political science, and religion—needed as foundations for sound policy decisions. I believe that interdisciplinary research institutes should be developed deliberately for the purpose of dealing with social, political and religious problems at national and, especially, global levels. These differences in emphases may turn out to be differences in kind, if I have misunderstood Laszlo's intentions.

WORLD ORDER MODELS

A second international movement endeavoring to understand and improve our world predicaments, the World Order Models Project (WOMP), originated under the guidance of Saul H. Mendlovitz. He first established the World Law Fund and then the Institute for International Order, which became the Institute for World Order. The World Law Fund aimed to influence "world educational effort" to bring about a "system of international relations in which war has been eliminated and world wide economic welfare and social justice have been achieved." This movement originated among political scientists, whereas the Club of Rome membership consists primarily of industrialists.

Common aims of WOMP participants center around five problems. The original problem, prevention of war, was supplemented in 1966 by concern for economic well-being and social justice, since, without these, war could not be eliminated. By 1974, pollution problems had become so severe that the ideal of ecological stability was added. To these Mendlovitz added a fifth problem, "alienation" (or the "identity crisis").

WOMP operates through meetings in different countries, regional research groups, and publication of books and periodicals. Its first two books were Jagdish Bhagwati's *Economics and World Order* (1972) and Ali Mazrui's *Africa and World Affairs* (1973). In 1974,

Mendlovitz edited *On the Creation of a Just World Order*, introducing a series on "Preferred Worlds for the 1990s." This series includes Rajni Kothari's *Footsteps into the Future* (1974), Richard A. Falk's *A Study of Future Worlds* (1975), Ali Mazrui's *A Federation of World Cultures* (1976), and Johan Galtung's *The True Worlds: A Transnational Perspective* (1977).

Its periodicals include *Transition*, a bimonthly progress report of institute news, and *Alternatives: A Journal of World Policy*, a quarterly edited by Rajni Kothari at the Centre for the Study of Developing Countries in New Delhi. *Alternatives* includes annually a "state of the globe message," evaluating local, regional, and global developments relative to the world order ideals and making recommendations for future action.

On the Creation of a Just World Order

Cooperative efforts to deal with world crises seems best exemplified by *On the Creation of a Just World Order*, edited by Saul H. Mendlovitz and eight contributers. Ali A. Mazrui, "World Culture and the Search for Human Consensus," examines obstacles to achieving consensus and recommends seeing "world order in terms of a federation of human culture contributions, combining in a global pool of shared achievement with local pools of distinctive innovation and tradition." Rajni Kothari, "World Politics and World Order: The Issue of Autonomy," explores issues of dominance of developing countries by developed countries and recommends "the realization of the dignity and autonomy of men, and hence of states. Other values—justice, nonviolence, participation—follow from this basic concern."[32]

Gustavos Lagos, "The Revolution of Being," points out that those living in underdeveloped countries experience inferior being and advocates an "integral development of man" through the "elimination of economic underdevelopment and external dependence," with special reference to Latin America. Carl-Friedrich von Wiezsaker, "A Skeptical Contribution," attributes world modeling efforts to "intellectual activism," claims that "what this world cannot master are the realities in man that are not present in his expressed ideas," and expects "growing crises culminating in catastrophe."[33]

Johan Galtung, "Nonterritorial Actors and the Problems of Peace," surveys multiplicities of international organizations, evaluates their potential for influencing world peace, and prefers a world with "a balance between association and dissociation, to conquer the evils of structural and direct violence." Yoshikazu Sakamoto, "Toward Global Identity," examines kinds of positive and negative identity, trends relative to transnational identification, and how a person can "identify himself with humanity without the depersonalizing effects that a big global organization . . . might bring forth."[34]

Richard A. Falk, "Toward a New World Order: Modest Methods and Drastic Revisions," is convinced that "the existing system does not deal adequately with individual and social problems and will become less capable . . . in the future," believes that "a new order will be born no later than early in the next century," and urges "a spontaneous mass movement for world-order reform." Paul T. K. Lin, "Development Guided by Values: Comments of China's Road and Its Implications," observes, "The inevitable and principal trend today is revolutionary change, towards the full emancipation of countries, nations and classes." He views "China's dynamic society" as "an enormously instructive paradigm of fundamental change."[35]

This work is significant for its warnings about drift toward catastrophe and "lack of creative thinking" about the "major crises, e.g., war, social injustice, widespread poverty, ecological imbalance and alienation" that "defy national solutions" and for its urging acceptance of responsibility for bringing about "a human and just world order." Its primary solution to world crisis problems consists of redistributing wealth and power. But awareness of the gap between adequate understanding of philosophical presuppositions and political practices is missing, and the significance of demoralization and the need for axiological and ethical science research as a necessary means for remoralization is not mentioned by any of the contributers. One Mendlovitz remark has a quantum-leap quality about it: "The fact that the overwhelming majority of mankind understands for the first time in history that human society encompasses the entire globe is a phenomenon equivalent to mankind's understanding that the globe is round rather than flat."[36] But awareness of globalism alone does not go far toward the quantum-leap conceptions needed to provide guidance for cooperative living on a global scale.

Footsteps into the Future

Rajni Kothari of the Centre for the Study of Developing Countries in New Delhi, wrote the learned and cautious *Footsteps into the Future: A Diagnosis of the Present World and a Design for an Alternative.* He claims that "the autonomy and dignity of man, and, as a necessary condition thereof, the autonomy and dignity of states as well" are necessary bases for justice and nonviolence in the world. [37]

Admittedly expressing a Third World viewpoint, Kothari sees the main problem as "the economic gap between rich and poor," which "continues to widen." Although it "arises out of an exponential growth in the number of human beings," Kothari claims that living conditions would be better if present technology had not spread over the earth since it has contributed to "this surfeit of human beings." Although actual colonialism has virtually ceased, economic and cultural colonialism persists. "The most relevant revolution that needs to be carried out has to be directed against the overpowering culture, the dominant world view," prevailing in First World countries. First World countries will not voluntarily surrender dominance, so Third World countries must take initiative. [38]

His solution includes a reduction of First World technological growth, the transfer of much technology from developed to underdeveloped nations but not to present First World levels, increasing autonomy for Third World nations, and retention of the nation-state as "integral to any movement toward a better world." He would reduce the multiplicities of nations to about twenty or twenty-five political units, each aiming at self-sufficiency and autonomy, because "a world state is not the answer to this crisis." His vision is one of "creative anarchy" in which changes from dependence to independence will then evolve to interdependence in ways to be brought about by the Third World. [39]

My criticisms of Kothari's alternative all focus on his world model as seen from a Third World perspective, which he has ably presented. He seems unaware that the same technology that has promoted population growth by improving health can, by other methods, aid in population reduction. Not only does population decline as standards of living rise, but also deliberate use of birth control methods, including the millions of vasectomies performed in India since Kothari's book was written, can reduce population. He neglects to blame the persisting cultural tyranny of ancient religions that refuse to recognize truths that have been scientifically demonstrated. The evils of obsolete false doctrines seem much more debilitating to underdeveloped than to overdeveloped nations.

His fear that any world government will become an "insufferable leviathan" grows naturally from his feeling tyrannized by First World power and culture. But that any anarchic association of twenty-five nations can solve world crises by benevolent interaction appears to me naive. In a world where intricate interdependence already exists, idealizing twenty-five autonomous self-sufficient regions as a solution seems unrealistic. The deterioration of strength, both political and cultural, in leading First and Second World nations (Great Britain is now a most obvious example) is a factor Kothari has not taken into account.

The growth in numbers of nuclear reactors and nuclear bombs, and the availability of these to terrorists as well as to national armies, is generating a critical mass that brings us ever closer to the threatened holocaust. Nothing short of a world government with the power to control all world-endangering armaments will save us. Although Kothari rightly represents Third World concern for getting a bigger slice of the pie, he fails to see that there may be no pie to slice if we do not take effective measures to develop the needed world self-control. I believe the Third World peoples have more to gain from the development of a world government than do First and Second World countries, and that cooperative initiative by Third World leaders can bring about a system more favorable to their interests than waiting for the collapse of First and Second World institutions and an emergency concoction of a world-control system by desperate antagonists. But Third World leaders will have to achieve a whole-world perspective if they are to succeed in proposing what will be needed to overcome world crises.

A Study of Future Worlds

Richard A. Falk's *A Study of Future Worlds* is an extensive study of alternative world order systems for realizing WOMP values. [40] In addition to the first four—peace, well-being, justice, and ecological quality—he adds eight of his own: social conditions promoting harmony, joy, creativity; elimination of coercive governmental authority; conditions conducive to beauty, privacy, and dignity; a conception of ethics as including man-and-nature relations; experiments with organizing human activities; an affirmation of the diversity of life types and humanistic belief systems; a better appreciation of differences in male and female value perspectives; and the use of science and technology in ways that ensure the realization of human values.

Falk argues that "state sovereignty impedes rational management of these issue-areas at present" and that we need "some greatly augmented capacity for central guidance in affairs, including some increase in coercive authority," if these values are to be realized. We may not need a "world government," but "central guidance implies a unified capacity for policy-formation, -coordination and -implication." He examines the logic of a world order constituted exclusively by the sovereign states, the logic of transnationalism and the logic of supranationalism and notes exponential growths of international institutions supported by cooperating governments, of international movements of goods, ideas, and people without government participation, and of multinational corporations. [41]

But he is "not optimistic" about prospects. "Governing groups are locked into an obsolete system of values and beliefs and are, therefore, not capable of defining the interests of their populations." He observes that "vested interest groups are now pondering global reform options; the American public is not." Yet if energy and food shortages are "persuasively interpreted as world order storm warnings, there exists an unprecedented opportunity for rapid mass education on the need for global reform." Falk is more concerned about what conditions would be required for the adoption of which policy than about making a specific proposal. He invites "each one of us . . . to assist in his grave but exhilarating struggle to achieve global reform at the eleventh hour of the human race." [42]

Falk's cautious survey of options is primarily from an American perspective and does not consider how Asian preconceptions must be accommodated in the emerging world culture and reflected in needed world government policies. He seems not to be fully aware of the seriousness of progressing demoralization. Although he recognizes the debilitating effects of obsolete belief systems, he seems not to foresee the need for the emergence of a world belief system involving quantum-leap conceptions. We are indebted to Falk for seriously surveying our "bleak" prospects, for examining the merits and demerits of many possible options, and for expressing faith that "global humanism . . . can be achieved" if "its pursuit is the highest priority of people everywhere."[43]

A Federation of World Cultures

Ali A. Mazrui deserves my highest recommendation for his competently written wide-ranging study, *A Federation of World Cultures: An African Perspective*, fairly presenting many complexities inherent in African and Third World perspectives. The work is enlightening, scholarly, frank, considerate, and benevolent in its factual surveys and evaluative comparisons. I share Mazrui's faith that "the world of tomorrow can be tamed either through outright force or through shared values" (preferably the latter) and that "mankind is on the verge of a great empathetic leap."[44]

But I disagree that the emerging culture can best be discerned from a deliberately African perspective, or from an intentionally Indian, Chinese, Marxist, American, or any other national or regional perspective. Particularized perspectives are inherently reductionistic. This is why the Philosopher's World Model is needed. Its aim is to be comprehensive, universal, and global in perspective in a way that incorporates the truths as seen from particular perspectives as much as possible. Mazrui may condemn my perspective as American rather than as global. To a certain extent he would be correct; but it is also philosophical in a way that intends to represent a human global perspective genuinely concerned with the welfare of mankind as a whole.

Mazrui's aim is that there "should not be a world government but a world culture." I object; the aim should be both a world government and a world culture. The two interdepend. But Mazrui's aim is not at a world culture immediately, but at a world federation of cultures. "The Third World first needs to generate its own nationalistic momentum" and "a sense of nationalism . . . by which to rebel against encroachments of a Euro-centric cultural universe." He is much disturbed about Third World feelings of dependency, both structural and cultural, and proposes creating a "cultural parity as a basis for mutual respect." "The restoration of balance in the cultural arrangements of the world requires a combination of two approaches. First, the formerly colonized societies must seek to protect more effectively their own cultural heritages. Second, Western culture must be infiltrated by non-Western values to help make the global pool of shared culture less Euro-centric and more diversified." "Regional African autonomy . . . would help provide a climate for both cultural and structural independence in the years ahead."[45]

Mazrui is aware of the importance of interdependence as an essential characteristic of human association. Yet his preoccupation with overcoming feelings of dependency causes him to rationalize three stages of interdependence: primitive interdependence, feudoimperial interdependence, and mature interdependence. "Only a combination of an egalitarian ethic and reciprocal vulnerability, within a framework of wider technological and intellectual frontiers, can provide the foundation for mature interdependence." "Reciprocal vulnerability" must be a precondition of maturity because "the emotions required for the rebellion against dependency will have to look for their ultimate sustenancy to the still relatively dormant reserves of dignity and national pride, especially among the colored peoples of Asia and Africa."[46]

Mazrui seems to be trying to reconstruct the world from the viewpoint of his feudoimperialistic stage and expecting "mature interdependence" only after national pride has been aroused from dormancy and satisfied that equality of esteem has been achieved. Such feelings of equal esteem would be supported by a balance of armaments.[47] I object to his conception of "mature interdependence" as consisting ultimately of a world federation of regional or national cultures. There is one more, still higher, stage of interdependence that he neglects: interdependence between a world culture and the various regional, national, and more local cultures. In a whole-part interdependence, the whole depends upon the parts, as well as the parts upon the whole. Each, the whole and each of the parts, is partly dependent on and partly independent of all of the others. Not until we achieve "organic interdependence" will a genuinely mature interdependence be attained.

I have no objection to Mazrui's presentation of his "African perspective," but I cannot accredit it as an adequate world order model. The world is missing from his perspective, as I see it; so it is up to the Philosopher's World Model to supply what is missing.

I believe that black Africans will gain more from efforts to establish a minimal world government immediately than from efforts to unfreeze the "frozen war" necessitated by racial and cultural pride and to suffer from interregional struggles as well as from costs of "counterpenetration into the ranks of the powerful."[48]

OTHER MODELS

In addition to the Club of Rome series and the World Order Models series, many other world models have been proposed by individuals working alone or with research institute staff assistance. The number has become extensive. Space limitations require selections.

The Year 2000

Herman Kahn and Anthony J. Wiener, authors of *The Year 2000; A Framework for Speculation on the Next Thirty-Three Years*, [49] exemplify managers of a financially successful private interdisciplinary research institute with considerable experience. The Hudson Institute, headquartered in New York, has branches in Paris, Hudson Research Europe, Ltd., Montreal, Hudson Institute of Canada, Inc., and Tokyo, Hudson Institute-East Asia. It is a nonprofit institute with sixty-six public members, sixty-two fellows, a staff of fifty-three members, and an income from all sources of more than $3 million according to its 1974 *Report to Members*.

Kahn and his colleagues expertly explore varieties of alternatives relative to their problems and give arguments for each, always carefully qualifying prospects by citing arguments against it. When called on by clients to predict the future, they claim that although "it will be worth while to try to improve our understanding of future possibilities . . . the problem is ultimately too difficult, and these efforts can never be entirely successful."[50] Although a major work in progress, *Prospects for Mankind*, may tell a different story, Kahn's general attitude seems to be summed up in the title of a memorandum, "A Slightly Optimistic World Context for 1975-2000."[51] He expects the economic growth increase to extend far into the next century and believes that the United States will continue to lead other nations in gross national product. He expects most people will be well off by 2000, and the rest will become so soon after. Although the Hudson Institute has published the three-volume *American Values: Past and Future* (1974) for the National Endowment for the Humanities, and has submitted a work identifying national objectives and choices to be faced regarding the quality of life in the United States to the Commission on Critical Choices for Americans, I have found no hint that the best way to reach decisions about values is to ground ourselves soundly in a science of values and a science of ethics so that we may then have a basis on which to build reliable arguments regarding choices. I find myself in the uncomfortable position of admiring an institute that has done much worthy interdisciplinary work and of regretting that it does not recognize axiology and ethics as basic disciplines.

World Without Borders

Lester A. Brown, in his *World Without Borders*, hopes for cooperation between nations and a sense of world community.[52] He reviews our environmental crises, the widening rich-poor gap, urbanization, unemployment, and hunger and proposes some keys to the future, including stabilizing population, reducing armament dangers, and improving education. He examines the increasing economic interdependence of nations, the expansion of multinational corporations, the processes restructuring global economy, growth in global communications, and transportation, and numerous new supranational institutions. He calls for a new social ethic incorporating a global minimum standard of living and recognizing that well-being in an interdependent world requires higher levels of cooperation.

We cannot expect to surmount our crises only by reversing some global trends. A workable world order will become possible only if we "reorder global priorities,"[53] especially by reducing military expenditures and shifting from "superaffluence to the elimination of poverty." We are handicapped in trying to go in new directions because we are still "formulating policies and making decisions on the basis of a world that existed some time in the past." But since we must regard a "unified global society . . . as the inevitable reality," we should take steps now to bring it about. [54]

Brown's warnings about the need for an integrated overview if we are to surmount global crises is not accompanied by suggestions that a new, more complex, more dynamic, more intricately conceived philosophy is needed to understand the multidimensional interdependencies and multicultural complexities of the world which we must overview. He sees need for a new ethic but not for a science of ethics providing demonstrable foundations for the new ethic. The Philosopher's World Model calls for a world without philosophical borders, or at least a world philosophy that sees that common goals for human survival and improvement have a basis in human nature present in people in all countries and all cultures.

The Coming of Post-Industrial Society

Daniel Bell, in *The Coming of Post-Industrial Society*, ably interprets trends. [55] He summarizes his comparison of preindustrial, industrial, and postindustrial society relative to six factors: most important resources (land, machinery, knowledge); social location (farm or plantation, business firm, university or research institute); dominant figures (landowner, military generals; businessmen; scientists, and researchers); means of power (direct control of force, indirect influence on politics, balance of technical and political forces and franchises and rights); class base (property, military power; property, political organization, or technical skill; technical skill, political organization); access (inheritance, military seizure; inheritance, patronage, or education; education, mobilization, or cooptation).

Bell is aware that "we in America are moving away from a society based on a private-enterprise market system toward one in which the most important economic decisions will be made at the political level. . . . We now move to a communal ethic, without that community being, as yet, defined. In a sense, the movement . . . is a turn to non-capitalistic modes of social thought." "The post-industrial society is primarily a change in the character of social structure—a dimension, not the total configuration of society." Bell recognizes that "we have moved completely into a world economy." "The world horizon becomes a single canvas, as financial capital increasingly sensitive to differentials in yields, quickly crosses national boundaries in order to obtain better returns on its money." But he offers no plan for world organization. He presents impressive statistics on the knowledge industry but neglects the importance of interdisciplinary science management and of axiology and ethics as sciences and the role of philosophy as a comprehensive discipline. [56]

He observes that growth in specialization has resulted in a multiplication of languages condemning specialists to being increasingly unable to understand each other. We are experiencing a new tower of Babal. If the postindustrial knowledge society involves its own communication crisis, then, I suggest, the quantum-leap system gestalt must find some way to refine techniques for more common utilization of specialized knowledge when needed partly by making specialists more conscious of the larger significance of their work.

In spite of the depth, and breadth, and soundness of Bell's interpretations, the best his "agenda for the future" comes up with is "a reaffirmation of liberalism." His reformed liberalism is based on observations that business, because of inherent contradictions, is unable to sustain itself. Because it fails to meet public needs, it is coming increasingly under public control. But the philosophy of state capitalism has still not been worked out, for we need "a new socio-economic bill of rights which defines for our times the needs that the polity must try to satisfy." [57] He offers no suggestions for a needed world philosophy.

The New American Ideology

George Cabot Lodge, in *The New American Ideology*, describes "how the ideological bases of legitimate authority in America [are] being radically transformed," with shifts from atomism to holism and from specialization to generalization. "The time has come to part from the romance of specialization." He recognizes that "the new planning role of the state is virtually upon us, but its ideological underpinnings are still missing." "The vital tasks for this society are to recognize the ideological meaning of the changes that have already occurred in the real world" and "to work toward the formulation of a new, coherent, and generally acceptable ideology to take the place of the old." "The process of redefinition has already begun." Awareness is developing that "the concept of integrity and independence in the smallest unit (the atom, the individual) suddenly appeared to us as ultimately important about three hundred years ago; but that this concept seems to have yielded to that of the relative importance of the whole and of wholes within wholes—the community, the universe." We are participating in a trend "toward an organic vision."[58]

Lodge adds to the richness of analyses of changing conceptions; but he does not yet see that what we need is not merely a shift in emphasis from parts to wholes (a shift that has other dangers inherent in it) but also one recognizing the need for constant attention to that organic whole which is inclusive of both whole and parts and their dynamic interdependencies. He recognizes a trend "toward organic vision." Yet those who understand the organic by looking from parts to whole see the parts controlled by the whole. A more mature understanding of the organic sees parts and whole as interdepending, both controlling and being controlled by each other partly. Holism is not enough; organicism is needed. Having overemphasized specialization, we now need to reemphasize generalization; even more, we need newly emergent emphases on the interdependence of specialization and generalization and of deliberate dialectical development of each through awareness of how each also becomes modified by means of its own influences in modifying the other.

A Strategy for the Future

Ervin Laszlo, in *A Strategy for the Future*, is less disturbed about crises and more concerned with recognizing that there is already only "one global eco-system." "The next level to be reached in human societal development is that of the world system." To help us understand that world, Laszlo proposes an "anatomy of the next conceptual synthesis."[59]

His inspiration comes from biologist Ludwig von Bertalanffy, an integrative philosopher surpassing the insights previously obtained from Hegelian, Marxian, positivist, and Whiteheadian philosophy. By replacing Whitehead's "notion of 'organism' and its Platonic correlates with the concept of a dynamic, self-sustaining system," he extended general systems theory "into a general systems philosophy."[60] Although seeing the world as an organization, Laszlo adopted many cybernetic ideas, such as homeostasis and feedback, which seem to me to picture processes in a more mechanical and less organic way than seems desirable.

"A global homeostasis defined in reference to complex, both regionally and temporally variable, steady-states is such a preferable pathway. The optimum-state which the World Homeostat System is to maintain through the principle of minimum interference with the political principles and domestic affairs of societies is not a stationary state, arbitrarily frozen at a given level. . . . This state is (i) partially changing, (ii) never fully attained, (iii) a variable yet enduring goal of human striving."[61]

My sympathies for Laszlo's views are great. I, too, believe that "the Whiteheadian synthesis has to be done over again," that Bertalanffy's organicistic conceptions of natural systems provide useful insights, that we should recognize "the growing interdependence of all vital processes on this planet," and that "our conceptual synthesis will have to be scientific at its core."[62] But, I am not yet fully convinced that general systems theory, especially when interpreted cybernetically, is able to meet our challenge. As a movement, systems theory appears to me to involve an irreconcilable split between two conflicting conceptions of the nature of systems. One conception originated from observing interactions between wholes and parts organically interdepending (biological wholes, social wholes, psychological wholes such as "gestalts") and thus presupposes some internal relations. The other conception originated from digital computer programming and presupposes a doctrine of completely external relations exhibited in Boolean algebra and the symbolic logic developed in *Principia Mathematica*.

Since I fear domination of systems societies by persons with financial interests in computer manufacture, operation, and use, I remain uncertain whether the artificial and inadequate conceptions of systems presupposing external relatedness will be properly subordinated as means to understanding and controlling natural systems involving organic relations (including both some internal and some external relatedness).[63]

Another related difference is Laszlo's preference for cybernetic language, which seems to me to be unduly mechanistic when compared with dialectic properly understood as naming natural growth processes involving interactions, transactions, and mutual incorporations of different but complementary processes. His exploration and adoption of "interexistence," while pursuing the *Goals for Mankind* project, places his thinking much closer to mine than does his cybernetic language. [64]

Laszlo's synthesis is primarily Western. He does not attempt to understand and incorporate Asian ideals and to show how their oppositions to Western ideals can be interpreted as complementary and thus as integratable organically into a world system. Hence he does not deal as directly with the dangers of too much idealization of internal relatedness as with those of too much external relatedness. Hence he seems to me unaware of how much of a quantum leap will be needed to comprehend the probably emerging world culture, even though many of his ideas, such as interexistence, are of the kind needed in the proposed quantum-leap philosophy.

Building the City of Man

Historian W. Warren Wager, in *Building the City of Man; Outlines of a World Civilization*, calls the crisis in civilization "The Great Explosion"; it resulted, he says, from accelerating changes bringing human civilization to "its critical mass." "The enemy is change." "The villian is . . . the logic of technique," which has despiritualized man. "The most spectacular fossils in the twentieth century's museum of dead faiths are those of the traditional religions, such as Christianity, Islam, and Buddhism." "As a society we have lost power to . . . create new systems of our own," so we face "the final catastrophe," "the crack of Doom," unless we accept "the inescapable task" of building "a new civilization. . . . We must totalize the search for world order. . . . Anything less is too little." So we must "develop a master strategy for world revolution."[65]

What strategy is needed for building the new cosmopolis, the city of man? "Cosmopolitanism can achieve nothing until it faces a full-blown ideology." It "will demand unqualified loyalty to mankind, against the claims of all segmental polities, tribes and churches. It must be an *integral humanism*." It "explicitly rejects the liberal goals of cultural pluralism and international federalism." "The desirability of a unified world culture is unarguable." However, cosmopolitanism will respect "the freedom, dignity and integrity of the person to the maximum extent compatible with societal need." It will be "in some degree socialist and democratic." It will need a world government "to ensure the democratic distribution of wealth, to prevent crime and rehabilitate criminals, to educate the world citizenry, to curtail population growth, to plan and administer the world industrial complex, to manage the natural environment responsibly, to guard against counterrevolution and civil warfare, and to sponsor mankind's exploration of the universe." "Even a socialist commonwealth can gladly grant the right of enterprise," provided the entrepreneur does not "take more than his share of the world's wealth."[66]

The new society will require the "creation of a new morality," which includes three principles: "reverence for life" (a "yea-saying" to the beings of persons, mankind, and the cosmos), "self-determination" (including freedoms of "belief, speech, publication, artistic expression, association and assembly"), and "union" ("love" and the "will to agree"). It will end patriarchal society, liberate eros, and encourage education ("not less than half of the work of the world will consist of education"). "Hundreds of thousands of universities will exist . . . , with perhaps a quarter of the world's population associated with their communal life."[67]

Critical evaluations of Wager's work are difficult because this historian, behaving like a philosopher, obviously has a fuller grasp of the comprehensive understanding needed for discerning crisis problems and essentials required for a solution than most other world modelers. I find many points of agreement. He does recognize the need for a new "cognitive synthesis" to be accomplished "by facilitating authentically interdisciplinary studies" and by developing a "new race of specialists" with "fields of concentration in a multidimensional world of thought." "We advance dialectically the fuller truth of the coming world culture, toward a synthesis that gave us civilization itself more than six thousand years ago." "The world civilization will indeed constitute a new higher organic manifestation of personal consciousness." He believes that "as many as ten percent of the world's population will consist of professional research and development workers" and that "we shall not reach the organic world civilization without the help of a new living religious faith."[68]

Our differences are perhaps minor. Tempermentally, I am democratic, but he is an elitist. "In all revolutions, a few pre-eminent minds do most of the thinking and planning." "The formation of revolutionary elites is therefore imperative." "We must first bring into being an authentic world political party . . . , with underground as well as above-ground organizations." I do not foresee the course of world revolution and the consequences of probable violence. I hope only for a minimal world government to begin with. Wager classifies "minimalism" among his "myths." He prefers "the policy of the whole hog," "a revolutionary doctrine of cultural monism," and a dissolution of "most of the political frontiers of the old civilizations, and begin afresh." I hope for demonstrable knowledge, emphasizing comprehensive interdisciplinary research as a necessary means. Wager condemns "salvation by science" as "unintelligent" unless supported by a "party of evangelists" willfully motivated. He does not include me among his elite.[69]

Despite his awareness of the need for new morality and of scientific research as a means, I detect no sensitivity relative to axiology and ethics as basic general sciences urgently needing attention. I believe that our utter neglect of the problem of understanding the ultimate bases for moral appeals constitutes a major cause of our crises, and attention to this problem should have top priority. Until reliable knowledge about the ultimate nature of values and obligations can be demonstrated and popularized, efforts toward a "cognitive synthesis" for a world religion or evangelical politics will remain without solid footing. Existential will to project a new ethics cannot succeed without a groundwork of demonstrable reasons. Wager emphasized lack of will. I stress lack of reason. My complaint is that we lack the will to find the reasons.

THE WORLD MODEL.
WHY IS IT NEEDED?

Human survival depends upon a fuller understanding of our present predicament. This predicament consists in part of accelerating crises tending toward human extinction if we do not intelligently modify the course of future trends. Recent and current efforts by responsible leaders to cope with our crises by proposing research-based models have failed because they are insufficient. The development of a sufficient model, a plan adequate for dealing effectively with our predicament, requires the greater comprehension and comprehensiveness that can come only with a philosophical perspective.

WHAT IS PHILOSOPHY?

Our question is an old one. It arose when a human being first wondered: "What is life?" and "Why live?" Our question is also a common one. It recurs today in every life that inquires: "What am I here for?" "Does life have meaning?" Philosophy originates in questions, which prod persons to seek answers. Thus philosophy continues as a quest for answers, an inquiry into the nature and meaning of life. Philosophy, said my teacher, Roy Wood Sellars, "is a persistent attempt to gain insight into the nature of the world and of ourselves by means of systematic reflection."[1] When we achieve answers to our philosophical questions, they too can be called *philosophy*. So our view of life is our philosophy. The view of a group, a culture, a civilization, a *weltanschauung*, is a philosophy. Philosophy thus consists, first of all, of questions, the quest for answers, and the answers one gives to these questions. But there is more, much more.

The simplest way to present a clear picture of the extent and complexity of philosophy is to summarize systematically six components essential to full understanding: problems, attitudes, methods, activities, conclusions, and effects.

Problems

Although not every person who asks questions about life raises all of the following, the task of professional philosophers remains unfinished until they have faced and struggled with at least the following problems. The problems are of two sorts—comprehensive and specialized. Or perhaps we should call them *more comprehensive* and *less comprehensive* because all are very general in nature. Since scientific methods may be used in dealing with these problems, we are justified in calling them *philosophical sciences*, including one increasingly neglected: philosophy as a comprehensive science.

The philosophical sciences originate when persons ask certain typical questions about life and the universe. Inquiry about the nature of existence and its universal characteristics is called *metaphysics*. Whenever someone proposes an observed trait as universal—as present in everything that exists—that proposal becomes a problem in metaphysics. Examples of such proposals, or questions, are: What is space? What is time? What is cause? What is substance? What are relations? What is permanence? What is change? What is process? What are universals? What kinds of beings are there? What is the nature of self? How are mind and body related? Is there a god or gods and, if so, what is the nature of god? (Some regard this question as sufficiently significant to originate a still different science, called *theology*.)[2]

Discovering that some of one's beliefs do not serve satisfactorily, that doubts arise, that certainty is not assured, persons ask, What is truth? What is certainty? What is knowledge? Problems faced in answering these questions serve to originate *epistemology*, or *theory of knowledge*. Since some seek certainty through inference, inquiries into the nature of valid inference, and into the structure of thought and of what thought is about as bases for such inference, have come to be called *logic*. Since physicists, biologists, economists, and others make claims, some of which later turn out to be false, inquiry into the nature of science and methods used by scientists in conducting their inquiries has itself become a science called *philosophy of science*. As difficulties with language provoke problems in communication, including scientific communication, further inquiries into the nature of language are now called *philosophy of language*.

Whoever asks, Is life worthwhile? wants to know whether it is good or bad and whether it may become better or worse. Questions about the nature of values, which occur daily to most people, I suspect, are among the most important questions we can ask. Unfortunately our cultural heritage is suffused with confusions, and a major cause of our incapacity thus far to deal intelligently with our crises, I believe, is not merely lack of understanding but positive misunderstandings about the nature of values. Unfortunately also some movements have vested interests in perpetuating and increasing such misunderstandings. But such confusions can be clarified if we reexamine the basic presuppositions inherent in asking questions about value in the first place.

Four closely related sciences grow out of our value inquiries. The most general, and the most basic, consists of inquiries into the general nature of good and bad. These quickly become inquiries into the distinction between ends and means, or intrinsic values (ends-in-themselves) and instrumental values (means-to-ends). Until one can locate and understand the intrinsic values of life, he cannot understand life's meaning and how to act so as to maximize life's value. The most general science of values is called *axiology*.

Intrinsic values appearing as objects are experienced as aesthetic, and the objects are called "beautiful" or "ugly." Inquiries concerning beauty and ugliness constitute the science called *aesthetics*, together with inquiries about instruments employed in producing them, usually referred to as *art* or, more specifically, as *fine art*.

When faced with two alternatives, one of which appears better than the other, what ought one to do? Choose the better. Why? Because it is better. Oughtness, I propose, consists in the power that an apparently greater good has over an apparently lesser good in compelling our choices. Inquiries into the nature of oughtness, obligation, duty, rightness, justice, and conscience originate, and continue to constitute, *ethics* as a science. Failure to understand the simple, fundamental, and pervasive nature of oughtness and rightness and morality persists as a continuing cause of our crises and of our inabilities to deal with them effectively.

The fourth value science, consisting of a field of questions even more pervaded with misunderstanding than ethics, if that is possible, is *philosophy of religion* (our culture has refused to adopt the word *religionology*). Religion is concern for ultimate values, for the value of life as a whole. The religion adopted by a culture represents its endeavor to understand not merely the nature of self, society, and the universe but also how values originated, why they persist and can be achieved and maximized, and what can be expected of them in the future. Without a sound axiology, there cannot be a sound religion.

In addition to the foregoing three groups of philosophical sciences, those related to questions about the nature of existence, knowledge, and values are questions about the nature of society and its major constituents. One who inquires into the nature of human association, groups, and culture is engaging in *social philosophy*. When you ask about the nature of wealth, income, production, consumption, exchange, and distribution of wealth, you are entering the field of *economic philosophy*. When you pose questions about the nature of social control, governance, or regulating the behavior of persons and groups, you put yourself in the arena of *political philosophy*. What is education, teaching, learning? This question is the source of *philosophy of education*. The question, "What is history?" initiates *philosophy of history*. All of these can be regarded also as value sciences to the extent that their questions and answers presuppose value questions and answers. But they are metaphysical also when one asks whether groups, culture, exchange, control, and learning exist. They extend to epistemology by inquiring how one knows about groups, culture, exchange, and control.

Without completing a list of philosophical subsciences, and more specialized sciences, such as those called *philosophy of marriage, philosophy of business, philosophy of war, and philosophy of recreation*, I turn to all of the other sciences constituting human inquiries about the way things are. Physics, chemistry, astronomy, geography, geology, biology, physiology, psychology, anthropology, sociology, economics, political science, and so forth originated with specific questions. Geology, the science of the earth, astronomy, the science of the stars, psychology, the science of the soul (original-ly), began with questions about the nature of the earth, the stars, and the soul. When these questions are most general, they too can be re-garded as philosophical. Philosophy of physics, for example, and metaphysics sometimes ask the same questions. Any failure to find the same answers constitutes a gap in our understanding, which may function as a disability in formulating the comprehensive philos-ophy needed for dealing with our crises.

Philosophy as a comprehensive science grows out of the natural need to fit the answers produced by all of the specialized sciences into a general picture. The questions constituting it arise as naturally as the distinction between some and all, or between parts and the whole. Today when questions and answers have become increas-ingly specialized, their relations with questions about the whole have become more difficult to answer. And they have been increas-ingly neglected. Questions about the whole of life too often have gone unanswered, or people have remained saddled, if not satisfied, with answers originating in simpler societies when simpler views of the universe had to serve.

Since parts and whole naturally interdepend, the growing neglect of attention to how our comprehensive views and our specialized views fit, or fail to fit, together has resulted in an increasing, and in-creasingly important, area of ignorance. The blame for perpetu-ating, and even promoting, such neglect falls on both professional philosophers and professional scientists. But regardless of blame, the growing importance of the necessary guidance of specialists seeking to cope with our crises by a sound, intelligible, relevant, and re-vealing comprehensive philosophy constitutes part of the need for the Philosopher's World Model.

Among the most troublesome, and most important, problems of philosophers trying to understand and deal with today's philosophi-cal crises are those of discovering, recognizing, testing, and keeping in mind presuppositions. When conclusions are drawn from prem-ises, either these premises are conclusions drawn from other prem-ises or they function as first premises. Traditionally philosophers have called them *first principles*. Earlier philosophers regarded them as axioms, or self-evident principles, from which deductions can be made but which themselves are not deduced from any other principles. Since some interpreted axioms as not only primitive or primary but also as unquestionable, many recent philosophers who propose that any principle can be criticized rejected the idea of first principles as axioms and replaced them with *postulates*, propositions proposed as true for the sake of starting an argument.

Regardless of how one stands in this controversy, the problem of discovering which principles must be assumed if certain other deduced principles are true continues to be most fundamental. Someone has said that "philosophy is a quest for the questions you must beg." Without most basic principles, one lacks a foundation upon which to build the structure of a philosophical system. The problem is complicated by the fact that each of the sciences, including the philosophical sciences, has its own specific set of presuppositions, as well as being involved in those general presuppositions inherent in any comprehensive philosophy. A major task of the comprehensive philosopher is to achieve assurance that presuppositions in the various sciences are consistent not only with each other but also with those of philosophy as comprehensive.

Today different philosophies, some of which have shifted answers without revising their presuppositions, contend for acceptance. But confusion prevails because of a prevailing ignorance of these shifts. For example, individualism assuming direct communication between God and each individual soul gave way to individualism assuming that each person had his own private store of perceptions with which to judge what is true. It in turn gave way to individualism assuming the rugged self-reliance of the frontiersman, which gave way to individualism assuming individual rights guaranteed by the Constitution, which gave way to an individualism (existentialism) assuming the ultimacy of each person's act of will (*existenz*), which, when authentic, is freed from all responsibility to anyone for anything except what one may whimsically choose to accept. Individualism as a philosophy is praised today for many different, often conflicting, reasons.

Loss of confidence in our philosophies has arisen because we have habitually neglected to discover and keep in mind their basic prem-

ises. Clarification of conflicting presuppositions and elimination
of those that have become obsolete in our dynamic organic society is
the most important problem facing our culture today. We lack confidence in our officials partly because they are incapable of demonstrating to us the soundness of their policies in terms of demonstrably sound principles. Resort to power (political, economic, military)
is all that is left for those who have lost the power to control (both
themselves and others) through rational appeal to fundamental principles. Prevention of human extinction in a nuclear holocaust depends on rediscovery of the first principles actually operating in
megalopolitan global society and then of guiding our policy decisions in terms of them and demonstrating to all how and why our
own interests are best served by accepting them and embodying
them in our own living practices. This is the philosopher's most important problem. This is mankind's most important problem.

Attitude

Although the popular definition of one's philosophy of life consists of whatever views he holds about it, regardless of how he arrived at them, something more is needed to describe an attitude that
has come to be regarded as necessary in our quest for reliable knowledge. Some call this *objectivity*, or an effort to see things the way
they are, without injecting one's own desires or wishes into the process leading to conclusions. Some call this *the scientific attitude*, and
indeed it is. It is equally as essential to philosophical as to nonphilo-
sophical sciences. Sometimes it is spoken of as the willingness to
follow the argument wherever it may lead. Such an attitude requires
open-mindedness about entertaining unfamiliar answers. It requires
a willingness to remain uncertain and to suspend judgment when evidence needed for deciding an issue is not all in. It involves a willingness to be guided by experience and reason. It involves a willingness
to remain tentative and undogmatic about conclusions, since it is
always possible that future evidence may indicate a different conclusion.

Closed-mindedness and intolerance of differing answers to questions about self, society, and the universe have troubled mankind
since early times. But faced with extinction, mankind must dispense

with the luxury of remaining sure about the utility of solutions devised for nomadic, agricultural, feudal, or early modern problems when coping with much more complex problems today. Also the assurance some specialists acquire in achieving specialized results often extends to their specialized view of their relations to other specialists and to the universe as a whole. Dogmatism among specialists regarding comprehensive problems can be as debilitating as dogmatism about obsolete solutions. I believe that reviving and extending the scientific attitude is necessary if we are to achieve intelligent solutions to problems of human survival.

Method

The philosophical method and the scientific method are the same in general, and I will spend no time here developing details. In addition to having problems, proposing hypotheses, testing hypotheses, revising hypotheses, and retesting them, sometimes devising crucial experiments when issues have become clear-cut, each scientist often has to devise methods peculiarly suited to his kind of problem and even to each particular problem. The philosophical sciences thus share with all other sciences something general, called *the scientific method*, and something specific, which may be called *scientific methods*, which is the need for devising specialized methods for dealing with specific problems.

Since the methodology for dealing with current problems calling for solution by philosophy as a comprehensive science is not well developed, I shall have to propose my own hypotheses about it for consideration. My proposals are more drastic than might have seemed necessary when it appeared that mankind had an indefinite future in which to work its way through to more intelligent and happier solutions. When future shock becomes chronic, philosophical method must adapt itself to ways for designing a philosophical solution incorporating both ideals and techniques for surmounting accelerating changes in a practical philosophy of life.

Activity

Philosophical activity consists of whatever goes on in the minds of persons when they ask philosophical questions, when they formulate answers to their questions, when they search for evidence and valid inference in testing their solutions, and when they communicate with others about such questions, formulations, and tests. Childish questions, youthful wishes, mature convictions, and aging faiths all function philosophically. Professional papers and comments in philosophical meetings, preparing and reading contentious articles, and writing and reading more systematic claims in books also constitute philosophy.

Those who worry about the fate of mankind, explore the prospects and the possibilities, and propose alternative models of possible futures for mankind may be philosophizing. As doomsday evidence magnifies, more existing philosophical activity may consist in fretting about human fate and in speculating about hypotheses that may yet, even if miraculously, save mankind.

Conclusions

For many, philosophy consists of answers to philosophical questions, no matter how they were acquired. One's philosophy of life consists of the views he holds about his life. Often such views are acquired from others—parents, teachers, preachers, companions—without much critical reflection. Professional teachers of philosophy often point to the history of the philosophies of ancient, medieval, and modern thinkers that have survived in literature.

I propose that conclusions deserve to be called *philosophical* in the fullest sense of that term only when they are intended as solutions to philosophical problems reached by means of the philosophical (or scientific) attitude and method. This means that they continue to be held tentatively as working hypotheses to be modified whenever additional evidence indicates need for a change.

Today, when changes accelerate so rapidly that modifications are called for more frequently, more people encounter the incapacity to change their philosophies fast enough to keep up with factual changes. Thus the practical importance of retaining an attitude of tentativity regarding conclusions has reached critical proportions. But also when neglect of concern for keeping practice and presuppositions consistent has resulted in loss of morale, and loss of confidence that we can cope with our problems, the earnest and urgent search for needed relevant presuppositions becomes increasingly important.

The need for reliable conclusions about life in intricately interdependent, dialectically dynamic organic society is so great that the survival of mankind may depend on our achieving them. Drastic revisions are needed more now because of prolonged neglect.

Effects

Philosophy is what philosophy does. Philosophical problems, attitudes, methods, activities, and conclusions influence the lives of persons and of societies. John Dewey claimed that philosophy consists primarily of how it behaves in shaping a civilization.[3]

If, as I claim, one's religion is the practice of one's philosophy, then one's religious behavior is an effect of one's philosophy. If philosophy is love of wisdom (which presupposes some understanding), then religion is trying to live wisely. If the purpose of life is happiness, then no one is wise until he is happy.

But if we have permitted our philosophies to decay, to become obsolete, to become irrelevant, to admit deceptions, and to be neglected, then we deserve the unhappiness brought upon us by current crises. Loss of morale, fear of extinction, distrust of officials, increasing crime rates and nuclear armaments, overpopulation, overrapid use of resources, maldistribution of wealth and income, pollution, racism, and short-sighted nationalism all result partly from philosophical incompetence. There is evidence that not only official and popular philosophy but also professional philosophy is becoming increasingly incompetent. The effect of such incompetence is appalling.[4]

OUR PRESENT PHILOSOPHICAL PREDICAMENT

The complexities in our philosophical crises cannot be fully understood apart from the issues that arose and survived in the history of philosophy, both Western and Asian, and from the major theses contending for supremacy in human consciousness. Philosophical issues interact with political and economic conditions, so globalization of our other crises contributes to additional complexities in-

herent in the need for a world philosophy able to grapple with basic
issues in Asian philosophies as well as with conflicts growing out of
contradictory presuppositions.

Problems Inherited from Our Past

Many complexities of existence were recognized long ago. But existence is so complex that the human mind, which is less complex
than the existence it seeks to understand, has to abstract from its experiences comparatively simple ideas that it then uses to symbolize
general traits of existence. Some persons in some circumstances discover general traits that seem of primary importance for such understandings, whereas others select different traits as primary.

Western civilization has two major taproots, which may be called
Greek and Hebraic. The contributions of Greek thinkers have been
so significant that some historians claim that Western civilization
began in Greece. (Greek civilization, of course, had its own antecedents.) Prominent Greek philosophers idealized law and order,
including natural laws, laws of reasoning, and political laws. We
recognize their important contributions to the origins of mathematics, logic, philosophy of science, metaphysics, axiology, aesthetics,
ethics, and political philosophy.

Greek philosophers recognized some ways in which existence is
complex. Among the problems they studied are "the one and the
many," permanence and change, universals and particulars, genus
and species, form and matter, perfect and imperfect, temporal and
eternal, essence and accident, actual and potential, caused causes
and uncaused causes, possible and necessary, good and bad, and
means and ends. Greek philosophers struggled with the problem of
the unity of opposites and came up with ideas of harmony and of a
mean between extremes. They developed a logic with both contradictory and noncontradictory opposites. They expressed views
ranging from Platonic claims about the ultimate reality of eternally
perfect Forms (Ideas), including the Idea of the Good, to the claims
of Heraclitus that change is so common that "one cannot even step
into the same river twice" and of Epicurus, the hedonist, that intrinsic value consists in momentary, subjective, pleasant feeling. Reac-

tions to claims seeming to be dogmatic resulted in schools proclaiming skepticism and agnosticism.

These problems and views are still with us. Two millenia of exploration of these problems have demonstrated some dangers of carrying partial explanations to reductive extremes, but time has also added new dimensions of these problems. Any philosophy adequate for our needs will have to provide satisfactory solutions to metaphysical, axiological, and ethical problems. As long as these problems are not solved in ways consistently supporting a workable, coherent, general perspective, they remain unsolved and call urgently for solution today.

Hebraism had its own kinds of complexities. The issue of whether there are many gods or only one took centuries to work out. The same was true of questions about whether god is a person or a nature power, like a jealous tribal chieftain or like a caring father, powerful enough to win local battles or powerful enough to have created the whole world. Evolution from the ethics of vengeance (seventy of theirs for one of ours) through the ethics of justice ("eye for an eye," "son for a son") to "justice tempered with mercy" accompanied the development of the ideal of ethical monotheism. Idealizing a god who created the world and mankind by an act of will, who contracted with Jews to lead men to do his will, and promised punishment for those who refuse (and thus sin), and exhibited repeatedly mercifulness to Jews and others who did not deserve it finally developed. The will of God revealed from time to time and recorded in scriptures, together with multitudes of interpretive comments (Talmud and Torah), provide authoritative sources of knowledge. Hebraic theism and scriptures continue to contribute influentially to our present predicament, both directly through Jewish religious teachings and practices (and Zionist and Israeli military budgets and political policies) and indirectly through influences on Christian and Islamic doctrines and practices.[5]

Two Jews, Jesus and Paul, are credited with originating Christianity. Jesus taught that "love casteth out fear," "Heaven is here within you or among you," and "God is love." Paul taught "Christ and him crucified, and risen from the dead" and repentance for sins in readiness for the return ("second coming") of Christ. Differing in-

terpretations by New Testament writers were complicated by difficulties expressing Jesus' Aramaic ideas in the Greek language
shaped somewhat by philosophical controversies. Early church
fathers disagreed among themselves so much that King Constantine,
converted on a battlefield when promised victory, called them together to settle their differences. The creed drafted at Nicaea and
modified at Chalcedon became orthodox. Conflicting interpretations were declared heresies. Although demanding credal acceptance
brought some unity, diversities of views expressed in the books of
the Old and New Testaments constituting the church-authorized
Bible continue to serve as sources of conflicting interpretations.[6]

Christian theology shaped up in the mind of Augustine, a Roman
Catholic bishop who had previously been converted to Manichae-
ism (belief in the two gods of light and darkness) and then to the neo-
Platonism of Plotinus (who had absorbed Hindu ideals of ultimate
reality without distinctions). Augustine ingeniously reconciled conflicting Greek and Hebrew ideals of reason and will respectively. For
Plato, the Ideal or Universal Man subsisted eternally and perfectly
prior to creation. Particular persons were created after this pattern
and thus were essentially good; but they were also imperfect and
thus not wholly good. Hebraic ideals included original sin, an inherited tendency of persons to willfully go against the will of God.

Augustine's theology reconciled conflicting Greek ideals of the ultimacy of Reason, which is necessitarian and determined, with Hebraic ideals of the ultimacy of Will, which is free, by means of the
Greek ideal of perfection. Whatever is reasonable God wills, freely
because of his own rational nature. Will and Reason are identical in
God, who is perfect, but not always identical in men who are imperfect. Thus the Hebraic original sin of willfulness and the Platonic
imperfection of created men as rational coalesce in Augustinian, and
thus in much of Christian, thinking. Augustine's synthesis proved
lastingly influential, and an awareness of conflicts between the numerous opposites that he reconciled have received continuing reconsideration.[7]

The Reason-Will controversy has continued to plague Western
thought to the present time. Medieval philosophers split over the
issue: Thomists, influenced by Aristotle, favored Reason, while
Scotists perferred Will. The Protestant Reformation was divided be-

tween Calvinists, rationalists deducing predestinarianism from
God's perfection, and Lutherans, insisting on salvation by faith (act
of will) because created imperfection ("total depravity") made sufficient rational assent impossible. Descartes, Spinoza, Leibniz, and
Kant were rationalists. Although opposed by Locke, Berkeley,
Hume, Benthan, and Mill as empiricists regarding the origin of
knowledge, they were more directly opposed to the romanticists—
Rousseau, Fichte, Schelling, Schleiermacher, and Nietzsche, including many British poets and American transcendentalists, not-
ably Emerson. Rationalism took the form of logical positivism and
now linguistic analysis, while romanticism continued as existentialism, represented by Kierkegaard and Sartre. There is no more serious unresolved controversy in contemporary Western thinking than
this Reason-Will issue. Disagreements about it often subtly subvert
disputes over other issues.

Fourteen centuries elapsed between Augustine's synthesis of opposites inherited from Greek and Hebraic ideals and Hegel's synthesis of many more opposites inherited from centuries of philosophical
controversies. The Hegelian system is perhaps the second greatest
original synthesis to have a major impact on Western thought. Of
course, like Augustine, Hegel had help from predecessors. Significant for our purposes is his development of dialectical logic, presupposing existing opposites that flow into each other, combine in a
hierarchy, and participate both structurally and historically in a
totality of reality that he called the Absolute. Critics regarded his
system as too idealistic. Karl Marx, who "turned the system upside
down," developed dialectical materialism and a dialectical interpretation of history. Marx, more a political economist than philosopher, turned out to be more influential. Marxian opposition of capitalistic and communistic ideals persists as an unresolved part of our
present theoretical and practical predicament.

Although ideals of a static universe inherited from Greek, medieval, and many modern philosophers had already been challenged
by romanticism and by Hegelian and Marxian dialectic, the evolutionism stemming from Charles Darwin's *Origin of Species* (1857),
developed by Herbert Spencer, and flowering in the pragmatism of
William James and John Dewey (and other pragmatists as well—
Charles Sanders Peirce, F. C. S. Schiller, George Herbert Mead, Max

Otto, Charles Morris, Sidney Hook, Lewis Hahn, and H. S. Thayer) and the emergentists (Roy Wood Sellars, C. Lloyd Morgan, S. Alexander, Jan Christian Smuts), contributed a new dimension, and many pairs of opposing ideals to philosophical discussion. Pragmatic logic, the instrumentalism of John Dewey, interpreted life in terms of problem solving in a world characterized by a struggle for existence and survival of the fit.[8] Dewey's influence, especially through philosophy and practice of education, resulted in much confusion because many misinterpreted his solving-life-problems advice with Rousseau's romanticistic advice that children should follow their own whims. Evolutionism and pragmatism were both indebted to, and in turn helped to reinforce, the philosophy of progress that has pervaded Western thought.

The philosophy of progress idealized an unlimited future of growth in quantities, complexity, and improvement. Stimulating, and in turn stimulated by, more and more scientific discoveries, technological inventions, industrial production, expanding commerce, growth of cities, geographical discoveries, conquest and settlement, and increasing wealth, health, and education, this philosophy pervaded most of Western civilization. Combined with ideals of individual initiative, democratic government, laissez-faire economic policies, and the rights of individuals, this philosophy inspired frontiersmen, entrepreneurs, scientists, and politicians, pervaded the expanding educational system (the Horatio Alger, Jr., books are examples), and inspired World War I soldiers to help "make the world safe for democracy."

World War II, which left not only devastation but also a world divided almost as much as before, and demonstrated atomic bomb potentialities for extinguishing mankind, raised questions about the reality of progress. The Vietnam debacle, increasing frustrations from rising expectations regarding income and political power of a more highly educated populace, general failure to attain happiness in spite of affluence, billion-dollar armaments budgets increasing while millions of persons starve, growing incapacity of public officials to deal with increasingly complex problems, and increasing evidence of white-collar crime defrauding public interests have contributed doubts about possibilities for futher progress. Watergate publicly displayed American philosophy in practice. Seemingly uncontrollable stagflation is being experienced by more and more as a kind of progressive end to hopes for further progress.

Recent philosophical movements have contributed to growing demoralization. Logical positivism proclaimed itself the most superior philosophy of science. It distinguished between "factual" and "value" statements, declaring the latter "meaningless" and thus outside the realm of science. Holding that science is, or ought to be, completely value free, it contributed to attitudes that regard values, and consequently obligations, as inferior. Building on previous materialistic philosophies of science that also denigrated value, this view has developed a virtual stranglehold on the attitudes of policy-determining scientists, and thus has made the scientific community tend to abhor the prospect of having to deal with the value-saturated aspects of our crises. The self-declared incompetence of many scientists to deal with value problems is a major contribution to the hopelessness that is beginning to pervade our predicament.

Linguistic analysts, starting with the plausible proposition that thought cannot be clear if language is unclear, propose principles of clarification that result in alleged demonstrations that the meanings of commonly accepted words are inherently unclear or meaningless. One professor in a theological school reasoned thus: You cannot understand theology unless you understand the language of theology. Theological language can be demonstrated to be meaningless. Therefore it is unnecessary to study theology. Similar attempts have been made on most significant terms, such as value, government, science, mind, life, self, and philosophy. The net effect of this process has been to reduce problems of life to problems of language and thus to retreat from the problems of life. I await pronouncement by some linguistic analyst that *crisis* is a meaningless word so people are foolish to bother themselves about it.

Existentialism, originating as a revolt against excessive rationalism and drawing inspiration from voluntaristic philosophers ranging from ancient Hebraism, Greek worship of Dionysius, Persian Sufism, Lutheran pietism, and French and German romanticism, idealizes each spontaneous act of will (*existenz*) as ultimate reality that is free to form itself in any way it chooses. It creates its own essence. Therefore it is entirely responsible for its own choices and its own nature. Also it is not responsible to anyone else or even to its own previous or later self. A self is "authentic" only if it does not permit its act of will to be imposed upon (influenced) by any law (logical, legislated, moral, or natural), by any other will, or even by its own previous acts of will. To promise and then to feel obligated to keep the promise renders a will "inauthentic." Such a philosophy is antiethical because it is antisocial. It contributed to the proclamation by spokesmen for a second after-World-War-II generation of a new freedom, or a new right—the freedom from responsibility.

Contemporary Chaos

Philosophy today is a chaos of claims. Our sampling of some of the more obvious diversities in the United States includes the following: sectarian philosophies, humanistic philosophies, philosophies of scientists, New Left philosophies, university administrative philosophies, research institute philosophies, philosophies of teachers of philosophy, and Asian philosophies. (To include further diversities among the varieties of Marxist followers, Third World traditionalists and revolutionaries, Indian, Buddhist, Chinese, Japanese, and Islamic religions, and minority thinkers everywhere, to say nothing of individual variations, would require a volume in itself without exhausting actual types.)

SECTARIAN PHILOSOPHIES

Political toleration of sectarian religious doctrines in the United States has made it a home for hundreds of religious organizations, both imported and home grown. Most obvious are the multitudes of Christian Protestant denominations, conservative and liberal, Roman Catholicism with growing numbers of partial dissenters; Eastern Orthodoxy, with its Greek, Russian, and Polish divisions and offshoots; and Judaism, with its orthodox, conservative, and reform branches. Recent ecumenical efforts have met with stubborn sectarian resistance. Any partial success, should it occur, would, I shall argue, be much too little and too late.

HUMANISTIC PHILOSOPHIES

Humanistic philosophies, all holding that there is something ultimate and irreducible about each person and that the value and goal of life is to be found inside life, and not outside it, continue to differ from each other, sometimes violently. Greek ideals of rationality have inspired many, but some of these have also despised will, feeling, and emotion, thereby subordinating the whole person to one prominent part. British empiricists laud each person's private stock of experiences as bases for his beliefs; but some of them also reject reason as unempirical, thereby eliminating an important part of a whole person. Mechanistic materialists interpret man as a machine with an electronically coordinated nervous system responding to external and internal conditions in ways producing behavior. But behaviorism, depicting persons as complicated stimulus-response mechanisms, is one of the most reductionistic of humanisms. Romanticists and existentialists also claim to be humanists, but reducing a person to intense desire or to a momentary act of will omits too much of what is essential to being human.

Some humanists are extremely individualistic, advocating frank and consistent selfishness; they overlook the fact that to be human is to be social. Some humanists love other persons so completely that they habitually sacrifice themselves for them. Some humanists identify themselves closely with their family, community, race, and/or nation and see themselves fulfilled through family, community, racial, or national service. Some humanists become officers, public or private, and find human fulfillment primarily in performing official functions. Our needed world philosophy should be humanistic, I shall argue. But so many different kinds of reductionistic claims have been made in the name of humanism that my use of this word will have to be clarified. My point here is that our present predicament is a mess of our own unwitting making and that multiplying humanistic philosophies contributes to our chaos. None has yet appeared that is sufficiently wholesome and convincing to guide us to successful solution of current critical problems.

THE SCIENCES

Growth of science should increase our understanding; indeed it already has. Yet growth of the sciences has also increased our misunderstandings in many ways. The sciences are by their very nature specialized, and advancement in each tends to require further specialization. The more specialized a scientist becomes, the narrower his interests, the focus of his efforts, and the center of his perspective tend to become. Despite the omnipresence of whole-part relationships, the more devoted a specialist is to parts, the more larger wholes will fade from his vision.[9] What he does not see does not exist for him functionally. In this way, science tends to be disintegrative, and our understanding, even when scientific, tends to be reductionistic.

Such reductionism can be experienced by almost any person consulting his physician. Where can one find a physician willing to examine him as a whole person? My physician is a cardiologist. When he has checked my electrocardiogram and tests requested regarding glandular problems brought from my previous physician, he feels satisfactorily finished with me. Although my digestive, nervous, muscular, respiratory, skeletal, cutaneous, and glandular systems all interdepend with my circulatory system, they receive no significant consideration. Wholeness and wholesomeness, something we need as an inspiring and guiding ideal, is missing from science.

It is missing from education too. The ideal of a well-rounded education, instilled in my youth, is no longer feasible. The quantities and complexities of specialties have become so great that even the ideal of a well-rounded specialist is becoming unrealistic. Few specialists can keep up with current literature published in their field. Computer assistance is needed for locating subjects in three thousand medical journals, for example. Much technical knowledge rapidly becomes obsolete. The absence of comprehensive perspectives in terms of which to interpret specialized developments means that the specialist is ignorant of how what he does serves and is served by larger wholes.

Unfortunately scientists' needs for a philosophy of science have been met mainly by sectarian philosophies, often under the influence of peer group pressures. Physical sciences, stressing analytic methods, tend to accept a materialistic philosophy holding that existence consists ultimately of some indivisible particles. Evolution from static particles idealized by the Greek atomists to dynamic atoms (of more than a hundred kinds) to subatomic particles (more than forty kinds identified) has not changed the view that such ultimate particles are more important in understanding existence than are larger wholes. Recent ideas of interdependence of particles and fields, and of complementarity, seem to have challenged this view. But prejudice in favor of analyticial ideals condemns many scientists to persisting reductionism.

The influence of materialistic and logical positivistic philosophies on scientists has eliminated questions of value from science. Axiology, the science of values, is excluded from among the sciences by leading scientific institutions. Antipathy regarding factual versus value factors in understanding has so divided people in different fields that some have come to regard the sciences and the humanities as two different and conflicting kinds of culture.[10]

Two sciences, sociology and anthropology, tend to accept cultural relativism as a fact. As long as each culture, or each geographical unit, has its own coherent authority regarding morals, people can manage to associate reliably. But as megalopolitan melting pots progressively erode particular cultures, increasingly more people are caught in cultural conflicts that raise doubts about the reliability of each. Especially when supported by ideals of religious, and thus cultural, toleration, and by ideals of individualism, cultural relativism becomes transformed into individual relativism. Now that existentialism pressures more persons into accepting a relativism of the moment, morality is becoming progressively chaotic. Our society seems to be moving toward a moral vacuum. I believe that there are limits to demoralization before a society itself disintegrates. The more rapidly morality degenerates, the greater the need for a new morality. Since moral degeneration and the human predicament have become worldwide, the need has become one for a new world morality.

NEW LEFT PHILOSOPHIES

Nothing epitomizes contemporary chaos better than New Left philosophies. Demoralization, sparked by Vietnam war drafts and deaths, created antipathies mistrusting "anyone over thirty," the "military-industrial-educational complex," universities, and then all institutions. Nonconforming modes of dress, hair, language, and life-styles were designed to provoke conformists. Hippies, refusing regimented work, drifted in automobiles supported by social welfare checks. The use of halucinogenic drugs—from peyote and marijuana to heroin—started as nonconformist ventures and hardened for many into a symbolic necessity of a peer group life-style. Anti-institutional attitudes extended to marriage and sexual practices. Students demanded unlimited dormitory visiting hours and then co-educational dormitories. Oral contraceptives, repeal of antiabortion laws, increase in no-fault divorce systems, open practice of homosexuality, and the spread of pornographic stores and hard-core movie houses all intermingled with New Left philosophies. Anti-establishment music rose to the self-assured "revolution now" theme, persisted through many subtly self-righteous antiestablishment theses, intermingled with minority-group messages, and now seems to have returned to more typical youthful self-pity. Electric guitars, strobe lights, and even incense contribute to feelings of fuller participation in movemental rebellion.

Once New Leftists demonstrated that they could successfully taunt the establishment without much penalty, minority groups arose with their own rebellious demands. "Power to the people" turned into "Black power," "Chicano power," "Native American power," and finally "Women's liberation." These groups, less concerned about damning the pie as rotten, were more interested in getting a larger slice of the pie. Thus numerous kinds of confusion were added to rebellious trends contributing to our demoralizing predicament.

A positive side to these numerous rebellious philosophies should be noted. The rejection of a status quo presupposes idealizing something better. New Leftists tended to be political, moral, and intellectual anarchists. The existentialism of Sartre and Camus was antiphilosophical. Literature, not philosophy, was the primary mode for existentialist expression. Yet somehow even extremely momentary individualism was intended to express ideals of a better world. Existentialism in its pure form was hard to accept even by the most rebellious under strenuous peer group pressure. Furthermore, because it idealized absurdity, it was easily misunderstood. Consequently, many semi- and pseudo-existentialist philosophies appeared, and youthful minds poetized love for mankind, economic and political justice for all, guaranteed incomes from completely automated industries, freedom from all responsibilities, and utopia without restrictions. They condemned as hypocritical elders who proclaimed humanitarian ideals and yet participated in and supported antihumanitarian institutions. Some conscience-stricken elders aided many minor youth-proposed reforms.

As riots, communes, vagabondage, drugs, and sexual excesses gradually produced greater frustrations (as the Vietnam war ended and compulsory draft was replaced by an all-volunteer army), some turned to political activities. But vested interests were too strong; costs in time, effort, and money were too great; and the power of huge corporations to influence final outcomes legitimately or fraudulently, were too overwhelming. Youthful reformers were too divided among themselves to have very much effect at all.

UNIVERSITIES

The most obvious positive effects of youthful efforts appeared in the form of student representation on faculty committees, administrative committees, and even university boards of trustees. To understand why universities accepted the idea of admitting relatively inexperienced students to positions of trust where experience is needed, consider an example from my own university. When students complained about degree requirements, a bachelor of university studies was proposed by a faculty committee. Except for 128 semester hours of course work, forty of which must be upper division courses, and a grade average of C, there are no requirements. The student is free to choose any course in any department in any college at any level if he gains the instructor's permission. No major, minor, language, physical education, or minimum distribution requirements exist. The program partially exemplifies the ideal of eliminating institutional restrictions. But the point I want to make is that when the chairman of the faculty committee advocating adoption of the program presented his arguments, he asserted that, given the uncertainties of our time, we as faculty members do not know what is best for our students. Some of them, he said, know better what is good for them than we do. Certainly if they are free to choose and then regard their efforts as wasted, at least they will not blame the faculty for imposing useless requirements on them. When a vacancy occurred in the deanship of the College of Arts and Sciences, this man, who asserted that we do not know what we are here for, was selected for the position. If faculty do not know and students do know why they are in the university, ought not faculty committees and administrative boards avail themselves of the advice of those who know?

Practice seems to have demonstrated that students do not know more and are subject to the same pressures, dilemmas, and prejudicial choices as are faculty and administration. Disillusion with unrestricted choices has appeared when employers discover that graduates cannot spell and multiply enough to serve them reliably. My university faculty has just restored previously dropped entrance requirements in an effort to restore their degenerated product. This reform is not inspired by a new high idealism, a world vision, a new morale; it is merely a confession that recognizes that, in our complex and confused world, students cannot be counted on to guide themselves to achieve the minimum essentials of education necessary for ordinary living. But, except for such minimums, our university faculties still do not know very much about what curricula are best for students. If the leaders of our universities have lost their own bearings in our confused and confusing present predicament, we can hardly look to them for guidance.

RESEARCH INSTITUTES

Growing complexities of factors and more rapid and more pervasive changes, combined with increasing uncertainty resulting from chaotic confusion, have prompted corporations, private and public, to seek expert advice. Many have turned to interdisciplinary research institutes claiming the ability to assemble needed information, to discern its implications, and to formulate models of possible alternative futures depending on how stably and variably past and present trends continue. Spurred by the advent of rapid data-processing and computing technology, some institute personnel have promoted their services with unabashed enthusiasm. Marvelous advances in computer capacities have fanned optimism until some devotees have begun to expect magical results. But overenthusiasm resulted in some overselling; thinner results at higher costs are causing considerable reassessment and retrenching. Computers cannot think; they merely respond quickly and complexly to data programmed into them. If the programmers are confused or incompetent, computer products are confused and incompetent and, in addition, very expensive.

Computer technology requires the training of experts called *systems engineers*, some specializing in hardware (machinery) and some in software (program designing). Most computers operate on a two-valued logic. The rapid training of most systems engineers permitted no time for critical evaluation of the logic employed. Limitations inherent in the symbolic logic used became limitations of computers and of all computer programs. Too often these limitations are unwittingly overlooked, often resulting in unwarranted claims.[11]

The need for understanding the structure of systems in general after programmers had constructed many different kinds of specialized systems resulted in the development of general systems theory (and the Society for General Systems Research, which is also an International Organization for the Development of Theoretical Systems, headquartered in Washington, D.C.). Programmers responsible for designing systems to be used as bases for important policy decisions needed a more comprehensive perspective and understanding of their enterprise. Consequently general systems theory was called on to perform the functions of philosophy, even though their formulators were inexperienced in philosophical thinking. Many mistakes were made, and still-unsettled controversies regarding whether the general nature of systems can be defined rigorously in terms of symbolic logic or needs to be understood in terms of organic relations exhibited in organisms and organizations continue to rage.[12] The philosophical controversies arising out of the needs and efforts of computer programmers have added some new dimensions to our contemporary chaos.

Research institutes themselves have contributed their own share of influences to present philosophical chaos. Trying to overcome inadequacies in advice by specialists in single disciplines, many have become deliberately interdisciplinary. Even though not all difficulties in communication between persons with the thought and language patterns of different specialties can be overcome, some can be with sufficient effort. Interdisciplinary approaches to our complex economic, social, political, and ecological problems should be superior to those of single disciplines. Yet partly because of a lack of financing, awareness, and demand, not all relevant disciplines are consulted. Philosophy as concern for first principles or foundational presuppositions, and the special philosophical sciences of axiology, aesthetics, ethics, philosophy of religion, and logic tend to be ignored completely. Thus interdisciplinary research institutes contribute new dimensions of unreliability and misunderstanding to the present human predicament by continuing to ignore the philosophical disciplines. As long as these disciplines suffer from incompetence and irrelevance, however, consulting them may not improve reliability or understanding.

INCOMPETENT PHILOSOPHERS

If research institutes do turn to philosophers, including axiologists and ethicists, for interdisciplinary assistance, they find that the vast majority have training interests and abilities causing them to be incompetent to deal adequately with the problem of providing the philosophy needed to restore morale to America and/or to the world. There are many reasons for this incompetence.

Philosophy itself has become more complex and continues to become more so every day. Its history of published thinkers grows longer. The numbers of problems, theories, and critical evaluations become greater. The numbers of philosophical books, journals, articles, and interdisciplinary studies involving philosophy continue to increase. Surely no one can keep up with all that is written in philosophy today. New varieties of philosophy, like old ones, tend to have peculiar intricacies and specialized vocabularies that often require tremendous effort to master. Where bilingual or multilingual abilities are needed for understanding philosophies, the problems become still more complicated because meaning systems in different languages do not always permit literal translation.

Some philosophers remain committed to sectarian doctrines for which they are paid propagandists. Some entered philosophy with prejudicial intent, to support or attack a particular ideology. Many are devoted to studying and teaching the history of philosophy or some portion of it, especially its ancient, medieval, or modern philosophies, in ways preventing sufficient attention to contemporary trends. Almost all tend to specialize, either in some historical period, some particular philosopher or philosophical movement, or in logic, philosophy of language, or some other special field of philosophy. College enrollment increases during the Vietnam war period created vacancies for teachers whose interests are primarily those of job holders. All of these factors contribute to a lack of interest and ability for confronting the philosophical needs of the present human predicament effectively.

Worst of all, however, are the prevalence and promotion of particular philosophies (and antiphilosophies) claiming that grappling with the needs of comprehensive philosophy is not the philosophy teacher's job. Logical positivism emphasized logical analysis and interpreted philosophical and scientific investigations as excluding both value judgments and metaphysical statements, including those about the world as a whole. Linguistic analysis followed with the doctrine that philosophy consists in "ostentation"—in showing what is meant—for the purpose of clarifying meanings. Its function is not to pass judgments but merely to clarify meanings. Its purpose is not to seek wisdom or to advocate the good life or even to understand the external world. When meanings have been clarified, its job is done. Existentialism rejects all explanations of the world as inauthentic except when spontaneously whimsied by a self-assertive will uninfluenced by anything. The possibility, even actuality, of world philosophies is admitted, but only as an external, and thus evil, imposition on the freedom of unfettered wills. Existentialism aims not to create a better philosophy but to free man from philosophy. Thus it functions as a major enemy of intelligent efforts to understand our world and to formulate the world philosophy needed for human survival.

The incompetence of philosophers is not a deficiency resulting from within the field of philosophy alone. Philosophy is not popular. Part of the reason is that its problems and minimal modes of treatment require high-level abstractions that are difficult for many people to understand. Part of the reason is that business, government, education, and religion make little or no demands on philosophy. And, as we have already seen, interdisciplinary research institutes seldom call on them. Each person tends to be satisfied with the philosophy he already has; if he were not, he would already have replaced it with one that is satisfactory. Only those who are lost, perplexed, wondering, or seeking for sounder beliefs appeal to philosophy. How many people consult a professional ethicist when they are faced with a difficult ethical question? I put this question to a successful corporation insurance man recently. He replied: "I didn't know there was one." Few people know—or care—about the thousands of persons teaching philosophy in United States colleges. Does America have any outstanding philosophers? No Nobel Prize has ever been awarded to an American philosopher.

When teachers of philosophy are not called on to function significantly in American life, such neglect does not inspire them to unselfish service. When they are thus neglected, nothing stops them from pursuing their personal interests, specializing in topics, persons, movements, or problems of their own choosing. Even in managed departments, some have been captured by sectarians; some claiming to be represented by many different viewpoints often permit, even encourage, each to pursue his own preferences; and some are so torn by antipathies by persons holding antagonistic views that enduring emotional turbulence exhausts much of the available energy. Philosophers come to believe that solving the world's philosophical problems is not their task partly because those who support them, those who surround them, and those who could make use of their services make no demands on them. Thus others as well as philosophers must be blamed for much contemporary philosophical incompetence.

ASIAN PHILOSOPHIES

Persons rebelling against Western philosophies, whether sectarian, professional, or popular, and holding that current crises constituting the human predicament are products of Western culture including Western philosophy, often seek something better elsewhere. The slow growth in Western understanding of Asian philosophies has suddenly changed by a flood of missionaries, both Asian and Western converts. Some valuable insights in Asian philosophies have been missed or neglected in the West. Studying Asian philosophies is usually rewarding. But also it can be perplexing, mystifying, and repugnant. Indian and Chinese civilizations have their own long history of emphases and neglects, of true insights and mistaken understandings, of conflicts resulting from exaggerations, and their own kinds of reductionisms. Translation problems are especially numerous with Asian languages.

Growth in expert scholarship has been helpful, though vast libraries of resources remain untranslated, so our knowledge of Asian philosophies is still limited. But popular movements promoting Yoga, [13] Zen, and Taoism seem to have mushroomed everywhere. In addition to the more scholarly Vedanta centers, numerous yoga institutes and transcendental meditation and Hare Krishna centers have popularized Indian philosophies. Attention to Japanese philosophies, influenced by Japanese architecture, flower arrangement, kamikaze pilots, jujitsu, and karate, has stimulated interest in Zen, to say nothing of the eighty thousand native-born Shin Buddhists of Japanese ancestry. Soka Gakai, a militantly aggressive form of Buddhism, has made many converts, and the Korean minister, Sun Myung Moon, has established a colony for his numerous American followers in Barrytown, New York.

Taoism has become sufficiently popular that, on an average, a new English translation of the *Tao Teh Ching* is published every year. [14] The *I Ching* (*Book of Changes*) has aroused much interest, and Tai Chi, a naturalistic, worshipful, ritualistic form of exercise, has appealed to many health fans. Alan Watts, an Americanized British Anglican priest, ably translated Taoistic and Zen ideas into the American idiom in ways that have been widely appreciated. [15]

Broadening and enriching American experience through acquaintance with Asian philosophies has been a very healthy development; an adequate world philosophy must include all of the true insights and useful practices originating in Asia. But much misunderstanding has resulted also, both from hasty enthusiasms and credulous adoption of partly mistaken interpretations. Even when understood doctrines are developed, they often prove to be reductionistic, appealing to some aspect of human nature as if it were the only essential or the primary essential. The flood of doctrines enriching American experience also contributes to the chaos and the confusion resulting from an unrestricted proliferation of increasingly incompatible alternatives.

The more kinds of differing philosophies entering our culture, the more confused people tend to become. Increasing the plethora of alternatives does not thereby provide the guidance needed for co-operative action in solving the critical problems of mankind. There are limits to both the number of influential alternatives and to the complexities of such alternatives before the enormity of their intricacies cripples our abilities to respond intelligently. Have we passed those limits? If so, then the need for reducing such complexities and so many varieties is itself a characteristic of our contemporary philosophical predicament. Yet there is some truth in each of them. An intelligent humanity will manage to keep such truths by gathering them up in a newer larger synthesis. It is too late in history to achieve another primarily Western synthesis of the magnitude and ingenuity exemplified in the Augustinian and Hegelian syntheses. Now we need a new worldwide synthesis, incorporating Asian as well as Western riches into a more complicated but still integrated world philosophy.

Global Disorder

At the world level we face an even more formidable task of seeking a philosophy that incorporates the obvious and explicitly contradictory assumptions and ideals of Asian and Western philosophies, in addition to the historical and contemporary varieties and modifications developed in each. Many visions of world community remain unrealistically ignorant of fundamental differences, not merely in surface mores but in foundational presuppositions functioning as persisting bases for prejudicial ideals. Some Westerners dismiss Asian views as exotic. But enough competence has been achieved by scholars so that we now can discuss these differences knowingly, clearly, confidently. [16]

Permit me to sketch some main differences between Western and Indian philosophies first and then to show how both Western and Indian ideals differ from Chinese ideals. I shall not take time to review the complex histories of Indian and Chinese philosophies, each having its own varieties of significant issues that also contribute to the whole picture of disorder from which world culture is emerging. Summarizing whole civilizations in terms of key ideals that have received special emphases in them is to postulate theses of very high-level abstraction. But comparative philosophy, a relatively new field of specialization, has already advanced to the point where several volumes have been published and several different hypotheses have been presented for further research consideration. [17]

The extreme opposition between two pervasive types of ideals in Indian and Western philosophy leads many to believe that they can

never be reconciled. In particular Reason and Will, the two characteristics of ultimate reality persistently present in Western ideals, are
denied ultimacy in much of Indian thought. For example, Nirguna
Brahman, ultimate reality as conceived by Advaita Vedanta, is entirely without distinction and entirely without desire or will. Westerners have idealized sharp, clear, precise distinctions; Indians have
idealized pure or perfect indistinctness. Westerners have idealized
will, or desire (emphasizing free will, desire as a precondition of
satisfaction, wanting as the beginning of getting); Indians have
idealized extinction of desire (*moksha*) because desire is the source of
frustration, anxiety and disturbance. Yogic practices aim at eliminating both distinct objects, even all objects, and desire, including
the desire to eliminate desire. [18]

These general differences pervade specific ideals. Western philosophers tend to be realistic and to seek reality in objects or behind
apparent objects, so they seek understanding through information
about real things. Western inquiry tends to be analytic, assuming
that parts are more real than wholes and that differences are more
real, or at least more important, than similarities. Indian philosophers tend to be subjectivistic and spiritualistic, and to seek reality
within self or in a spirit from which self emerges (*atman* is *Brahman*).
So they seek to eliminate interest in objects that distract attention
from concentrated intuition of the ultimate reality that constitutes
one's own self or with which one's self is intrinsically united. Indian
inquiry (*jhana yoga*) idealizes intuition of ultimate reality as pure indistinctness, assuming that identity (sameness without difference) is
more real than difference.

Western thought encourages desire, activity, effort, and production of goods. It idealizes improvement and thus being progressive.
The future is expected to be better than the present. Indian thought
encourages suppression of desire, enjoying passivity, idealizing the
eternality of present being. Ultimate reality never changes; it merely
appears and disappears. Change is illusory, so progress is illusory.
The ultimate goal of life is to be gained not by producing things but
by withdrawing from things.

To our previous criticisms of Western thought, we must now add
criticisms of Indian thought as contributing to contemporary predicaments. If our crises result from overpopulation, pollution, over-

rapid use of resources, nuclear war dangers, poverty, and maldistribution, then it seems that Hindu ideals of desirelessness and indistinctness have nothing to contribute to overcoming them. One can argue that if we can succeed in suppressing desire, we can succeed in suppressing desire for war, more children, more technology, and more industrialization. The world crises have been brought about by persons inspired by Western philosophies, not by persons inspired by Indian philosophies. Therefore if we can convert the world to Indian ideals, our crises will disappear. But the urgency of world crises makes impossible any such conversion, and the absorption of Western (Islamic, Christian, democratic, scientific, and technological) ideals in India has partially Westernized its people. Conflicts between Western and Indian ideals within India and other Southeast Asian countries are themselves part of our present predicament. Awareness of the extremities to which opposing Indian and Western ideals are sometimes carried is essential to understanding our global philosophical disorder.

Turning to Chinese ideas embedded in the *Tao Te Ching* attributed to Lao Tzu and in the works associated with Confucius, we find ideals that have persisted through twenty-five centuries of thought and action. The history of Chinese thought has its own series of conflicting issues, some of which persist at present.[19] Some interpreters find the ideals of Confucius and Lao Tzu in sharp opposition with each other and with Sinicized versions of the foreign import, Buddhism. My own view is that the naturalism (Taoism) of Lao Tzu and the humanism of Confucius are partly identical and otherwise largely complementary.[20] In any case, I contend that, except for its Buddhist import, Chinese thought tends to be as different from Indian as from Western so far as emphasizing certain typical ideals is concerned.

The idea of *Tao* (nature), which acts naturally without artificial compulsions, is as different from *Nirguna Brahman*, perfect inactive ground for all illusory actions, as it is from God, eternally omniscient personal creator of a world external to himself. Tao consists entirely of *taos* (natures), which change more or less regularly through stages of initiation (*yang*) and completion (*yin*). Yang and yin are opposites, so Tao and taos consist of opposites, complementary opposites, that succeed each other as dominant characteristics. But as the Tao symbol depicts, each tao includes both yang and yin, and even though each succeeds the other in dominating it, some yin remains present when yang dominates and some yang persists when yin dominates. Thus the Chinese have idealized distinctions (yang and yin are different and opposite) that are not completely distinct (some of both are always present).

Things have more complex natures, so several pairs of yin-yang symbols are required for appropriate representation. The *I Ching* (*Book of Changes*) consists of sixty-four hexigrams, or six pairs of yin-yang symbols. These hexigrams function as types of analogies that serve for interpreting the nature of existing things and processes, such as each day, each year of seasons, each lifetime, and each dynasty, and so they provide a basis for comparisons and predictions. Useful as these have been in the history of Chinese culture, and complex as they may seem to unaided minds, in a world strangling itself by confused usage of computer complexities, the sixty-four hexigrams are certainly not complex enough to be of much use in dealing with world crises. Yet the *I Ching* involves some principles missing from current symbolic logic and necessary for the logic needed for resolving our crises and difficulties.

Comparing Chinese ideals with Western and Indian ideas relative to Will and Reason, I see Chinese accepting desire as natural. Desire is something to be accepted when it comes, not something to be stimulated artificially by advertising and other motivators and not something to be suppressed or extinguished by yogic efforts. Desire begets satisfactions sometimes and frustrations sometimes. Each should be accepted when it comes. Whereas Westerners idealize willfulness and Indians willessness, Chinese tend to idealize willingness. One who is willing to accept what comes tends to be more present oriented. One should enjoy the present, since not to do so is to waste it. Any future enjoyment will have to be enjoyed as present or not enjoyed at all. The Taoism of Lao Tzu does not prepare us for dealing with global crises. His advice regarding local crises is summed up as follows: "When opposing armies meet for open battle, he who runs away to hide is the one who wins." But threatened with global holocaust, where will one hide?

The issue of preferring distinctness or indistinctness separating Western and Indian thought does not bother Chinese thinkers much.

Instead of seeking clear distinctions or pure indistinctness, Chinese tend to accept appearances, most of which combine elements of both. Instead of analyzing things into their parts or of seeking an intuition of the universal whole without parts, Chinese tend be content with apprehending their participation in nature, including their social nature. Instead of seeking reality behind objects (as atoms or God) or reality within the self, Chinese tend to be naively realistic and accept as real what is directly apprehended in things as they appear.

These Chinese ideals do not seem useful as guides to global crisis solutions. Granted that we need to recognize ourselves as participating in nature, we have discovered that nature has become too intricately complex to yield much understanding through naive realism. The emerging world culture has much to gain from understanding and accepting many Chinese ideals, but they do not themselves help our predicament much. Their differences from Indian and Western ideals constitute part of the pluralism, and in some ways the antagonism, that must be overcome if we are to achieve a new quantum-leap system gestalt needed to bring a viable order out of present global disorder.

I have omitted the insights of Confucius, misunderstood as a formalizer because his teachings became formalistically institutionalized. Although Confucius derived his ideas from simpler societies, he captured some essentials of human association that every healthy society, including the emerging world culture, must understand, accept, and practice if it is to remain healthy. Yet his insights are not enough, for life in complex, multileveled, dynamic, increasingly impersonal megalopolis requires additional essentials. But controversies about Confucius, including Maoist condemnations of Confucianism, function as part of our global disorder.

There is much more to global philosophical disorder than the contrasting, and conflicting, ideals prevailing in Western, Indian, and Chinese civilizations. (I lack competence to survey contributions from black Africa and other cultures not participating in the three mainstreams.) Difficulties to be faced in formulating the philosophy we need are great enough when grappling with these more general types of conflicts. When intermingled with the philosophies of particular political, religious, and racist traditions and movements, they contribute to both the philosophical and practical difficulties occurring in concrete situations.

Many of these philosophical conflicts may be observed in action as parts of current Israeli-Arab (Moslem) wars, Hindu-Moslem division of India by separating Pakistan and Bangladesh, Christian-Moslem fighting in Lebanon, and Buddhist-Hindu friction in Sri Lanka, for example. Marxist opposition to capitalistic philosophies is backed by one of the mightiest military capabilities the world has ever seen. As atheistic, it opposes all theistic philosophies and societies. Differences between Marxist (or at least U.S.S.R.) and Maoist philosophies participate in the military confrontations between the U.S.S.R. and the People's Republic of China. Yugoslavian and other Soviet satellites propound still other varying versions of the communist doctrine. These varieties too contribute to the general philosophical confusion at the world level.

The multilingual barriers to communication function as barriers to philosophical intercourse. The best efforts to solve human crises at the world level continue to be seriously handicapped by translation problems. The interdependence of political and philosophical tendencies is complicated by both nationalistic and private efforts to subvert the interests of religious groups for their own ends. Billions of dollars in armaments loaned or given by the United States and U.S.S.R. to Middle Eastern countries influence the survival and propagative fortunes of Jewish, Moslem, Christian, and Marxist philosophies. Wars have determining effects on what philosophies prevail; so do famines, floods, earthquakes, fires, and abundant crops and utilizable resources. Inflation, fraud, dictatorship, and demoralization all have bearings on the course of philosophies.

At the same time, the stability and support continuing for Jewish synagogues, Christian seminaries, Islamic, Hindu, Jain, Buddhist, and Marxist educational systems stand as obstacles to an easy achievement of the needed world philosophy. A list of Roman Catholic universities in Latin American alone provokes dismay. How the multitudes of indigenous African philosophies contribute to the world disorder continues to be amazing.

How are the philosophers of the world meeting our world predicament? The UNESCO-related International Federation of Philosophical Societies has difficulties enough in coping with internal jealousies, personal, religious, political, and other philosophical antipathies, and distrust and fears in electing officers and meeting locations so that little energy or appetite remains for larger problems. The dominating political leaders of this federation are the members of the smaller International Institute of Philosophy. This institute, although a needed step when it was organized in 1937, now functions as a feudal house of lords, consisting of a restricted (to one hundred), self-elected membership. By influencing UNESCO-appropriated funds for international meetings, the institute is able to assist favored colleagues with travel funds not available to others. Although UNESCO officials urge certain minimums of worldwide democratic representation in international meetings it sponsors, the influential power of a continuing group tends to dominate elections and policy decision.

The federation has issued no policy statements regarding world crises and the role of philosophy in causing them or in proposing solutions for them. It is explicit in refusing to participate actively in attempts to solve practical global problems. According to its Secretary General, André Mercier, who describes it as "the most complete philosophical organization in the world," it can intervene with its moral authority in cases of injustices "to individual philosophers, groups, and associations." But it "will not launch projects that can be called applied philosophy."[21] When rapid changes and mounting crises require immediate attention, refusal by our most representative philosophical organization to concern itself with them demonstrates that it is incompetent to contribute constructively to the world philosophy which we need. It, too, thus exemplifies our global disorder.

The Need for a New World Philosophy

Although I believe that living together in the world will call for a new world philosophy even if our crises should somehow disappear, the existence of our crises, some of which threaten human extinction, raises questions about what contributions philosophy has made to causing them and what contribution it can and should make to over-coming them.

Our crises are caused by pursuing policies contributing to their de-velopment. Policies practiced have explanations, and explanations eventually rest on foundational assumptions, called *presupposi-tions*. Some of these presuppositions are philosophical (metaphysi-cal, epistemological, logical, axiological, aesthetic, ethical, relig-ious, social, economic, political, and educational and philosophy as comprehensive understanding). Sometimes philosophical presup-positions are deduced as necessary premises of practices. Some-times practices are justified as deductions from accepted presupposi-tions. That is, sometimes practice precedes and leads to formulated presuppositions, and sometimes practice is led by previously formu-lated presuppositions.[22]

Philosophical presuppositions become faulty or inadequate in three kinds of ways: obsolescence, present neglect, and failure to re-solve conflicting assumptions.

OBSOLESCENCE

Philosophies and doctrines embedded in religions, cultures, mores, laws, and political proclamations, originating long ago as adaptations to situations then calling for explanation, cannot be ex-pected to be adequate for today. The persistence today of the influ-ence of ancient doctrines, especially those hallowed as sacred re-vealed scriptures, exemplifies our willingness to attempt to solve to-day's problems in the way ancients adapted to their ancient situa-tions. These ancient ideas, no matter how useful then, have become inadequate because conditions have changed. The vast expansion of our knowledge, the advent and development of the sciences, and the accumulation of many kinds of experience with newer conditions provide us with additional capacities for dealing with our changed situations. To impose on or to appeal to obsolete doctrines as abso-lute truths requiring acceptance in determining present policy de-cisions is a very fundamental kind of mistake. To the extent that practices guided by obsolete philosophies have contributed to pre-sent crises, we may properly regard them as causes. The extent to which such appeals prevail, quantitatively and in crucial decision circumstances, is itself a measure of the need for a new world philosophy.

PRESENT NEGLECT

New conditions arise, new practices develop, and new problems occur without an awareness that new presuppositions, some of them philosophical, are involved. There are many reasons for such lack of awareness. People satisfied with previously accepted philosophy feel no need to look for new assumptions. Those grappling with more complex problems have their energies so fully exhausted by practical aspects that theoretical presuppositions fail to get attention. The growth of specialization tends to give attention primarily, or only, to those presuppositions on which specialized practice immediately depends. Specialists having difficulty communicating with even neighboring specialists tend to ignore the difficulties in discovering more general presuppositions common to all specialties.

Neglect of philosophical assumptions has become acculturated. When those who neglect philosophical assumptions become teachers, they, in effect, teach their followers to ignore the assumptions. Philosophies advocating the neglect or denial of some kinds of philosophical assumptions have been developed to rationalize the neglect. Most philosophies tend to be reductionistic, even when not intended to be so. The separation of philosophy from science and its inclusion among the humanities, which are often opposed to the sciences, has tended to isolate scientists from concerns about philosophical presuppositions and to add to further ignorance about such presuppositions by policy deciders who rely on such scientists. Democratic ideals of freedom of speech and publication imply toleration of all philosophies regardless of how well founded and in effect they conduce to a climate of opinion in which concern for presuppositions is purely optional.

Neglect by sectarians, scientists, administrators, and the public to call on philosophers for expert assistance in examining and rectifying presuppositions further institutionalizes the neglect of philosophical presuppositions. Teachers of philosophy themselves tend to become more and more specialized and often regard the problem of the nature of presuppositions as a very specialized kind of problem, which may not be included in their own area of interests. We now have existentialism, which repudiates all presuppositions. Thus contemporary philosophers, by contributing to the neglect, or denial, of presuppositions have contributed to, and are continuing to contribute to, our present predicament causally.

Thus we pursue practices presupposing unrecognized presuppositions. In doing so, we remain ignorant about the basic reasons for our actions and thus are unguided and undirected by such reasons.

FAILURE TO RESOLVE CONFLICTING ASSUMPTIONS

When problems pertaining to particular parts or aspects of human nature, society, or the universe are solved by hypotheses claiming that some trait or principle is essential and then, as a result of questioning by doubters, are reasserted as very essential or as the essential, dogmas develop. When different problems focusing attention on other parts or aspects of human nature, society, or the universe are solved similarly, other dogmas develop. To increase the apparent adequacy of each dogma, its proponents tend to interweave it into the larger fabric of a cultural perspective. If proponents of different dogmas are unable (and this is so often the case) to recognize the origins of their doctrines in different but complementary aspects of human nature, then they tend to defend their own dogmas by trying to refute the others. In such circumstances, what may in fact involve bases for complementarity tend to be interpreted as contradictory opposites.

Conflicting assumptions may arise in the thinking of a particular person, in a community or a nation, in a religious or philosophical sect, in a civilization, or in a world in which different civilizations intermingle in an emerging world civilization. Conflicting assumptions often arise as a result of the perspectives of different functionaries, officers, classes, or castes within a society. Today the different perspectives of different specialists, in the sciences and in various technologies, are conducive to such conflicts. Generally the more isolated each functionary is from the others, the more likely that such conflicting assumptions will become institutionalized. Conflicting assumptions tend to beget conflicting practices. When conflicting practices endanger the welfare of either, or both, or many, then their conflicting assumptions function causally. Conflicting as-

sumptions sometimes cause conflicting practices, which are sometimes disastrous.

Whether the conflicts between assumptions are obvious (as when
each contender deliberately appeals to the truth, even exclusive
truth, of his assumptions) or have been neglected and only vaguely
felt (as when disputants disagree without being able to give any un-
derlying reasons for their disagreements), when conflicts reach crisis
proportions, peaceful and intelligent resolution of the crises may depend on recognizing and understanding that their conflicting assumptions can and should be reexamined, reconsidered, and possibly reconstructed. Some of the more obvious conflicting assumptions in our present predicament are those among different civilizations, among different religious sects in each civilization, among
different philosophies growing out of different caste, class, or functionary perspectives, and—increasingly in a world favorable to the
development of individual philosophies evolved in highly unique
situations—among creative intellectuals. Prevalence of a plethora of
conflicting assumptions in our contemporary world is conducive to
growths in conflicting practices. As we become more intimately interdependent and interact more often and in more vital ways, our
conflicts become sharper, more effective, and more urgently in need
of resolution.

The degeneration of the powers within nations to maintain citizen
morale because of conflicting practices due to differing assumptions
leads to a dictatorship in which such practices—and sometimes
thought and talk about conflicting assumptions—are suppressed.
The emerging world community involves even larger numbers and
varieties of conflicting assumptions. So unless some way can be devised to induce people to recognize a common source of their ideas in
human nature and human society in ways that reveal key interpretive ideas as complementary to each other rather than as inherently
contradictory, we can expect world dictatorship as a necessary development if mankind is to survive. This is why we need a new world
philosophy. Prevailing philosophies are reductionistic because each
regards some part or parts of truths discovered about human nature
as wholes warranting exclusion of other parts. Reductionistic philosophies are not adequate. The more reductionistic a philosophy is,
the more inadequate it is.

If deficiencies in our present philosophies have caused and are causing present crises, then we need to remove them. The way to overcome inadequate philosophy is by achieving a more adequate philosophy. "Without a public philosophy, explicitly stated, we lack the fundamental condition whereby a modern polity can live by consensus (and without it there is only continuing conflict) and justice."[23]

THE KIND OF PHILOSOPHY NEEDED

Arthur W. Bronwell had stated that our society needs a philosophy "that can transform a jumbled mass of confusing intellectuality into a comprehensive, understandable, guiding philosophy of the creative society."[24] We need a philosophy that will interpret for us our present predicament, including our contemporary philosophical chaos, in America and in the world, and the philosophical aspects of all our contemporary crises, thereby throwing additional light on their full nature and seriousness. We need a philosophy that will guide us out of our present predicament, its chaos and crises, or at least will provide us with principles of understanding that can be used for developing such guidance. It should offer hope for human survival beyond recent doomsday predictions. It should restore confidence in human intelligence by demonstrating that the fuller understanding which it provides is sufficient to grapple successfully with present crisis problems. It should enable us to restore morale by locating the ultimate bases for moral appeals where they exist actually and by demonstrating how and why humanization requires several varieties of socialization as a means to fuller, richer, happier self-realization. The kind of philosophy we need should be humanitarian, humanistic, scientific, comprehensive, adequate, and quantum-leaping.

Humanitarian

The philosophy we need should be humanitarian; its goal should be what is best for human beings and thus what is best for mankind. Its aims should be human survival and happiness. How much more should be included in the humanitarian ideal, such as ideals pertaining to justice, equality, peace, minimum standard of living, dignity, rights, opportunities, freedoms, responsibilities, and quality of

life, have been debated and formulated in bills of rights, in the
United Nations charter and amendments, and in the Universal Declaration of Human Rights. Variable conditions affect the kinds of
values that are available and thus the kinds of ideals that are realistic. Progress of some toward affluence has produced unrealistic
ideals in both those favored and those not favored by the course of
developments. Thus although the general meaning of *humanitarian*
is clear, what the word can mean in particular situations and in particular periods in history is clearly variable. Thus a more complex,
flexible, and sensitive conception of what is best for mankind is
needed.

Present overpopulation and overconsumption-of-resources trends
force a reconsideration of what is needed to make plans humanitarian. Suppose, for example, that conditions become such that
what is best for mankind will require either (or both) reduction of
population by half or reduction of essential resources by half. Is a
recommendation to pursue such a requirement humanitarian? Assuming for the sake of argument that the reducing process itself
would be humanitarian, would aiming at such a goal be humanitarian? Some would say no. Each life has a unique, irreducible value.
To reduce the population by half is to reduce the amount of such
unique, irreducible value by half. The world would be only half as
good. But there is a counter argument: The continuation of present
needs will result in the extinction of mankind. Is it not better to reduce population by half if we can thereby save half, not only now
but for a much longer future? If we refuse to depopulate by half, we,
in effect, consent to total depopulation. Therefore true humanitarianism calls for depopulation by half. A similar argument can be
formulated regarding resource consumption.

The philosophy we need will be much more complexly and sensi-
tively discriminating in its ideas regarding population and resource-
consumption controls in order to fulfill its ideal of being humanitarian.

Humanistic

Humanism is a philosophy recognizing that there is something
ultimate and irreducible about each person, that each person has intrinsic value as an end-in-itself, which requires no external justifica-

tion for its existence and its optimum self-realization. Humanists differ widely in their interpretation of the nature of persons and of humanity; but all insist that to be human is to embody intrinsic value, and such being and value is irreducible.

Temptations to reduce seem perpetual, however. Two kinds of reductionism have plagued humanism: reduction of human beings to something nonhuman and reduction of the human to some part of the human (less than human). Whenever the human is conceived as completely submerged or completely dependent on something non-human, such as Aquinas's God, Hegel's absolute, LaMettrie's matter, Mussolini's state, or Marx's dialectic, antihumanism is present. Whenever the human is conceived as consisting of some part primarily, so that the whole as well as other parts are dominated by that part, antihumanism is also present, even if less obviously so. Whoever selects, for example, either Reason, or Will, or diet, or sex, or association, all essential to human nature, as alone essential or alone predominant thereby denies the other essentials or subordinates them unwholesomely. People who do this may still call themselves humanists. But reductionistic humanism lacks something, sometimes very much, that is essential to the being and value of a person as a whole. [25]

The humanism we need should be unreductionistic. As more complex, multileveled, multidimensional, organically related conditions of wholesome personality are revealed by new discoveries, our humanism should accept an enriched conception of potentialities (as well as dangers to them). As personality functions interdepend with more persons, groups, cultures, and ecological and astronomical conditions, each with both opportunities for personality enrichment and dangers to personality overextension, our humanistic conceptions should become more complex, more flexible, and yet more organically integrated. There are limits to the growth of complexities in personalities, no doubt; but we have not yet reached them. It is true that some may suffer from future shock, but such shock tends to disappear as more static, fixed-value conceptions of personality are replaced by more flexible, developmental-value conceptions.

Humanism, as the philosophy locating human value inside rather than outside of personality and in the whole as well as in the parts of personality rather than in some one or two parts of personality, also idealizes optimum realization of such value. Hence to be fully humanistic is to be humanitarian. And being wholesomely humanitarian can be aided best by being fully humanistic.

Scientific

Science aims to understand the way things are. We thus speak of it as being realistic (aiming to understand the way things really are) and as objective (aiming to reach warranted conclusions in terms of the evidence presented to us rather than subjectively influencing the outcome in terms of our preferences). Unfortunately for simplicity, being objective is itself a subjective attitude, and the reason why we advocate being scientific is that we believe this is the best way to reliable conclusions. Hence although it may seem paradoxical since subjectivity is essential to an attitude of objectivity, a completely objective philosophy of science will recognize that such subjectivity is essential to it.

Are not those who believe that scientists, in seeking to be completely objective, thereby eliminate all subjectivity, all preference, and all values from themselves as scientists mistaken? Science is not value-free.[26] Science that is so fully objective that it recognizes the necessity of subjective factors in attitudes of objectivity is believed to be the best way of achieving the understanding needed for coping with present and future crises.

Philosophies of science also tend to be reductionistic. Expansion of knowledge has necessitated specialization and division of labor among scientists. By selecting some part of existence, the physical as against the biological, for example, or the geological as against the mathematical, a scientist may so immerse himself in his own subject matter that he ignores, or at least underestimates, the significance of other sciences that are investigating problems in other fields. When he formulates his philosophy of science, he formulates it in terms he knows best, and so often unwittingly incorporates a specialized bias into a general theory about the nature of science. The kind of philosophy we need will include a philosophy of science that takes the viewpoints inherent in each of the sciences into account in formulating a general theory of science. This includes all of the philosophical sciences.

Especially important for scientific wholesomeness is attention to interscientific, interdisciplinary, interspecialized knowledge. The more we learn, the more specialization will be required, and the more important will become the problem of not merely closing the gaps but of organically integrating the knowledge of each into a more revealing whole. In this way more about each part is revealed because each naturally functions interdependently with the whole and with other parts in more ways than mere specialists can discover. Also interrelations among science, pure and applied, and technology, industry, government, education, and religion need to be clarified and the resulting knowledge utilized in improving mankind by improving all of these fields. Such an interdisciplinary effort will involve language sciences in ways needed to improve communication between sciences.

Comprehensive

The philosophy we need should be comprehensive. Our predicament is global, so it should take into consideration all of the world—geographically, populationally, politically. As humanitarian, it should comprehend all of humanity. As humanistic, its conception should include the whole personality, and all of the ways to improve its wholesomeness. As scientific, it should include all of the sciences. It should comprehend all of the cultures, including all languages, all mores and institutions, and all histories.

Failure to be comprehensive is to be reductionistic. Since there is some truth in all philosophies and in all religions, a fully comprehensive philosophy will incorporate all such truths within itself. Many will say that this cannot be done; we can catalog the varieties, but we cannot synthesize them into one consistent whole, they say. Yet the need of our time is a philosophy that can show how all of these differences have emerged within one world and in ways that do not require that the existence of that world be split apart. Granted that no simple, single-level, single-dimension, single-process gestalt will do. We need a quantum-leap kind of system to achieve the comprehensiveness suited to the rapidly increasing complexities of our day that is at least proportionately greater than the comprehensiveness of the Hegelian synthesis when compared with the Augustinian synthesis.

Adequate

The philosophy we need has to be able to solve all of the philosophical problems inherited from the past (and better than Hegel and Augustine did) as well as those constituting our contemporary chaos and world disorder, and do it better than other models. Too many proposals are inadequate because they are reductionistic; they aim to solve only some of our problems and claim, or imply, that once these problems are solved, then the others will somehow solve themselves or diminish in importance. The philosophy we need should show why the solution of interdependent problems requires their being solved together.

We suffer from a persisting failure to become and remain aware that obvious changes in practice have not been accompanied by ardent attention to the changes needed in theory when theory and practice interdepend. We commonly fail to be aware that our practice presupposes fundamental assumptions that need to be true if our deductions, implicit when not explicit, are to be reliable. Ignoring them ignores their truth. Ignoring them commits us to practicing without certainty. But also keeping obsolete presuppositions leaves us without adequate guidance, not only during practices when we ignore them but also when crisis shock demands that we ask, and try to answer, the question, What is really happening? The philosophy we need will be adequate only if it reveals both the presuppositions contributing to present crises and the presuppositions needed to recover from them.

Our philosophy will not be adequate until it is freed from inconsistency. We have shown how the Reason-Will controversies have plagued Western civilization and how conflicting Reason-Intuition and Willfulness-Willessness ideals divide Western and Indian philosophies and how traditional Chinese ideals differ from both. How can truths from competing religions, overspecialized sciences, and opposing philosophies be reconciled? Principles of consistency themselves vary depending on narrowness or breadth of assumptions. Since the philosophy we need must reconcile more complex, multileveled, and multidimensional kinds of oppositions, it will require a more complex principle of consistency derived from understanding existing complex, multileveled, multidimensional, multiprocess interdependencies.

Existing limits need to be recognized by any philosophy that is adequate. This study was inspired by attention called to doomsday prospects by the Club of Rome's *The Limits to Growth*. The evils of overpopulation, rapid consumption of irreplaceable resources, and the pollution of earth, water, and air have been effectively explained. But others limits, equally real and equally evil, have not yet been made so obvious. There are limits to plurification, fragmentation, differentiation, independence, and isolation before disintegration occurs. Some unity, some interdependence, some sharing are necessary for existence. Limits of unification also exist, for too much unity, too much integrity, is destructive of the plurality and variety essential to existence. But the problems facing us today are more those of achieving greater unity, through a new complex organic synthesis, than of achieving more diversity.

There are limits to which obsolete philosophies (of religion, government, science, education) can guide us today. There are limits to demoralization if human society is to continue. There are limits to complexity in human interdependencies before developing evils outweigh the goods. There are limits to comprehensiveness in the sense that the human mind doubtless will continue to try to comprehend everything. There are limits to irresponsibility and limits to responsibility. There can be too much planning as well as too little, even though too little planning is what troubles us most now. So the philosophy we need will advocate perpetual alertness to all of the kinds of limits conditioning existence. There are limits to progress, but we have not yet reached all of them, because there remain many different ways in which to progress.

The reversal of demoralization, doubt, distrust, and fear of futility is needed. Our philosophy will be adequate only if it can restore confidence that mankind is capable of utilizing scientific methods on a sufficiently large scale to deal effectively with our global crises. This will include capacity to demonstrate enough about the nature of values and obligations in ways that people will again find convincing and worthy of loyalty and continuing participation. It must demonstrate how each person is rightly self-interested and also ways and extents to which each person has rich, complex, and enduring interests (self-interests) in the welfare of others, including all mankind.

Quantum Leaping

Mankind's present inabilities to cope with current global crises are due in part to incompetencies inherent in trying to solve new problems with old methods. These old and no longer adequate methods are guided by conceptions derived from efforts and successes in dealing with past problems. Our new problems call for new conceptions. The new conceptions must enable us to comprehend growing complexities, greater interdependencies, more numerous dimensions, more extensive ranges of levels, more intricate specializations, more rapid and more variable changes in each, the organizability of more varieties of cultural divergencies, and the approaching of more kinds of limits inherent in each tendency.

The new conceptions needed will involve a quantum leap to some new system gestalt. It will have its own key ideas. It will hold together in its own way. It will have its own principle of coherence. It will have its own way of making sense and its own common sense. It will generate its own conception of intelligence, its own morale and spiritual morality, and its own ideals. It will also have its own limitations, deficiencies, and detrimental tendencies, though these may not become obvious until practitioners of the new philosophy begin to carry it to its own extremes. (I refer here not to what will appear to be deficiencies to those who cannot yet participate in the system but to deficiencies resulting from inadequacies in the new conceptions and from excesses of enthusiasts who transform a virtue into a vice. However, deficiencies resulting from nonparticipation and from partial, and thus partly confused, participation must also be reckoned with.)

The quantum leap we need in intellectual understanding of the nature of things, including atoms, cells, persons, societies, galaxies, and the universe, requires quantum leaps in each of the sciences, including philosophy as a comprehensive whole, interacting with each other in achieving the new interpretive gestalt. A quantum leap in only one discipline is not enough. The philosophy needed, being one in which whole and parts organically interdepend, requires active, positive, adequate participation by each of the parts. The philosophy needed will evolve through dialectical interactions, which may be thought of as mutual proddings of parts and whole, as well as emerging reembodiments of contributions by parts to the whole and by the whole to each part. Minds attuned to the philosophy we need will become more constantly aware of interlevel causation, interdimensional causation, and interfunctional causation as factors in understanding, and acting upon, every major problem. If it can be shown how humanitarianism, humanism, science, comprehensiveness, and adequacy all interinvolve each other in new quantum-leap conceptions, our needed philosophy will be underway already.

A WORLD PHILOSOPHY? HOW TO FORMULATE IT

The needed philosophy cannot be formulated fully without significant contributions from each of the major disciplines. It should be a product of multidisciplinary and interdisciplinary research. It should be humanitarian, humanistic, scientific, comprehensive, adequate, and quantum leaping. It should explain and interpret the nature of existence and its processes, or self, society, and the universe and their processes, better than any of its predecessors—both the great Augustinian and Hegelian syntheses and the more limited models of recent design. It should be not only understandable and believable by people in all cultures but should appear able to answer in novel ways, realistically and satisfactorily, questions troubling all persons disturbed by contemporary crises, global and personal. It should serve as a guide to those who are suspended between a decaying or decayed consensus and a new consensus needed as a basis for a new morale providing confidence in the worthwhileness of working for a better future for mankind and for oneself.

KNOWLEDGE

Much knowing will occur as it always did, and true understanding of the nature of knowledge prevailing now will continue to be useful.

The new conceptual system gestalt will have a nature of its own, however. The new must build on the old, but the new is so different from the old that some of its features could not have been predicted from previous knowledge. On the one hand, human nature remains much the same and any new knowledge is conditioned by that nature. But the new kind of knowledge introduces something genuinely new into human nature so that, those whose lives are guided by it embody a somewhat modified nature. Thus, what is new is not absolutely new. It depends on that from which it emerged. Yet what is novel about it did not exist before. So something new has been added, not merely to knowledge but to the nature of knowledge.

The question *What is knowledge?* is a complex one, having at least four parts. These four distinguishable parts are the questions *What is knowing? What is truth? What is certainty?* and *What is science?* Answering each involves a host of other problems.

Knowing

Knowing involves knower and known, often called subject and object. Persisting issues regarding the nature of each and the importance of each in constituting knowledge perpetuate debates among theorists. The most troublesome issue pertains to whether objects of knowledge are apparent or real, though issues regarding whether the knowing subjects are real or apparent also make the picture more complex. What appears is intuited or immediately apprehended. What is real (exists in addition to intuited appearance) must be inferred. Inferences, perceptual or conceptual, may be false, and inferential reasoning about percepts and concepts may be invalid.

Realistic theories emphasize knowledge as information; that is, knowledge reveals the form or nature of real things in ideas about them existing in minds. Subjectivistic theorists emphasize knowledge as ideas in minds, whether as products of minds alone or as products of minds influenced by external sources whose real natures may not be reproducible in minds. Quantum-leap conceptions of knowledge must include not only complex, dynamic variations in both subject and objects but also principles describing constancies and variations in their intricate interactions.

Objects of knowledge may be things or processes existing at any of the multiplicities of levels of existence. All of the sciences that contribute to understanding any such objects have a contribution to make to the nature of knowledge as involving such objects. Physics, chemistry, astronomy, geology, geography, agriculture, architecture, and economics all have contributions to make. When the objects are living or manufactured, then biology, physiology, psychology, and aesthetics all have roles to play in understanding objects.

The subject of knowing is also a multicomplex process produced by its own biological evolutions and cultural histories with genetic, dietetic, environmental, and linguistic influences upon its nature. So biology, physiology, psychology, sociology, and anthropology, all have contributions to make to understanding each subject and thus to understanding the nature of knowledge.

Epistemology, the science of knowledge, is a complex interdisciplinary science. Its special problems begin after all of the other sciences have made their contributions. I do not mean that persons face problems of knowledge only after such contributions. I mean that our quantum-leap conceptions of the nature of knowledge can be expected to reveal understanding adequately only after the essential contributions from all other sciences have been included among needed data. Knowing involves a continuing interaction between knower and known such that dialogical or dialectical developments tend to change both subject and object somewhat as ideas become more adequately adapted to the things known.

Issues regarding appearance versus reality persist and, in contrast with those theories favoring reducing knowledge to appearances or phenomena and with those favoring naive or direct realistic revelation of definite forms, our quantum-leap conceptions should demonstrate an ability to deal adequately with both appearances and realities. American pragmatists have shown us ways for coping with these issues, and their contributions to epistemology should be recognized and utilized in evolving further developments needed. Knowledge results from being confronted with problems, formulating hypotheses about what will solve them, efforts to test the hypotheses, and retention of successful hypotheses for possible future use.

Some problems pertain to appearances, even to dreams, but most practical problems involve inferences about the nature of something real. We need an increased sensitivity to both the inferential character of knowing and the need for devising plans for acting intelligently in the absence of assurance that our only-partly-adequate realistic hypotheses will work. Both subjective and real limitations need to be kept in mind. A knower cannot know what is beyond the capacity of his mind to know. Real things or processes that cannot influence a knower or cannot be represented by appearances cannot be known. But within these limitations, possibilities for increasing capacities of minds and for facilitating influences (through microscopes, telescopes, telephones, computers, and other instruments) should be exploited.

Although the superiority of quantum-leap epistemology may seem more obviously a result of its indebtedness to quantum-leap developments in all the other sciences contributing to greater understanding of the natures of things functioning as objects and of persons acting as subjects, awareness of the intimate interdependence between the nature of knowledge and its conditions as described by other sciences should lead to constant attention to such interdependencies rather than to a systematic ignorance of them. Attentiveness to the ever-present role of values in knowing promotes a capacity for discriminating variations in shades as well as for distinguishing differences in kind.

Truth

Despite the simplicity and seeming convenience of copy and correspondence theories of truth, they must be given up as inadequate. In spite of laudable interest in comprehensiveness of those proposing phenomenal coherence as constituting truth, it too is inadequate. Truth, having its locus in knower-known contexts, is double ended. Beliefs have two essential conditions: what is believed to be (usually called *idea*, contributed by the knower) and what is (an object of attention, which exists as something known). The truth of a belief depends upon both what is believed to be and what is and upon how closely these are related (for example, the same, completely, partly, in some respects, or not at all).

"Believers vary in their intentions from time to time, sometimes intending that 'what is believed to be' depends more on what 'is' and sometimes intending that the relevant 'is' depends more upon 'what is believed to be.' For example, when I study a new subject, such as a map of Tibet, I normally intend that the map should serve as the basis on which the truth of my belief will depend. But when I desire to draw plans for a house I wish to build, then it is my desire that provides the primary basis on which the truth of my belief depends; what is desired functions as the criterion for truth rather than the plans to be drawn."[1]

Some theories emphasize dependence of what is on belief. "Truth is a property of a belief when what is believed to be is."[2] Others emphasize dependence of what is believed to be on what is: "To say of what is that it is is true."[3] The organicist theory of truth, here proposed as a contributor to the quantum-leap conceptions about truth, claims that in spite of, or rather through, differing emphases regarding the relative importance of what is and what is believed to be, both are essential where beliefs exist. Instead of claiming that either correspondence, coherence, workability, authority, intuition, custom, or any other specific criterion conditions all truth, the organicist theory remains systematically ambiguous about criteria: "Each judgment is made with such specifications as are required by its peculiar set of conditions. . . . The truth of each judgment depends on whether there are whatever specifications are judged to be."[4]

Additional problems arise during communication between two or more persons, when groups adopt standardized interpretations, when words, printed or spoken, intervene, and when ideas are translated from one language to another. The organicist theory intends its generalizations to be relevant to all of the foregoing problems and to any additional complexities, interdependencies, dynamic variations, and dialectical developments that may appear for attention. Its systematic ambiguity in subjective-versus-objective emphases enables it to adapt automatically to whatever new gestalts, whatever newly discovered particles appear, and whatever new levels, dimensions, interdisciplinary relations, comprehensive syntheses, or kinds of interexistence emerge.

Any generalization about the nature of truth, when trueness of beliefs interdepends with the somewhat flexible natures of both knowers and what is known, should be stated in terms of such natures, flexibilities and interdependencies. And as our knowledge of the natures of things and processes (both knowers and known) develops, it should have its influence on our understanding of the nature of truth. Truth, in its fuller concrete sense, includes both its systematically ambiguous general nature and all of the particular beliefs of all people (and I have no reason for doubting that animals also have true and false beliefs).

Certainty

Only after doubts arise in a naive believer who then fears that he may not solve his problems, does the problem of assurance that beliefs are true occur. Charles Sanders Peirce is credited with alerting us to the insight that certainty is a feeling of belief or conviction resulting from settling a doubt. Some doubts can be settled completely. A clerk shows me shoes that appear to be too small for me. I doubt that they will fit. I try them on. They fit comfortably. My doubt is gone. Certainty—all that was required to settle that particular doubt—prevails. But some doubts can never be settled completely. In fact, all inferences regarding the nature of what appears to be real can and, in all but the naive and credulous, should remain uncertain. Certainty and uncertainty, belief and doubt, tend to occur as more or less. When our beliefs prove trustworthy in practice, we tend to continue to trust them. But we also learn that beliefs work sometimes and not others and that policies that usually bring satisfactory results sometimes produce frustrations.

The quest for certainty is so strong in some that once they have doubts, they refuse to be quieted short of authoritative assurance of absolute certainty. Some students of philosophy who encounter the skepticism of David Hume, after studying systems proclaiming eternal truths and deducible necessary implications in Platonic, Aristotelian, and Thomistic views, refuse to recover a willingness to venture uncertain inferences. They go from absolute certainty to absolute uncertainty. They insist on doubting everything continuously, unaware that their insistence involves a kind of dogmatism, i.e., claim to certainty, that no beliefs can be certain.

A saner view avoids extremes of both dogmatism and agnosticism by adopting an attitude of tentativity—holding beliefs that work as long as they work but not holding them so tightly that they will not be released when they do not work. Our quantum-leap conceptions must be held with sufficient faith to try them out and to give them a

fair trial. But especially since we can expect that a complex of multicomplex hypotheses will not solve all problems in our complexly
multicomplex world perfectly immediately, we must expect to modify them in light of additional evidence derived from practice with
them. We must expect to give up some of what we are holding so that
we can hold on to a more satisfactory hypothesis more firmly. Since
our problematic world is expected to keep changing, not only in
ways consistent with the natural developments of many different
kinds of natures but also in ways that are new in kind and complexity, new in varieties of flexibility, and new in degree of incomprehen-
sibility, we must be ready with multiplicities of beliefs each held with
some different degree of tentativeness while at the same time looking
for evidence expected to modify such degrees.

Thus our quantum-leap system gestalt will be filled with uncertainties drawn from each science, from interdisciplinary inabilities,
from ambiguities inherent in any comprehensive picture of a whole
that is both the same as and different from its parts, from variable
rates of change creating new problems, from incapacities for complete communication, from incapacities of minds to grasp intricate
complexities and multidimensional dynamics sufficiently, and from
suspicions that the task of understanding enough to survive is beyond our capacities. Even if we succeed with our quantum-leap conceptions, how soon will growing complexities require still another
quantum leap also necessary for survival?

Our quantum-leap gestalt will also be filled with confidence, for
when it enables us to overcome current crises, we will embody it in
our mentalities and characters and participate in it willingly to the
extent that it continues to sustain our hopes. By embodying it, we
become embodied in it. It becomes a second nature, guiding our interexistences with feelings of competence that we can meet and overcome still greater challenges and crises. As with all hypotheses, it is
characterized somewhat by a spirit of venture. Some persons will
find ways to stagnate in it, but the spirit of tentativeness to the system gestalt should make stagnation more difficult for many.

Science

Since present global predicaments result partly from deficiencies
caused by scientists and others who hold false or inadequate philoso-

phies of science, nothing is more central to our quantum-leap system gestalt than its philosophy of science. Many issues must be considered before an adequate philosophy of science can be achieved. Exploration here is limited to four issues: facts or values? method or methods? analytic or synthetic? and one superior science or many?

FACTS OR VALUES?

Does science presuppose values? Can science deal with problems of value? Unfortunately logical positivism, which has become the philosophy of science held by a majority of scientists and teachers of science in the United States, gave negative answers to both questions. Its answers were false.[5] Its influence has led not only to efforts to eliminate all references to values from scientific treatises but also to customary denial in scientific circles that axiology, the science of values, exists. It presupposes that science, which is completely objective, is incompetent to deal with values, since they are subjective. The truth is that science is permeated with values and that values can be dealt with by scientific methods just as surely as facts can.

Science aims to solve problems. In solving problems, is it better to use scientific methods or is it a matter of indifference whether such methods are used? If it makes no difference, then there is no need for using them. If it does make a difference, what is the difference? Using them is better than not using them.

The scientific attitude is characterized by objectivity. One should not permit personal prejudices to bias his conclusions. It is better to be objective than not, because it is better to reach conclusions without biasing influences.

In solving a problem, a scientist must formulate a hypothesis. Are some hypotheses better than others for dealing with this problem or are all equally good? If one is better than the others, which one ought the scientist choose? The better, or best, of course. Why? Because it is the best. In testing a hypothesis, are some tests better than others? If values were eliminated from science, no tests could be good or better. All would be alike in value or have no value. But all scientists know that some tests are better than others and that they ought to make the best one possible. Many more questions could be asked about different parts of science. Regarding each, scientists are forced to reply that, relative to each, they ought to choose the best. Values and obligations are present at every step in scientific processes.

Recognition of this fact is essential to our quantum-leap conceptions.

Axiology, the science of values, like physics, has existed from early Greek times. Its task is to understand the nature of values. Basically values are of two kinds—intrinsic and instrumental, more commonly called ends and means. Intrinsic values, such as feelings of pleasantness, exist. Every person has them. Each person intuits his feelings. Intuited feelings of pleasantness are intuited just as certainly as intuited sense data. So the empirical starting point of axiology is just as certain as the empirical starting point of physics. Scientific hypotheses usually are generalizations. Insofar as two or more things are alike in some respect, we have a basis for generalization. Insofar as they are different, we do not. Feelings of pleasantness are alike in some respects. When attended to directly, all are intuited as ends-in-themselves. When they participate in complex experiences, their ends-in-themselves quality may be more difficult to distinguish. But when any sense datum regarded as basic for a physicist is comingled in complex experiences, it too is more difficult to distinguish.

Continuous recognition of the numerous value aspects of all science and of axiology as a basic science will characterize our quantum-leap conceptual system. An absence of willingness and ability of political leaders to recognize and appeal to sound presuppositions and conclusions regarding values as bases for policy decisions cripples them in dealing with global crises when such bases for appeals are needed. Axiology should play an ever-present and foundational role in all interdisciplinary studies serving as bases for policy decisions.

METHOD OR METHODS?

A long-standing issue is whether there is one scientific method common to all sciences and all scientific problems, or whether each science designs its own methods for dealing with its own kinds of problems. The answer is that both are correct.

At least five common elements can be observed in all experimental sciences concerned with solving problems. The first is awareness of a problem. The second is examining the problem. Clarifying it and distinguishing relevant from irrelevant aspects should help in understanding the problem. Proposing solutions is third. Initial suggestions often prove inadequate. Such suggestions, functioning as working hypotheses, are tried out. Much trial-and-error thinking may be expected before a satisfactory hypothesis is achieved. Fourth is testing proposals. Hypotheses, especially more complex ones, tend to be tested mentally at first. Criteria, such as consistency, validity of interferences, and adequacy, should be employed. When deficiency appears, the hypothesis must be given up or reformulated. Last is solving the problem. Practical experiments should be performed where possible and, ideally, a crucial experiment that provides conclusive evidence should be sought.

But each science consists of problems of a particular kind and each tends to require methods peculiarly suited to its kind. Astronomers use telescopes. Biologists use microscopes. Chemists use test tubes. Archeologists use digging tools. Geologists drill holes. Social psychologists use public opinion polls. Some sciences use control groups. Astronomers, unable to control the stars, must be content with observations. Furthermore, each complex problem has some unique aspects requiring invention of a particular method for dealing with them. As problems become more complex, intricate, dynamic, and global, awareness of a multileveled approach to methodology becomes more important. Sound scientists will employ a method embodying all of those steps essential to scientific method in general, those methods considered essential for dealing with problems in his field, and whatever methods are needed for dealing with the peculiar aspects of his problem. Furthermore, as awareness of the interdependence of different kinds and levels of existence spreads, there is need for recognizing and utilizing both the methods of other sciences and the newly developing interdisciplinary methods when dealing with factors in other fields that bear upon one's problem.

Our quantum-leap system calls for increased sensitivities to the needs for general, specific, and particular methods and to reliance upon methods that have proved themselves in the past and new methods required by the novelties in problems emerging as a result of changes in our world. Furthermore, as problems become more complex, we need to devise more readily available methods for dealing with them, both with ways in which all complexities are alike and ways in which each complex is different and unique. Techniques for dealing with interdisciplinary problems and interdisciplinary aspects of problems in each discipline remain in their infancy. The importance of attending to the whole range of disciplines, to interdisciplinary interdependencies, to the comprehensive whole of knowledge, and to both the contributions from each for dealing with one's own problems and the implications of one's own solutions for each will become more obvious as we come to be more at home in our new gestalt system.

ANALYTIC OR SYNTHETIC?

Generally, contemporary scientists are used to thinking analytically and to seeking understanding by taking things apart into their essential constituent parts that analysis seems to be the main aim of science. Each science has to discover its own techniques for analyzing its own subject matter. Mathematics is a common useful tool because it can aid in analytical precision. Now electronic computers have magnified our capacities for quick quantitative analyses. Analytical habits presuppose that wholes depend on their parts, and that if the parts function as wholes, then these too depend on still smaller parts until we find some ultimate particles on which all else depend. The historical quest of physical scientists for smaller and smaller particles (for example, for molecules, atoms, and subatomic particles) has been remarkably successful. That the particles turned out to be dynamic and functioning as static aspects of waves has not discouraged the habit of looking for smaller or shorter waves.

Habits of thinking presupposing that parts, especially the most ultimate particles, are more real than wholes tend to ignore, and sometimes deny, existence to wholes. The apparent mountain, tree, person, and apple are unreal except insofar as they consist of the ultimate particles, the true ultimate realities. This way of thinking has serious difficulties. It implies that the subject matters of all other sciences, economics, psychology, biology, geology, and astronomy are less real than that of physics and chemistry and that these scientists can achieve their goal of understanding their subject matters fully only when it has been further analyzed into the physical and its ultimate particles. Such a view is clearly reductionistic. It is called materialistic because it locates ultimate reality in particles. But it demoralizes less materialistic sciences to the extent that they must believe that their own analyses can be only partial analyses. Although some reaction has set in to ideals of extremely reductionistic analysis, much more will be needed for acclimatization within our quantum-leap gestalt. Increasing difficulties facing physicists forced to reconceive the nature of particles in terms of wavicles [6] and of particle-field complementarities, to say nothing of reaching their limits of knowability referred to as a principle of indeterminancy, are encouraging other scientists to concentrate efforts on their own problems without worrying much about their inabilities to be more reductionistic.

Our quantum-leap gestalt calls both for more confidence in each science that it has something ultimate to deal with and, what is more difficult, that in having a significant contribution to make to the total picture, it also becomes involved in interdependent interactions with all of the other sciences in significant ways. The most troublesome kind of reductionism is the willingness of some scientists to see their own subject matter as having most ultimacy. Each specialized science tends to magnify itself beyond its true proportions in the larger picture. The need for multidisciplinary, comprehensive understanding and interdisciplinary understanding now becomes urgent. Retreat to some earlier unifying conception, such as Platonism, Aristotelianism, or Thomism, is inadequate. The evolutionists, emergentists, and process philosophers have located some new fundamentals that reconceivers ignore with jeopardy. Holistic conceptions are needed. But inexperience with thinking in terms of wholes opens the door for hasty speculations and ardent credulity. The problem is not merely one of understanding wholes, which has its own host of difficulties, but of understanding organic wholes embodying interdependencies of wholes and parts.

Despite the fact that we constantly function, variably, as both wholes and parts, our philosophies of science have tried to habituate us to believe that we are really parts without wholes (subatomic particles) or wholes (souls) without parts. I have tried to understand (using analytic methods) different aspects of the nature of organic wholeness. I have distinguished: "homotheses" and "henotheses" as parts of "syntheses," "partitheses," "holotheses," and "organitheses" and, stressing dynamic rather than structural aspects, synthetic dialectic, analytic dialectic and organitic dialectic. I have attempted to provide a preliminary glimpse of the nature of "organicity," that wholeness which includes both each whole and its parts while also functioning as part of other wholes multihierarchically.[7] Recent holisms rightly reject the presuppositions of extreme analytic ideals. But if they do not in turn reject the presuppositions of extreme wholistic ideals, their efforts at constructive contributions may mislead disastrously. Acceptance of complex dynamic part-whole interdependencies as ultimate realities seems necessary for quantum-leap science.

Replacing emphasis on analysis with emphasis on complementary cooperation of analysis and synthesis seems called for by our quantum leap conceptions. Inherent in such emphasis is an organic logic, one incorporating both analytic and synthetic logics and showing how extinction results from carrying either to its extreme. Work needed for clarifying and explaining simply (or as simply as a complex, interdependent, dynamic, multidimensional, multidialectical organic logic can be explained) remains to be done.

ONE SUPERIOR SCIENCE OR MANY?

Foolish claims are made about whether one science is superior to all others. Some regard physics as the basic science on which all others are founded. Some claim theology as prior to all other sciences. Marxists make political economy, as interpreted by Karl Marx, the foundation for all else. Historians recording all history, including the history of science, cannot see why others do not recognize their discipline as the most inclusive. Some mathematicians say that mathematics is the only science; it makes other sciences scientific. We await the final pronouncement by computer-based systems theorists: "What cannot be computerized is not science." Axiologists claim that the science of values is most basic because, without value, none of the other sciences can be any good. Philosophy in its comprehensive functioning systematically incorporates all the others as parts into a fullest whole. Persons in every science are likely to make similar claims. Persons in each such science can see their own as essential and believe that all others must depend on it.

Our quantum-leap system will both incorporate and deny each of the foregoing claims by showing how every science is superior to all of the others with respect to what it contributes and how each depends on all of the others for their contributions. Instead of relating the sciences in a single hierarchy and then locating one science at the bottom, or top, or in some other strategic location, and then proclaiming it king of the sciences, our quantum-leap system gestalt will depict each thing, each kind of thing, and certainly each science, as a pinnacle of development relative to what it is in itself. We must be able to grasp a multiplicity of interdependent hierarchies and understand that new hierarchies are constantly developing as interactions of variable processes create new kinds of existence. Since success in solving our critical problems by means of scientific methods will require mastery of both multidisciplinary and interdisciplinary insights, an infant study of multidisciplinary and interdisciplinary research may be the next science to claim essentiality and superiority. Scientists unwilling to grow in complexities of understanding by studying the contributions of all other sciences to their own are not ready for the quantum-leap conceptions.

What may make more scientists more willing to study contributions from other sciences is the fact that some sciences are engaged in their own quantum-leap problems. Astronomy's discovery of quasars and black holes, and new data and new puzzles from space exploration, provoke reconsideration of theories of the origin and nature of the universe. Physicists' discoveries of some unanticipated particles,[8] combined with growing dissatisfactions with particle theory, challenge reconception of fundamentals. Biologists experimenting with DNA and RNA structures and processes by producing gene recombinations open up a whole new era of both creativity and understanding that may revolutionize biological conceptions. Psychologists experimenting with brainwaves hope for a breakthrough soon in more adequate understanding of our mind-body problems. Technological advances in nuclear fission, lasers, and electronics present new problems that call for newer, more complex conceptions.

The course of development of our quantum-leap system gestalt may depend partly upon quantum-leap conceptions in each of several sciences since the system gestalt itself must both adapt to and integrate within itself all such developments. If global war can be postponed until this new system gestalt can guide educational and policy decision processes, it may be prevented completely. Thus the urgency for facilitating quantum-leap developments in each science

becomes evident. Lag in developing competent interdisciplinary research—research aiming to integrate quantum-leap developments in
many disciplines in our general quantum-leap system gestalt—may
prove to be our greatest deficit. Training for the management of
organizing quantum-leap conceptions in many disciplines in the new
system gestalt should have highest priority. If such training is successful, then educational programs designed to facilitate participatory embodiment of the gestalt sufficient to draw implications
needed for solutions to problems in all fields involving interdepen-
dences with other fields will develop naturally.

EXISTENCE

Mankind exists. The human predicament exists. Our crises exist.
Metaphysics is that science inquiring into the nature of existence,
especially its universal characteristics. Mankind, predicaments, and
crises embody such traits. We cannot here survey all claims and controversies about such traits.[9] But some, especially some probably
playing central roles in our quantum-leap conceptions, will be considered. I have selected twelve such traits, or trait complexes, to
show something of the direction that the kind of metaphysics needed
for our quantum-leap system will take.

Complexity

Existence is inherently complex. Continuing explorations in each
of the sciences and subsciences reveal greater complexity, and more
kinds of complexity, than we previously imagined. Understanding
such complexities had to await developing capacities for conceiving
them. These capacities have depended in part on developing instruments for distinguishing differences, measuring quantitative differences, and repeating observations and experiments to test hypotheses about them, and in part in cooperation among scientists, both
within and between various sciences, in accumulating, interpreting,
and integrating information. High-speed printing, satellite communication, electronic computation, rapid data processing and retrieval, research institutes, and billion-dollar funding will increase
our capacities to conceive complexities and to discover existence to
be still more complex.

One difficulty encountered in many efforts to comprehend greater complexity is the natural tendency to grasp newer and greater complexities by means of older conceptions. The advent of digital computers and their usefulness in astounding engineering achievements, such as landing men on the moon, encourages tendencies to conceive complexities in terms of more rapid quantitative measurements.[10] But there is more to increasing complexity than increasing quantity. Note that the word *complex* itself connotes both *plexity*, or plurality involving some interweaving, and *com*, consisting in union or unity. Until our conceptions and our methodologies reveal actual unities inherent in complexities, they remain inadequate. The symbolic logic used by digital computer programmers presupposes completely isolated entities and completely external relations between them. The *com* in complexity escapes both their conceptions and their computations completely. So our quantum-leap conception of complexity requires an organic logic based in an organic metaphysics. How much of such organicness can be captured by analog computers, I do not yet know.

Complexity interdepends with all other characteristics of existence, so one way of exploring needed quantum-leap conceptions of complexity is to examine other such characteristics. Details presented in treating the following topics should be interpreted as contributing to our fuller understanding of complexity.

Interdependence

Conceptions giving primacy to either independence or to dependence are inadequate for interpreting the nature of existence. Complexity involves interdependence, which in turn involves complexity. The concept of interdependence is a more complex concept than either independence or dependence because it presupposes both. When two or more things interdepend, each is both partly independent of and partly dependent on the other. As a general conception, interdependence is ambiguous relative to how much independence and how much dependence is involved in any particular interdepending situation, just as both independence and dependence, as general conceptions, are ambiguous relative to how much independence and how much dependence is involved in any particular situation.

Since existence is dynamic as well as complex and interdependent, interdependencies tend to vary. When two or more things interdepend, they may become more independent of each other or more dependent on each other. Some things vary in their ways of being dependent and independent regularly. Some evolve in ways that increase some of their kinds of independence and others in ways that increase some of their kinds of dependence. But the only way a thing could become completely independent of all else is by ceasing to exist; the only way a thing could become completely dependent on other things is by ceasing to exist as a thing. I propose as a candidate for inclusion among the quantum-leap conceptions needed for the system gestalt organizing the philosophy shaping our emerging world culture the concept of interdependence as a universal trait of existence.

Complementarity

Unless something can stand alone in complete isolation, it depends on all of the other things conditioning its existence in order for it to exist. These other things are complementary in the sense that they provide what is necessary to supply the conditions of its existence. No existing thing is complete merely in itself. Whatever else is necesdary to complete it is its complement. Thus complementarity is itself a condition of, or a universal characteristic of, existence.

There are many different kinds of complementarity. For each thing, there are as many different kinds of complementarity as there are kinds of existing things actually contributing to its existence. Complementarity characterizes all other universal characteristics of existence. Complexity embodies complementarity because complexity is such that its "com" is incomplete without its "plex" and its "plex" is incomplete without its "com." Each needs the other to complete it, and each helps complete the other. Interdependence embodies complementarity, for it requires both some independence and some dependence. The independence is incomplete without the dependence, and the dependence is incomplete without the independence. So each, independence and dependence, needs the other to complete it. Each complements the other.

We should not neglect negative complementarity. Each thing is both what it is and is not what it is not. For example, "I am a person" and "I am not a cow" are both true statements about me. If there were no cows, then, although I could not be a cow, actually I could not be "not a cow." I depend on the existence and nature of cows for my being not a cow. Although I am very complex and depend on everything else in the universe to complete the conditions of my existence in the universe, since I am also not most of the many things constituting the universe, my being not them and their being not me also characterizes me. Both statements about what I am and about what I am not are needed for any complete statement about me. They complement each other. This kind of complementarity may seem unduly technical or trivial, but I believe that more careful studies about the nature of existence reveal that the negative and positive aspects of each thing tend to complement each other symmetrically as well as asymmetrically (as depicted in the Tao symbol, for example).

The importance of complementarity, and of complemetarity of complementarities, as a quantum-leap conception may be suggested by its usefulness in replacing attitudes of antagonism between persons and between peoples whose antipathies result from conceiving their opposition as involving some essential exclusion. Emphasizing facts about complementarity, both positive and negative, will tend to diminish antipathies based on imbalanced estimations of actual complements. If Mazrui could see that more developed nations cannot exist as more developed unless less-developed nations exist, and that any attributed rating as "more" in any way depends for its existence as more in that way on the existence of what is less in that way, then he might not require artificaly induced pride, and efforts that seem to him needed to justify that pride, as a prerequisite to consenting to share feeling at home in a world community. The concept of complementarity does not by itself replace injustice with justice. But people are more likely to cooperate in preventing human extinction when they are aware of the universality of complementarity than when they are motivated by "reciprocal vulnerability."

The more complex world society becomes, the more important will become sensitivity regarding the multiplicities of ways in which private and public ownership complement each other essentially.

Although I do not yet see clearly how complementarism will replace or subordinate capitalism or communism in our quantum-leap system, current trends in both capitalistic and communistic countries caused by increasingly complex technological, megalopolitan, and global interdependencies appear to be forcing each away from extreme and exclusive claims about their differences. I suggest that the needed emerging world political economy will be forced to eliminate both capitalistic and communistic extremes and to recognize the in--herent complementarity of personal and social ownership as essential to human existence. Those who would explore and promote complementarity as a quantum-leap conception enlightening our understanding of political and economic affairs would do well to understand complementarity as a metaphysical concept and as a logical concept also, so that any essentials of its general nature will not be missing from the particular application of it in their field.

Polarity

Polarity is such a complex concept that I hesitate to introduce it here, yet it seems likely to play a central role among proposed quantum-leap concepts. [11] When opposites are complementary, each is not the other, yet each needs the other to complete it. Some opposites have more in common than others. For example, truth and goodness are opposites; each is not the other. And goodness and badness are opposites; each is not the other. But good and bad are both values, and thus they have more in common than goodness and truth, which has falsity as its direct opposite. Technological convenience has resulted in calling good and bad apposite opposites and good and true inapposite opposites. True and false are also apposite opposites, as are dependence and independence, wholes and parts, universals and particulars, cause and effect, internal and external relations, permanence and change, stability and novelty, and actuality and potentiality.

Apposite opposites are polarly related. Polarity involves two positive poles, each of which is negative relative to the other. But it also involves something that both poles have in common. I do not wish to explore the nature of polarity further here, but I wish to point out that more careful observations of different kinds of existences, including personal and social existences, will reveal more and more kinds of polarities embodied in their natures and that understanding these polarities can reveal more about such natures. For example, understanding the opposing ideals of willfulness and willessness characterizing Western and Indian civilizations as polar opposites rather than as contradictory opposites opens the way to incorporating both in a coherent system of ideals of the kind needed to guide mankind through its present critical conflicts.

Polar opposites not only complement each other but also share something in common that is essential to the natures of both. So looking for and discovering more existing polarities among different societies and cultures can serve as a basis for demonstrating the existence of common traits that tend to be overlooked when focusing on their negative aspects. Polar opposites already partly interexist. When polar oppositions develop dialectically, they come to interexist more fully because they interexist in more ways. I suspect that many contributors to our needed quantum-leap system gestalt will neglect the conception of polarity, but I believe that it can contribute powerfully to increasing quantities as well as qualities of feelings of mutuality among human beings and may become a necessary, if not sufficient, condition of continuing cooperation as our social world becomes more complex.

Organic Wholeness

No concept is closer to the core of our quantum-leap system gestalt than that of organic wholeness. It begins with the distinction between a whole and its parts. Each thing is a whole of parts. Each thing consists of both its whole and its parts. Both the whole of a thing and the parts of a thing are essential to its nature. But since the parts of a thing are not its whole and the whole of a thing is not its parts, the whole and the parts of a thing are not each other and are opposed to each other. This opposition between parts and whole is the basis for tendencies to separate parts from whole or whole from parts. It is the source of philosophies emphasizing pluralities of parts and particles and of analytical methods for seeking understanding, on the one hand, and of philosophies emphasizing unity and wholeness as more ultimate than parts, on the other. Thus it is the source of materialisms, spiritualisms, and dualisms, those philosophies separating parts from wholes but keeping both as ultimate. All three of these kinds of philosophy are inadequate.

In addition to the whole and parts of a thing, where that whole is understood as opposed to the parts, there is another whole that includes both that whole and the parts. This more inclusive whole is called an *organic whole*. Understanding it is necessary for understanding the nature of an organism, an organization, and organicism, the philosophy proposed here as a contributer to our needed quantum leap world philosophy. Organicism is a philosophy proposing that whatever exists involves organic wholeness. *Organic* here is a metaphysical term; it refers to all kinds of existence and not merely to those limited fields of investigation, such as biology and organic chemistry. Thus atoms and galaxies are organic wholes; so are cells and societies.

The concept of organic whole is more complex than that of a whole as opposed to its parts. It presupposes interdependence of whole and parts with each other, and it is partly constituted by an awareness of such interdependence. Parts and whole complement each other in it, and thus it is more complete than either because it embodies their complementation. A part and its whole are polarly related. Since each whole is polarly related to each of its many parts, each whole involves multipolarity. Organic wholeness incorporates such multipolarity within itself; thus something of its inherent complexity begins to be seen. The parts of a whole also complement each other because each requires every other part to fulfill its function as part of that whole of all of its parts. Thus each part involves multicomplementarity—the complementarity of every other part, as well as the complementarity of the whole. An organic whole embodies such multicomplementarity as inherent in its nature.

Since each part of a whole also embodies both its complementary relations with the whole and with each of the other parts, it unites all of these in such a way that it too is a kind of whole of them. Furthermore each thing that functions as part of a whole exists also as a whole with its own parts, each of which also helps to complete it, and thus embodies additional multicomplementarity. We could use the term *organic partness* or *organic wholeness*. Actually, the proper term is *organicness* or *organicity*, but since neither has popular currency, and *organic wholeness* does, I shall use the latter. The word *holism* has gained currency as a term used by those giving more emphasis to wholes than to parts. When too many philosophies overemphasize parts, holistic philosophies are needed as a counterbalance. But we would fail to be faithful to what seems to be our needed quantum-leap conceptions if we failed to make clear that organicness inherently embodies both parts and whole and left an impression that what is essentially both wholistic and partistic is more wholistic than partistic.

Of course, some things can lose parts, gain parts, or exchange parts. Sometimes things function more as wholes and sometimes more through their parts. Understanding organic wholeness thus involves understanding that great variation and variability exist relative to the importance of wholeness and partness in what is organic. Some things by nature function more as mechanical wholes—where the parts have greater independence and stability as parts—and some as more vital wholes—where the parts tend to cease functioning as parts as soon as the whole declines or ceases. The complexity of the conception of organic wholeness increases still more in its complexity when it embodies such variations.

Furthermore, not only do the parts of a whole exist as wholes with their own parts, but also the whole of parts functions as a part in a larger whole. As a larger whole, it participates in another complex of multi-interdependencies, multicomplimentarities, and multipolarities, and probably some multivariabilities. Thus we can see that leveledness is already inherent in organic wholeness.

Levels

The concept of levels is not new. Probably no primitive myth or ancient mandala failed to include levels of some kind. Each philosophy has included some account of levels, even if only to declare all illusory, evanescent, or subjective. Some thinkers have hypostatized levels as eternal. Today all specialists struggle with levels peculiar to their specialty. They often seem forced to seek to have their specialty recognized as high among the levels of specialization, since we have levels of rating as well as levels of existing.

Levels, the emergentists have emphasized, exist as levels of organization. Mendeleev's table of atomic elements revealed how chemicals exist as smaller and greater numbers and kinds of parts, with levels arranged somewhat correlatively to what we call their atomic number. Biologists have reconstructed much of the evolution of plant and animal life from single-celled organisms to hereditarily variable complexes of human species. Psychologists can trace levels of development from relatively simple stimuli to percepts, concepts, and conceptual systems, including the sciences, languages, and capacities for multicultural comparisons in human beings. Sociologists describe levels of groups ranging from the simplest two-person association (such as mother-child), through family, tribal, national, and global groups, with heirarchical levels obvious in political and other institutionalized functions. Geological layers and astronomical levels, from planets and solar systems to milky ways and galaxies, are well known.

The emergentists have also called attention to levels of levels. They distinguish major levels that are called *Matter*, *Life*, *Mind*, and *Society*. Although at each chemical level, some genuinely different kind of substantiality and functioning occurs, there is sufficient similarity between the levels so that generalizations about their similarities (as Matter) seem warranted. Furthermore, some actions result in changing an atom not merely into another atom of the same kind but into an atom of a different kind or of a different level. When Life emerged into existence for the first time, something new in the way of organization or wholeness developed that could not be explained merely in terms of constituent parts of lower levels.

Matter, Life, Mind, and Society are regarded as very different kinds of levels, even though levels exist within each of these kinds. Some investigators claim that the seeming greatness of differences between Matter and Life, Life and Mind, and Mind and Society are not as great as previously believed. At the same time, some investigators are demonstrating how apparently trivial changes at one level can causally influence what happens at distant levels. For example, a tiny bit of chemical functioning as a poison can kill the president of a government, which depends on him. Or the action of one governmental group can cause fear in another, resulting in increased military appropriations and actions, leading to explosions producing chemicals that never existed before. Not only do we have levels, and levels of levels, but we can observe how entities or events at one level can cause significant effects at other levels.

What happens to leveledness, an old and well-recognized characteristic of existence, when interpreted through our quantum-leap conceptions? Levels are not merely layers piled on top of each other and resting on some bottom layer. Levels interdepend. Each whole depends on its parts. Each higher level thus consists of entities functioning as wholes that continue to depend on their parts and also of organic wholes embodying the multi-interdependence, multicomplementarity, and multipolarities of wholes and parts. Also each lower level not only consists of entities functioning as parts continuing to function as parts of wholes but also participating in organic wholes embodying the multi-interdependence, multicomplementarity, and multipolarities of parts and wholes.

The interrelations between two closely interdependent levels are already complex. Further observation reveals that wholes exist also as parts of larger wholes, which are parts of larger wholes. Parts also exist as wholes of parts, which themselves are wholes of parts. Since a part interdepends with a whole that is also a part interdepending with a larger whole functioning as part of a still larger or higher whole, that part interdepends with several higher levels of wholes. It also interdepends with several lower levels of parts. Since each whole-part relationship differs somewhat from every other such relationship, the nature of interdependencies between units of one level and those of more distantly higher or lower levels is not something that can be generalized about with facility. But awareness of such multiplicities of kinds of interdependence that each thing embodies enriches the complexities of our conceptions of leveledness as inherent in organic wholeness and of organic wholeness as inherently levelistic.

Hierarchy

Levels already involve hierarchy and hierarchy involves levels. The issue considered here is whether, in any series of levels, there is always one central direction or many. Most traditional philosophies have been monohierarchical. The hierarchy rests on a stable bottom and rises tier after tier until the top tier. Some conceive the single hierarchy as originating in some top level from which succeeding levels descend until there is a last level that serves as a bottom. But such views are inadequate. Existence is organized in such a complex manner that one thing can participate as a part in several hierarchies and also participate as a whole serving as the pinnacle of several hierarchies.

A person, for example, can function as part of a family group, which is part of a community, which is part of a state, which is part of a nation, and so on. That same person might also be part of a school class, which is part of a school, which is part of a school system, which is part of an educational association, which is part of an association of professional societies. That same person functions also as a whole body of organs as parts that are wholes of cells, as parts that are wholes of molecules, as parts that are wholes of atoms. Although the organs of that body are all alike because they are all organs of that body, they are also different; they are differently specialized organs, each with cells, some of which have different specializations, each with molecules, including DNA and RNA structures, some of which are differently specialized. Hence several different kinds of hierarchy cooperate in constituting the body of that person.

Thus each person embodies several different hierarchies within its nature and participates in several other hierarchies as a constituent part of them. Such multihierarchicity should be kept in mind when trying to understand the quantum-leap system gestalt and its implications observed when drawing conclusions for practical purposes. The importance of such multihierarchical complexity should not be overlooked when we come to ethics, for example, where self-interest becomes a complex of interests in all of one's constituents, including those that are multihierarchical. Some of the practical difficulties to be faced in ethical decisions result from variations in the relative importance to a self of the varying interdependencies of its different parts and, especially, of the varying amounts of ignorance regarding the status and actual health of such parts when complexities are such that they cannot all be attended to at any one time or even during a time in which one has to decide.

Problems of understanding become much more difficult when things are conceived as embodying and participating in many hierarchies. But when it becomes evident that one's functioning as an officer in an international peace-keeping force is a cause of his absence from his wife and no resulting children with no resulting bodies, organs, cells, molecules, etc., hierarchically organized in such a child, negative hierarchy is exemplified. Negative complexities, including undeveloped potentialities for complexes of hierarchies, are part of organic wholeness as a generalized metaphysical concept.

The kinds of hierarchies emerging into existence are subject matter for specialized scientists. The division of sciences into physical, biological, psychological, and social seems somewhat in accord with major levels as depicted by emergentists. That bases exist for such observations and for such classifications of sciences need not be doubted. But the more we become aware of the kinds of complexities observable as multihierarchies, the more additional kinds of scientific specializations will become needed. Likewise there will be more need for attention to interscientific communication between sciences focusing on organisms more distantly related in hierarchies.

Traditional monohierarchical conceptions depict levels resting on some bottom (as in emergentism) or descending from some top (as in the emanationism of Plotinus) or both (as in the creationism of John E. Boodin). The quantum-leap conceptions proposed here both abandon any permanent bottom and any permanent top of any monohierarchy (partly because it abandons monohierarchy). It accepts each thing as functioning as the top of any hierarchy that contributes to it as an entity in ways that it is the highest level of the hierarchy. It accepts each thing as functioning as the bottom, or part of the bottom, of any hierarchy to which it contributes as a participating entity without depending on any of its parts for such participation.[12] Such tops and bottoms of hierarchies tend to function aspectivally as parts of complexes rather than absolutely.

Emergence

The emergentists claim that new levels of organization emerge when new organic unities come into being for a first time. The importance of their contributions, which have been mistakenly ignored by recent thinking, leads me to summarize ideas they have contrib-

uted. When a new emergent occurs in the world, what is it that is
new? It is a new substance in the sense that it has stability and endurance. It embodies a new nature, or structure, of its organization.
It has new properties, capacities, and functions over and above those
of its constituent parts. Its new functions enact the new laws occurring as regularities in its own behavior. It is a new center of causation, influence, and control. [13] Having emerged into existence, an
emergent continues to depend on the parts it has organized into it as
a whole. It may exercise some control over the behavior of its parts.
Hence emergentists conceive whole-part and interlevel causation as
two-directional. But since they tend to conceive parts as always
prior to emergent wholes, higher-level wholes are generally more
dependent on, and more effectively caused by, lower-level parts
than such lower-level parts are dependent on or caused by such
emergent wholes.

John E. Boodin partly accepted and partly rejected emergentist
doctrine. [14] His monohierarchical scheme accepted a bottom to the
hierarchy as did the emergentists, but it also had a top, similar to that
of Plotinus, which he called "God." Between top and bottom levels,
all other levels were generated through joint causation from above
and below. However, God as a more active principle permeates all
levels into the lowest. Particles of matter are more passive but not
completely so. At each level, whatever emerges is caused to emerge
both by higher, more formal, and more active influences and by
lower, more material, and more intertial influences. Boodin's contribution, for my purposes, is his emphasis on greater equality of
both higher-level and lower-level sources of causation at any level,
even though I reject his monohierarchism and both its top and bottom.

The nature and functions of each thing owe something to both its
whole and its parts. Sometimes, of course, the parts are more influential in determining the behavior of a thing and thus its nature as a
thing which behaves in that way, and sometimes the whole is more
influential. But the point I wish to stress is that we do not understand
the nature of anything until we understand how its nature has been
caused partly by its wholeness, and by higher-level influences, and
partly by its parts, and by lower-level influences. Those who proceed merely analytically in their quest for understanding are clearly
reductionistic in their devotions. Those who claim that the whole

(what in humans some call "the soul") is the primary source of the nature of person are equally mistaken. Our proposed quantum-leap conceptions of things interpret their natures as caused by both higher-level and lower-level, as well as same-level, causes. When we become aware of how all three cooperate in causing things and their natures, we can call our conceptions *organic*. If the word *emergence* refers to the emergentist conception of the occurrence of novelty, then, for the organicist, the term *emergence* is already obsolete. We need a term such as *organence* or *organicience* to connote the triple source of causation.

But we already have the word *organization*? Why not use it? One difficulty here is that most varieties of popular usage do not connote such triple causation, so a specification that *organization* means new embodiment of organicity will be required if communication is to avoid unclarity. I shall continue to use the word *emergence* in the more general sense of the occurrence of new organisms or organizations. When used in the context of our quantum-leap conceptions, I expect the word to connote novelty resulting from both higher-and lower-level, as well as same-level, sources. Until a more suitable organicistic word is adopted, *emergence* will have to serve.

Dynamism

That physical, biological, and cultural changes occur is well known. But how change can be conceived is not so well known. To change is to become different. To become different is to change. The opposite of change is permanence. To be permanent is to remain the same. To remain the same is to be permanent. So defined, change and permanence are very simple.

Many conceive change and permanence (and difference and sameness) as contradictory opposites. Change is not permanence and permanence is not change. But according to our proposed quantum-leap conceptions, permanence and change interdepend, are complementary, are polarly related, and participate in organic wholeness and the other universal traits of existence. Thus change and permanence are both complex.

How do change and permanence interdepend? Unless a change is instantaneous, so that the difference which becomes ceases to exist, change involves permanence. A thing that changes in any way cannot remain changed in that way without being permanent in that way. No thing can become changed without permanence—both the remaining of the thing which is changed and the remaining of the way in which the thing is changed.

Unless the permanence of anything is instantaneous, so that the sameness which remains does so during only an instant, permanence involves change. A thing that remains does so for more than an instant and hence more than one unit of time, however time occurs relative to it. Thus that thing changes in the sense that first it exists at one instant, or unit of time, and then at another instant, or unit of time. A thing can be permanent only by existing in and through different units of time, and its existing first at or in one unit and then at or in another unit constitutes it as existing differently at least that much. No thing can remain the same without becoming changed enough to exist at different units of time.

There are as many kinds of change as there are ways in which a thing can become different, and as many kinds of permanence as there are ways in which a thing can remain the same. A thing may change by gaining a part, by losing a part, or by exchanging parts. A thing can change completely only by ceasing to be. For as long as a thing remains in any way, it has not changed in that way. Some kinds of change are repetitious, some are cyclical, some are regular, some are variable and some are dialectical.

Since the whole and parts of a thing interdepend, when a part of a thing changes, the whole of that thing also changes by becoming different in the sense that it is now a whole with a changed part, i.e., in whatever way the part has changed. When a whole changes in any way, its parts also change in the sense that they become parts of a changed whole in whatever way that whole has changed. Just as a whole and its parts together constitute an organic whole, so the interdependence of changes in a whole and its parts participate in constituting that organic whole. To change is to be organic, and to be organic is to be changing (as well as remaining).

Temporality

Time, when measured by clocks and calendars, seems very regular in nature. But such time is quite artificial, and some of its units are very artificial (such as twenty-four hours in a day, sixty minutes in an hour and sixty seconds in a minute). Actual time consists in natural changes, such as a year (one cycle of earth about sun), a month (or moon-th, one cycle of moon about earth), and a day (one cycle of the earth about its axis). Understanding the nature of actual time may be facilitated by examing the more easily observable units of heartbeats or inhalations.

In order to understand time, a distinction needs to be made between events and duration. An event is the occurrence of a change. It can last as long as it takes for something to become different in any way. Thus there are as many different kinds of events as there are kinds of ways of becoming different. A duration involves something remaining the same. Whatever remains the same while some difference becomes endures at least from the beginning to the end of that becoming. Thus every actual unit of time involves both duration and event as two interdependent, complementary aspects.

After a heartbeat begins, it rises to its maximum pressure and then subsides gradually until it becomes replaced by the next beat. Each heartbeat is an event. It has a beginning, a pulse of pressure, and an ending. Each heartbeat has a duration. It endures from its beginning to its ending. Each heartbeat is a unit. It has unity or wholeness. It is the same heartbeat from beginning to end. As such, it is undivided. Some beats take longer to occur than others. Pulse rates vary. But these beats, and other events like them, are the actual units of time.

How long is the present? Each pulse is present from its beginning to its end. Its present is as long as it endures. Hence there are as many presents as there are events, and each present lasts as long as the event endures. So we have the present heartbeat, the present day, the present month, the present year. The presents of each wavelength of sound, light, radio and X rays are very short, comparatively. Each human life, remaining the same life from beginning to end, is also an event. The lifetime of a civilization, a star, and a galaxy is an event.

Some events include other events. My heart may beat several times during one inhalation cycle. A month includes twenty-eight days and a year more than thirteen lunar months. All twenty-eight days come and go, successively, during one month. On the first day of the month, the first day and the month are both present. On the second day, the first day is past and not present, but the month is still present. On the last day of the month, twenty-six days have passed, but the month is still present. On the fourteenth day of the month, the month is half past relative to that day and half future relative to that day. But all twenty-eight days occur within the present month.

Actual time can thus be observed as very complex, multileveled, and organically interrelated through many complementary interdependencies. The success human beings have had in discovering or inventing artificially precise systems and mechanisms for measurement and the multitudes of uses to which such measurements have been put have so conditioned us to think of time in terms of these mechanisms that we have forgotten about the complexities and organicities of existing time. I have no intention of diminishing the use of precision measurements, but I believe that our quantum-leap conceptions about the nature of existence will require us to become more fully aware of the nature of actual time also. Since other traits of dynamic existence interdepend and interact intimately, with the eventual and durational polar aspects of actual time, we cannot fully understand the actual nature of some traits unless we also understand something of the actual nature of others with which they interdepend. [15]

Causation

Physicists and engineers, assuming the principle of the uniformity of nature, often interpret causation mathematically in such a way that the cause equals the effect: $C = E$. This view is simple and convenient. However, causation is actually very complex. Each cause-effect situation involves a multiplicity of causal factors and a multiplicity of effects. A minimal symbolism for a cause-effect occurrence, I suggest, should be something like the following:

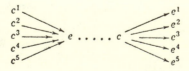

All of the causes, both those operating simultaneously and successively, that cooperate in producing a single effect, e, are symbolized by c^1, c^2, c^3, c^4, and c^5. If five c's are not enough, for any reason, one may add any number until the symbolism seems sufficient. The effect, e, is caused by all of its causes, and by no other causes and thus, in this sense, is completely caused. Yet something exists in e that did not exist in any of its causes, either singly or taken all together. The effect, as an effect having singleness, unity, or entitiveness about it, has something that is its own that did not exist in any or all of its causes. Its own unity is something new in existence even though caused to be entirely by its causes. C^1 is not the sole cause of e, since c^2, c^3, c^4 and c^5 are also its causes. Similarly c^2 cannot be the sole cause of e since c^1, c^3, c^4, and c^5 are also its causes. The same holds for c^3, c^4, and c^5. Thus e, as the joint effect of the five c's, has its own unity that was not contained in either of the five or in all of them together, because such togetherness involves a manyness and therefore external relatedness of each from the others that does not exist in the effect. Thus such novelty is necessarily caused. Thus does complex causation involve the emergence of such novelty.

The effect, as an existing entity, then also functions as a cause of still other effects. As c, it causes e^1, e^2, e^3, e^4, and e^5, taken as a minimal but sufficient symbolism. It joins other causes in contributing to each of these effects. To the extent that what existed in its causes continues to exist in it as effect and further continues to exist in its other effects, the effect-cause entity functions as a caused cause. In principle, such continuations might be calculated mathematically. But to the extent that the effect-cause entity has a new unitary entitiveness of its own that enters into its causing its effects, such novel causation is thus new and original with it. Emergent novelties function causally. Whether one cares to call such original causation *uncaused causation*, at least such original causation is held by organicism to account for all origination, or creativity, within a universe that had no absolute beginning.

Variations in causal complexities can account for variations of kinds of beings coming into, and persisting in, existence. The significance of multileveled causation is too often overlooked by single-discipline theories. A world philosophy capable of comprehending the present human predicament needs assistance not only from many disciplines and interdisciplinary studies but also of omnidisciplinary studies to the extent that each discipline has something essential to contribute to the total picture. Conceiving causation of particular events and processes as not only multileveled, but possibly even omnileveled, the complexities of semingly simple causation become obvious.16

Recognition that currently operating interdisciplinary institutes having competence in only a few disciplines cannot be expected to provide reliable knowledge of a comprehensive sort should spur those responsible for avoiding doomsday to expand their conceptions of what is needed in research competence in order to understand the more obvious causal processes. Not all problems require understanding interlevel causation. But some do, and understanding problems constituting contemporary crises endangering human survival do.

But even scientists and specialists indifferent to doomsday evidences become more fully aware of the significance of multilevel causation and recognize that they have a self-interested obligation to become informed about it. A cell biologist, for example, traces causes of processes in one cell to processes in other cells, whether antecedents or contemporaries. But he also has become concerned about the molecular and atomic constituents and their causal influences. He may become concerned about causal influences from a body as a whole. As social decisions (at many levels) influence bodily life, as earth resources diminish, as the solar system changes cause drought or cold, and perhaps as galactic trends vary light and other rays affecting life, the numbers of kinds of causal factors he must consider to understand cell behavior become enormous. Thus the cell biologist has an interest in the research quality and conclusions of both scientists dealing with kinds of causes at each level and with scientists dealing with interlevel causation.

Our quantum-leap conception of causation depicts cause and effect as partly different and partly the same, as interdependent, as complementary, as polarly related, as complex and yet organically unified, as multileveled, as temporal, as creative of novelty and destructive of some of what is old, and as unceasing, even though every passage from cause to effect involves some cessation. Focus of study on whole-part causation, instead of part-part and part-whole causation, could reveal to those fearful of world government how they may have more to gain than lose by its development. Of course, if whole-part causation is studied in isolation, it will be interpreted dictatorially. But when studied as an aspect of the quantum-leap conceptions of causation as organic, and as interdepending with part-part, part-whole, and multilevel causation, then the significance of its limitations as well as contributions to human survival and happiness may become obvious.

Dialectic

Dialectic is not a new idea, but it has been ignored, neglected, and denied for so long that many will find considering it a new experience. Preferences for ideas and ideals of independence, pluralism, seeking understanding through analytic methods, a mathematics in which a whole is equal to the sum of its parts, and a symbolic logic presupposing atomic propositions excluded middles and a theory of types illegitimizing any reference by a proposition to itself all imply dialectic as irrelevant. Most scientists and philosophers ignore the existence of dialectic. Association of dialectic with abstruse Hegelian idealism and with communist Marxist materialism classifies it as something foreign to most Americans. Marxist theoreticians themselves struggle unhappily with the apparent but obvious contradiction involved in having two logics: the antidialectical symbolic logic employed in putting Soviet spaceships on Mars and the dialectical logic presupposed in basic doctrine. [17]

Dialectic may be the least welcome candidate for a quantum-leap conception. But, since it interdepends with all of the other quantum-leap conceptions discussed thus far, those who achieve comprehension of it and familiarity with it should find all of the quantum-leap conceptions participating more smoothly in cohering processes. Comprehension can hardly be expected from a first acquaintance. But if dialectic pervades existence and thought and if comprehension of it is a prerequisite for adequate understanding of both personal and political processes, I must make an attempt to suggest something of its nature when proposing it as an ingredient in the quantum-leap system gestalt.

I distinguish three general types of dialectic: synthetic, analytic, and organitic. Synthetic dialectic is the best known, but a glance at organitic dialectic may reveal more quickly the multidynamic, tensely interinvolving creative processes compounding organic growth.

SYNTHETIC DIALECTIC

Consider, for example, two persons, a man and a woman, meeting for the first time. Each exists as something positive. Dialecticians say each is a thesis. But each is not the other. So each opposes the other or is an opposite to the other. Each is both something positive in itself and something oppositive in relation to the other. Dialecticians speak of such opposites as antitheses. Each is a thesis in itself and an antithesis relative to the other. (Two men meeting for a first time also function as antitheses. But I have selected a man and a woman because their additional biological differences may seem more difficult to overcome.)

In spite of their differences, oppositeness or antitheticialness, both are also alike in being human and in embodying humanity in their natures. Thus even before interacting in ways increasing their likeness, they are already alike in sharing their humanity in common. As male and female, they are by nature apposite opposites. In biological processes, both male and female are required for reproducing the race, and so each has already depended on both maleness and femaleness in order to come into existence in the first place. Humanity has such apposite oppositeness, or such antitheticalness, inherent in its nature.

Our pair, after meeting, fall in love and marry. When they marry, they participate together in constituting a family. The coming into existence of this family is a new emergent. It is a new level of organization of the behavior of these two persons that did not exist before. Dialecticians call it a synthesis, functioning as a new thesis. As it endures, it functions substantially (as a new substance). When the pair visits neighbors, not merely as persons but as a family, it performs functions that did not exist before. Any regular repetition of family functions can be observed as uniformities or laws of the behavior of this family. Any decision reached by the two functioning as participants in the family to act in relation to others constitutes that family as a source of authority or causal efficacy when the action is carried out. The family as an entity, substance, pattern of behavior, and causal agency has no existence apart from the two persons. Yet it is something more than either of them, and it adds something to each of them.

By marrying, a man becomes a husband and a woman becomes a wife. Each adds something to its own nature that it did not have before. By enduring, the family not only has a substance of its own but contributes something additional to the substance of each person. One's acquired trait as husband endures, and as it endures he thereby becomes more substantially a husband. Just as a person has duties to himself (such as to care for his health) so when married, he has additional duties to himself as husband. These duties derive from the nature of his family and from his own additional nature acquired by becoming a family member. His own nature has been changed somewhat by such additions.

Notice that each person remains the same person after marriage as before and becomes also somewhat different. His behavior becomes somewhat modified. So the emergence of the family as an entity influencing each of the members results in its functioning in ways that control the behavior of each member. Freely choosing to enter a family and then being influenced by that family is a form of self-control. But such self-control is somewhat indirect. A person who marries becomes more complex; he has more interests, including some shared with his wife. His own self-interest increases by adding interest both in the welfare of and the self-interests of his wife. To the extent that the two are opposites and antithetical, each adds and in-

corporates into his own nature some self-interestedness that is partly
antithetical to him. If tensions result from such antitheticalness, then
those tensions function as added complications within his personality.

For each of the two persons, dialectical interactions with each
other and through their family are only a small part of their dialectical developments. Each interacted with his mother after birth, with
siblings and neighbors, with cats, dogs, chickens, cows, with flow-
ers, vegetables, trees, with wind, water, ice, with earth, cement,
rubber, with sun, moon, stars, and with knives, pins, and shears.
Each interaction makes a dialectical contribution. An infant external
to its mother takes its first suck. Milk, part of the mother, enters the
child and becomes part of it. Later, the child receives more milk from
its mother. But now, in addition to being the same baby wanting
more milk, the baby embodying a part of the mother through milk
received returns to the mother, and in doing so brings back to the
mother some of her own milk embodied in the child.

When she feeds the child a second time, she is, in a sense, also feeding herself as already partly embodied in the child through previous
feedings. And the more milk the child drinks, the more something
other than itself becomes part of itself, and the more that which was
previously other than itself now functions as part of itself when it
goes for more milk. Selves, and bodies, are not simple. Through dialectical interactions, people exchange parts of themselves, and
these parts live on in others. The more we interact dialectically, the
more we interexist. To the extent that we are self-interested with respect to all of our interests, we become interested in all of those parts
of our selves living on in others.

When I converse with you and give you an idea you did not have
before, a part of me becomes embodied in you. You examine the idea
and find in it an implication I did not observe. You explain it to me.
Now I have received something additional—the implication just explained—from you. By giving something to you, and getting something back from you as a result of such giving, I have indirectly
caused myself to become different by adding this implication. Part of
what I am getting back is my own idea, but with something added
by you. Thus, through the dialectical interaction of my conversation
with you, I, though remaining the same person and with mostly the

same ideas, become different by adding the implication originating in you. The more one person interacts dialectically with more other things, persons, and groups, the richer becomes his development through adding to himself parts acquired from others. Some acquire much merely by reading. But the mutual enrichment achievable through conversation and through family living is often very rewarding.

Synthetic dialectic thus involves not merely the production of a new synthesis, and thus a new thesis, but also the perpetual evolution of the antitheses to the extent that each contributes to the other directly or indirectly. Some indirect contributions to each member come through functioning of the family in a community, which functions in a state, which functions in a nation, and so forth. So multi-leveled contributions may result from family activities or activities with other groups.

Synthetic dialectic may be illustrated also by the formation of a group composed of several members. Each member is an opposite to all of the others, so we have multiopposition. The group, as a new thesis, rests on many other theses, each antithetical to the others. Usually persons organize a group because they have some common interests that can be served by it. Each member both gives something as a participant and receives something. Usually he gives something, directly or indirectly, to other group members. Usually he receives something as a result of such membership and thus may be said to receive something from the group. Problems of unequal participation and benefit from membership tend to become greater as numbers of members increase, although such inequality tends to be a consequence of many different kinds of factors, so that this statement is only very generally true. But the dialectical processes present in interactions of people in larger groups tend to have additional complications.

Understanding group dialectics, and intergroup dialectics, should prove helpful in understanding both the metaphysics and the psychology of world government formation and operation. We have discussed thus far only constructive and beneficial dialectics. Competing with, quarreling with, fighting with, and killing another person also involve dialectical processes. When persons, as opposites, oppose each other, they may harm as well as benefit each other.

When genuine conflicts of interest operate dialectically, we may receive evil—a bullet, poison, false information, deception, disease—instead of good.

Increased awareness of the multitudes of kinds of dialectical processes inherent in existence, human nature, and human association is proposed not as something automatically beneficial but as increased insight into the nature of human and social processes. When dialectic is ignored, neglected, or denied, benefits of the process cannot be produced. Understanding dialectical processes is an additional intellectual tool for making more adequate and more satisfactory adaptations to predicaments and solutions to crises situations. When more people comprehend how they can be benefited by dialectical interaction through participation in world government, more will favor such participation. But dialectical evils as well as dialectical goods need to be explored before commitment to supporting a world government as a new thesis.[18]

ANALYTIC DIALECTIC

When two or more things functioning as antitheses produce a new thesis, the thesis is a new whole depending on previously existing parts. The process of organizing a new whole is called *synthetic dialectic*. When a thing as a whole functions in such a way as to produce a new part, so that the new part has its source in a previously existing whole, the process is called *analytic dialectic*. The conception, gestation, and birth of a child resulting from a marriage forming a family exemplifies, through the birth of the child as a third member of that family, how a new thesis, this time as a new part, is produced within a preexisting whole. This kind of dialectic has received much less attention by dialecticians, and further explorations should be helpful in understanding the nature of dialectic more fully.[19]

ORGANITIC DIALECTIC

Organitic dialectic, which exemplifies my own contributions to the theory of the nature of dialectic, involves synthetic and analytic dialectical processes proceeding interactively at the same time. Organitic dialectic involves the joint emergence of both a new synthesis (as in synthetic dialectic) and of two or more new analytheses (as in analytic dialectic) to constitute an "organithesis." The new synthesis (as in synthetic dialectic) and the new analytheses (as in analytic dialectic) function in the organithesis in two ways: first, they function together as antitheses constituting the new organithesis as a new synthesis; and, secondly, they appear as two new analytheses within the organithesis. Organitic dialectic, having synthetic and analytic dialectic as its own antitheses, functions both as a synthesis of them and as a source of them as analytheses.

Synthetic dialectic may itself be of two types or constitute a range between two typical extremes. The one type involves a tendency toward complete annulment (either destruction of or suppression of independence) of the two antitheses in the new synthesis (as a Marxian dialectic, where a classless society requires elimination of both capitalist and laboring classes as classes). The second type involves a tendency to preserve the independence of the antitheses, so that the new synthesis remains weak and dependent on the antitheses (as in a business partnership). If either of these tendencies was carried to its extreme, dialectic, relative to these tendencies, would terminate; however since there is a sense in which each thing remains implicit or actual in its own negation, it, and hence dialectic relative to it, can never be completely terminated. Between these two extremes is a range of degrees of interdependence of the new thesis and the two prior antitheses upon each other; all of these degrees are degrees of what is organic. Synthetic dialectic is organic to the extent that it avoids the extremes of complete annulment and of complete independence of the prior antitheses. (Note: "organic" here is to be distinguished from "organitic," the latter connoting interdependence of different, i.e., synthetic and analytic, dialectic trends.) Synthetic dialectic is organic to the extent that it both annuls some degree of independence, i.e., that degree required for their joint functioning substantially in and through their common synthesis, and preserves some degree of independence, i.e., that degree required by each to maintain its own substantial integrity. What is organic is always a matter of degree, a matter of variability or pliability, but also a matter of continuing integrity. What is organic may be destroyed (though not completely), but so long as it exists, it involves interdependence, i.e., partial independence and partial dependence, of its parts.

Analytic dialectic is also of two types. One type involves a tendency in the direction of complete annulment (either destruction or enslavement) of the original thesis within which the new analytheses are differentiated. (Examples: when a sovereign nation splits into two sovereign nations; or when a stone is broken into two unmendable parts.) The second type involves a differentiation or distinction, but in such a way that there is a tendency to neglect or minimize the distinction. (Examples: where differences are recognized but kept ineffectual, as in the North-South controversies resulting from the U.S. Civil War, or in "smother love.") If either of these tendencies were carried to its extreme, dialectic, relative to these tendencies, would terminate. Between such extremes is a range of degrees of interdependence between the new analytheses and the prior thesis, all of which are organic. Analytic dialectic is organic to the extent that it avoids the extremes of complete destruction or enslavement of the original thesis by the new analytheses, and of complete ineffectiveness of the new analythesis. Organic dialectic involves both some genuinely new substantial independence of the new analytheses and yet some continuing dependence of the new analythesis upon, hence interdependence with, their thetic sources. (Examples: in parturition, and in continuing physiological growth, where the original egg cell divides and yet remains a vital unity of body throughout multiplicities of further cell divisions—the persisting unity is so strong and sustained that some people then infer that a single, simple, substantial soul, independent of the body and its divisions, must have been present to keep the process together as a continuing whole.)

Organitic dialectic involves, or consists in, organic relations between synthetic and analytic dialectic. Organitic dialectic also may be thought of as being of two types with a range between them. The one type, or extreme, would exist if the synthetic and analytic processes were to take place independently of each other. (Example: in mixing and hardening concrete, interest may be focused solely upon the new solid whole with no interest in the emergence of new parts; or in breaking hardened concrete, interest may be focused solely on the resultant chunks.) Such synthetic and analytic processes, although differentiated, remain interactively joined to the extent that they are organically related. (Example: when, in the molding of steel, interest is directed both to the whole bar and also to the arrangements of particular molecules, or "impurities," affecting the strength of the whole, a two-fold interest is present.) The other type, or extreme, would exist if, somehow, no distinction were made between synthetic and analytic types of dialectic (as when one accepts developments as mystical), or if it were held that synthetic and analytic processes were strictly correlative (mechanically related) to each other. Such a process, in which synthetic and analytic aspects appear to have negligible independence, seems more organic as each aspect appears to have more independence.

Organitic dialectic involves constant interdependence of synthetic and analytic dialectic. Interdependence, involving both some independence and some mutual dependence of synthetic and analytic dialectic, implies that sometimes synthetic dialectic is more significant (as in the formation of a new group, e.g., by marriage) while at other times analytic dialectic is more dominant (as in cell division). Organitic dialectic is more organic as various synthetic and analytical dialectical processes proceed more interdependently. (Example: in the birth and growth of a child, its cells and functions continue to multiply and yet it retains integrity; it develops new and different, even opposing, capacities [analytheses] which may be joined in a single skill [synthesis], both [analytheses and syntheses] participating in constituting the child's personality [organithesis].) All vital growth is dialectical, and all actual dialectic is organic; but minds, having limited attentive, retentive, and reproductive capacities, have difficulty in comprehending dialectic fully.

The increasingly complex, interdependent, and dynamic life of persons and groups, local, national and global, calls for a philosophy recognizing complexity, interdependence, and dynamism as central concepts. Philosophies idealizing simplicity, independence, dependence, and unchangingness, whatever their earlier merits, are now clearly inadequate to serve as explanations of present conditions and as guides for crisis solution. The increases in complexity, interdependence, and dynamism are not merely quantitative; they involve increasing organicness. Increasing understanding of the nature of whole-part relations is necessary to understand the other concepts. Whole-part interrelations involve not only polarity but multipolarities, not merely with each whole but also between the whole and higher-level wholes of which it is a part and between its parts and lower-level parts of which each is a whole. Each person, each group, and mankind as a whole interdepend, interact, interexist, and interdevelop.

Wise self-interestedness on the part of each person calls for fuller understandings of the organic nature of self, groups, and mankind so that everyone can exploit their own multileveled, multihierarchical, multidimensional polarities to their fullest. Narrower conceptions of self and groups conducive to selfishness become more dangerous when life itself becomes more intricately interdependent. Failure to understand the nature of organic wholeness and implications of anti-organic behavior for destruction of self and society contribute to both increasing crises and incapacities for solution.

The necessity for understanding interlevel causation, if we are to organize multiscientific knowledge through interdisciplinary research effectively, should now receive our highest priority. Philosophy in its comprehensive functioning is the chief interdisciplinary science since its task is to achieve understanding of how existence is organized in all of the ways demonstrated by each science. Thus the philosopher's task, and the task of each science in making its contribution to comprehensive understanding, remains unfinished as long as interdisciplinary conflicts continue and interdisciplinary communication about interdisciplinary causation is incomplete.

I believe that *organicity*, the nature of organizations and other organisms, cannot be fully understood apart from concepts of complementarity, polarity, emergence, and dialectic. Our quantum-leap system gestalt will not be understood until we apprehend our participation in its concrete dialectical development as we grow interexistentially. The importance of the principle of reciprocity (and many other principles regarding values, ethics, economics, and government we have yet to discuss) in understanding complementarity, polarity, and dialectical development has come to be neglected. Fuller application of scientific methods to understanding complementarity, polarity, dialectic, and *organicity* should reveal richer opportunities for personal and social developments.

ORGANIC LOGIC

Logic as a science investigates the nature of structure. Logicians differ as to whether logic is concerned only with the structure of thought, or, more narrowly, only with the structure of inference or, still more narrowly, only with the structure of deductive influence, or also with the structure of existence and/or of experience. Interest in precision has led to the development of a symbolic logic so abstract that it no longer applies to existence. It is merely an intellectual game. Any application requires additional existential postulates. Without such additional postulates, involving existential structures, such logic would remain completely useless. The view adopted here is that philosophy, science, and those concerned with the survival of mankind are primarily interested in solving problems, and so its interest in structure is primarily an interest in problem-solving structures and in the structures of existence and experience as the locus of the problems to be solved.

The primary function of logic, more abstract than other sciences such as metaphysics and epistemology, is to aid in understanding the nature of existence and experience so that efforts to solve problems may succeed better through understanding the nature of the problems. The problems exist, and exist as experienced. So the more adequately a logic reveals the structure of existence as experienced, the more likely it is to contribute to problem-solving efforts. Thus logic, metaphysics, and epistemology interdepend. Their functions are complementary. They function as organic parts of philosophy as a comprehensive whole. Thus all of the concepts proposed as quantum-leap conceptions are already concepts included in the structure of logic as proposed here.

Most students of logic are introduced to only a single system of logic. Earlier that system, now called *traditional logic*, was based on conceptions derived primarily from Aristotelian concepts of the nature of existence, knowledge, and language. Now most are introduced to a symbolic logic having sources in Boolean algebra. Some introductions include chapters on definition of terms, logical paradoxes, inductive reasoning, and theory of probability. But few, even graduate students in philosophy, have been introduced to the whole history of logics. In addition to traditional logic indebted to Aristotelian metaphysics, with some revisions related to medieval theology relative to the comprehension of a term as known by an omniscient deity, and the numerous varieties of symbolic logics, one should know about inductive logic having debts to British empiricism, dialectical logic present in the absolute idealistic metaphysics of Hegel with variations in the dialectical materialism of Marx, and the pragmatic logic of John Dewey and followers.

Asian thought also has its own histories of logic. Jains have contributed *Syadvada*. Buddhists have developed a principle of fourfold negation and a tradition of subtle dialectical arguments. *Nyaya*, a general name for logic as well as the name of a major school of Indian thought, emphasizes logic. Vedanta, especially Advaita, idealizes ultimate reality as entirely without distinctions, hence entirely without structure. The goal of each yogin is to achieve intuitive awareness of pure indistinctness. Those who define logic as a science of structure are likely to interpret this view as antilogical; but I choose to see inherent in this view a very significant kind of logic, which I call *yogic logic*. From a perspective seeing complementary opposites as polarly related, I see perfect distinctness and pure indistinctness as terminal poles of a range of degrees from perfect distinctness, through less perfect distinctness, through being equally distinct and indistinct, through more indistinctness, to pure indistinctness. This range is a structure, and pure indistinctness is the endpoint of the structure. As such, the doctrine that ultimate reality consists in pure indistinctness illustrates that kind of structure that appears as the limit of the range from perfect distinctness to pure indistinctness. That distinctness also exists in Advaitic thought is recognized, even though it is described as illusory. Hence I not only regard yogic logic as something to be included in the history of logics but find a place for it in the all-encompassing grasp of organic logic. There is some truth to each of the historical logics that needs to be recognized when one endeavors to know all of the truth.

Chinese logic early crystallized in sixty-four hexigrams consisting of pairs of positive and negative, initiative and completive (yang-yin) symbols. Neither the extreme precision and the extreme exclusiveness idealized by Western logicians nor the extreme indefiniteness and extreme inclusiveness idealized by some Indian logicians seems to have troubled Chinese thinkers until influenced by Greek and Buddhist thought. But the both-and character of the yang-yin logic is fundamental to sound thinking and will be central to the organic logic needed for interpreting our quantum-leap system gestalt. However, in a day when we are dealing with actual complexities too intricate for our latest generation of electronic computers to handle, the analogical limitations of sixty-four hexigrams relegate them to historical museums.

If there is some truth to each of the historically developed logics, is there some way of organizing all of these truths together in some larger truth? Is there some whole of logic in which all of these numerous logics are parts? Any philosophy that seeks to be comprehensively adequate will try to discover some more comprehensive structure to serve as the structure of its comprehension.

My *Polarity, Dialectic, and Organicity* is prefatory to works on metaphysics, epistemology, and logic. It stands as a partial logic, and does explore and expound some concepts essential to organic logic. Its treatment of theories of polarity provides a clue to how the truth of many different kinds of theories can contribute to a larger, more adequate conception of truth relative to each issue. The chapter on "Theories of Polarity" is really an exposition of the organicist theory of polarity developed as a theory about theories of polarity. Organicism may be described as a philosophy about philosophies. It intends to be a philosophy about existence as experienced partly by way of being a philosophy about philosophies of existence, experience, logic, and so on.

Its diagram of types of philosophies provides a systematic means for demonstrating how to select what truths from each of many contending claims relative to each particular issue should be included in a more adequate understanding of that issue. These types were developed as part of the task of introducing beginning students to the major types of philosophical systems.[20] Comparisons of some types had become standard before I began teaching.[21] But the picture took final shape for me only after I had studied Asian philosophies, especially Advaita Vedanta,[22] and had struggled with deficiencies in earlier models.

An examination of a single diagram of types is laborious and can yield only what is most general and highly abstract. Like other logical abstractions, it requires further existential evidence to be useful. Nevertheless, it has an importance as a systematic way of precisely differentiating the possible kinds of variations, and ambiguities, normally found in a thorough investigation of issues regarding the existence and nature of complementary opposites. Each diagram is a kind of map of an area in which claims are staked. Organicism commits itself to the general policy of seeing some truth to each claim, proposes as a general policy to seeing some claims as naturally probably truer than others, and then leaves the question of actual truths to empirical investigation. The diagram is significant also because of its contributions to clarifying the nature of the organic—that is, of indicating definitely persisting ranges of indefiniteness that need to be recognized clearly as limits to the clarity possible.

Let us select for example the issue of which is better, private or public ownership, often called capitalism and socialism. These words have other, richer meanings, but the issue abstracted for consideration is limited for purposes of illustrating how twelve different types of theories tend to become distinguished when investigation proceeds to complete thoroughness. These twelve are logical types in the sense that they function as types of structure all needed for a complete understanding of each genuine issue.

1. *Extreme capitalism.* Capitalism alone is good. Therefore socialism is not good.

2. *Extreme socialism.* Socialism alone is good. Therefore capitalism is not good.

3. *Modified capitalism.* Capitalism is better than socialism. Therefore socialism is not better than capitalism.

4. *Modified socialism.* Socialism is better than capitalism. Therefore capitalism is not better than socialism.

5. *Extreme middlism.* Capitalism and socialism are equally good. Therefore it is false that either is better than the other.

6. *Modified middlism.* Capitalism is sometimes or in some ways better than socialism and socialism is sometimes or in some ways better than capitalism. Therefore capitalism and socialism are not equally good.

7. *Extreme dualism.* Capitalism and its goods and socialism and its goods are entirely different. Therefore the goods of capitalism and the goods of socialism are in no way the same.

8. *Extreme aspectism (nondualism).* Ownership and its goods is ownership and its goods regardless of whether such ownership is private or public. It is the ownership that is good, not the privateness or the publicness of the ownership that is good. Therefore the goods of capitalism and socialism are not entirely different.

9. *Modified dualism.* Capitalism and its goods and socialism and its goods are more different than alike. Therefore they are not more alike than different.

10. *Modified aspectism.* Capitalism and its goods and socialism and its goods are more alike than different. Therefore they are not more different than alike.

11. *Extreme equalism.* Capitalism and its goods and socialism and its goods are equally as much different as alike. Therefore they are not in some ways more alike and in some ways more different from each other.

12. *Modified equalism.* Capitalism and its goods and socialism and its goods are in some ways more alike than different and in some ways more different than alike. Therefore they are not equally as much different as alike.

Organicism, aiming to be antireductionistic and at the same time aiming to eliminate all false overstatements, systematically summarizes and affirms jointly twelve statements based on the foregoing twelve theories and affirms jointly the denials of twelve other statements based on the same twelve theories.

Ownership and its benefits are such that there is (1) a sense in which capitalism alone is good (there are some benefits to private ownership that are not benefits of public ownership). (2) a sense in which socialism alone is good (there are some benefits of public ownership that are not benefits of private ownership), (3) a sense in which capitalism is better than socialism, (4) a sense in which socialism is better than capitalism, (5) a sense in which capitalism and socialism are equally good, (6) a sense in which capitalism is better in some ways and socialism is better in some ways, (7) a sense in which the benefits of capitalism and socialism are entirely different, (8) a sense in which the benefits of capitalism and socialism are exactly alike (for example, alike in being kinds of ownership), (9) a sense in which their benefits are more different than alike, (10) a sense in which their benefits are more alike than different, (11) a sense in which their benefits are equally as much alike as different, and (12) a sense in which their benefits are in some ways more alike and in some ways more different.

Ownership and its benefits are such that: (1) it is false that there is no sense in which socialism is good; (2) it is false that there is no sense in which capitalism is good; (3) it is false that there is no sense in which socialism is better than capitalism; (4) it is false that there is no sense in which capitalism is better than socialism; (5) it is false that there is no sense in which capitalism is sometimes better than socialism and that socialism is sometimes better than capitalism; (6) it is false that there is no sense in which capitalism and socialism are equally good; (7) it is false that there is no sense in which the benefits of capitalism and of socialism are the same; (8) it is false that there is no sense in which the benefits of capitalism and socialism are different; (9) it is false that there is no sense in which the benefits of capitalism and socialism are more alike than different; (10) it is false that there is no sense in which the benefits of capitalism are more different than alike; (11) it is false that there is no sense in which the likenesses and differences of the benefits of capitalism and socialism are unequal; (12) it is false that there is no sense in which the likenesses and differences of the benefits of capitalism and socialism are equal.

These two sets of twelve statements jointly affirmed as constituting organicism's type of answer to a particular, very limited issue reveal how it succeeds in being antireductionistic. This does not mean that it accepts everything that anyone says but only that whenever an issue arises regarding a genuine opposition—between two posits functioning as complementary opposites—then care should be taken not to exclude any relevant truths or senses. Novices are likely to find the two sets difficult to formulate.

Those who would test the sets by standards in symbolic logic based on the principle of excluded middle may discover formal contradictions, but they will fail to understand that the purpose of organic logic is to reject that principle as central and to replace it with a both-and principle, here exemplified first as affirming all twelve sets. The diagram of types is a diagram of logical types; and that type of logic based on the principle of excluded middle is included among the twelve types and designated as extreme dualism. To interpret all twelve types and organicism as a theory of types in terms of merely one type would be to misinterpret it.

How organic logic and its diagram of types can serve in solving global crises can hardly be immediately clear. Logic is highly abstract. Global crises are very concrete. Yet to the extent that such crises are due to conflicts having bases in opposing philosophies that seem to their contenders to be irreconcilably opposed, awareness that organic logic is a more adequate, and in this sense truer, exposition of the nature of existence and existing oppositions, one may be able to demonstrate how some attitudes of irreconcilability are mistaken. If it can be shown that mistakes in attitude can be demonstrated by logical means, correction of such mistakes seems more likely. Although organic logic does contradict contradictory claims, it does show that many apparently contradictory claims also embody complementary aspects. Once these complementary aspects are revealed, reasons for the apparent sharpness of contradiction disappear. Without some means such as organic logic to reduce mistaken beliefs that opposites are always contradictory, how can our global crises be overcome.[23]

A mind conceiving issues shaped in terms of this diagram of types is an open mind, or a partly open mind. Although it is precommitted to eliminate extremists as serious contenders for truth, it sees its further task as that of exploring among the ranges of variables for the view that comes closest to fitting the actual situation.

This illustration of some technical aspects of organic logic should not overshadow other aspects of equal importance not developed here. The complexities of organic logic, including a shift from a two-valued to a twelve-valued logic, may be seen as results of efforts to adapt logic to the increasingly obvious complexities of physical, biological, social, political, and economic living. It should be especially useful in analyzing more complex multileveled complementarities, though the task of using it may be very time-consuming.

Minds habituated to other logics may not be able to see how the complexities of organic logic can contribute to interpreting our quantum-leap conceptions and system gestalt as a philosophy needed to solve megalopolitan and global problems. The following chapters will present proposals more easily grasped and more directly inspiring those concerned with formulating a world philosophy suited to the needs of our times.

WORLD ETHICS?
CAN IT BE ACHIEVED?

World ethics is possible if we become willing to do what is required to achieve it. What is required? Two interrelated essentials may be noted. First, ethics must be regarded as a science, a complex set of problems that can be dealt with by the use of scientific methods. Habituation in treating ethical problems scientifically on a global scale will be needed. Second, both the nature of science and of these ethical problems must be reconceived in terms of the quantum-leap system gestalt. Popular, scientific, and professional acceptance of persons participating in and sustaining the new morale generated by this system gestalt should become pervasive.

Identifying this quantum-leap conception is difficult. Readers not already partly oriented toward it are unlikely to understand, much less accept, it. I am not sure that even I fully understand it, since I believe that it will result from the work of many. The nature of the mature system gestalt is still in the making. My own suggestions thus are tentative. The leap is not from ethics to something nonethical, not from morality to amorality, not from principles to no principles. It retains concern for and understanding of the nature of rightness and wrongness, oughtness, obligation or duty, and the nature of goodness and badness as foundational to rightness and oughtness. Such concern is central to the nature of ethics.

The leap includes conceptions of complexity, interdependence, and multileveled and multidimensional dynamics, together with a

concern for both global extents and limits. Thus adequate understanding involves both multidisciplinary and interdisciplinary
acquaintance and attention to comprehensiveness when understanding details. The word *scientific* takes on a connotation of being multidisciplinary, interdisciplinary, and comprehensive, as well as
value saturated, in the quantum-leap gestalt. To be genuinely scientific in the most adequate sense is to be antireductionistic. Despite
the necessity for further specialization and more detailed analyses,
science remains inadequate whenever it overstates the claims of any
particular science or subscience. I judge that constant attention to
antireductionism will characterize the quantum-leap gestalt, even
though it will eventually age and develop new varieties of reductionism in its own way.

As the new system develops, comparisons with historical and
other contemporary systems occur naturally. My own comparative
evaluations may not be correct. But in my present perspective, the
new gestalt will be both antithetical to philosophies emphasizing reductionistic extremes and incorporate the partial truths of each.

It will be anti-Platonic in not postulating eternal forms and time-
less principles. It will be anti-Aristotelian in rejecting fixed species
and a fixed hierarchy. It will be anti-neo-Platonic because it rejects
unity as the sole source of plurality. It will be even more anti-Ad-
vaitan because Advaita rejects distinctness and plurality as having
no reality of their own. It rejects monotheisms that depict creation of
a preconceived universe by an act of will. It rejects Jain conceptions
of eternal souls and Theravada conceptions of impermanence (and
thus no soul). It rejects materialism as locating ultimate reality in
particles, whether static or dynamic, and as claiming that manyness
is fundamentally prior to unity. It rejects tychism and indeterminism
as excuses for ignorance. It rejects agnosticism and skepticism when
these cripple investigators from trying out new working hypotheses.
It rejects phenomenological bracketing (excluding or postponing
questions about the unknown from present scientific inquiry).

But it will also draw from all of these historical and contemporary
philosophies. Each philosophy that becomes reductionistic tends
first to hit upon something essential to understanding the nature of
self, society, and the universe. Thus not only openness to suggestions from conceptual developments in all civilizations and all types

of philosophy as well as from all of the sciences characterizes the new gestalt, but also the interest in thoroughness needed for comprehensiveness should motivate systematic search regarding what essential contributions each reductionistic theory may provide. One who rejects extremes and also rejects what is essential is acting reductionistically.

Issues regarding individual and social ethics in quantum-leap conceptions are caught up in the greater complexity, more intricate interdependence, more levels and dimensions of stability and change, and both global and multidisciplinary comprehensiveness and concern for limits of many kinds. First of all, individual and social ethics interdepend because persons and their group functions interdepend in many ways. The new system gestalt will reject as antireductionistic attempts to reduce social ethics to individual ethics and also to reduce individual ethics to social ethics. Each person is essentially social, and groups are made up entirely of persons. Institutions exist in persons and nowhere else. Thus despite genuine differences between persons and groups, to depict them as primarily opposed to each other is a mistake. Although I shall give separate emphases to individual and social ethics, anyone who fails to keep in mind the multileveled and multidimensional interdependent complexities interrelating both will misunderstand both.

Although there is some truth to all persisting theories of ethics, the principle of enlightened self-interest is foundational. Self-interest and enlightenment relative to it depend on how self is conceived. Thus I shall explore some issues relative to self-conceptions implicit in, and contributing to, the new system gestalt. I shall propose an ideal of luxuriant individualism in contrast to formerly viable eternalistic individualism, rugged individualism, and Buddhist and existentialist momentary individualisms as better suited to the quantum-leap gestalt.

ETHICS AS A SCIENCE

Just as distinction is made between pure and applied science in other fields, so ethics can be investigated both as a pure and as an applied science. As a pure science, ethics is inquiry into the nature of ethical behavior, of rightness and wrongness, of oughtness, of obligation and duty, and of numerous related problems pertaining to conscience, justice, and law, for the purpose of discovering universal principles inherent in such behavior. It presupposes axiology, the scientific inquiry into the nature of values, and involves scientific inquiries into many other fields, including psychology and the social sciences as well as other fields of philosophy, both as necessary resources regarding additional principles inherent in ethical problems and as areas in which ethical principles also apply.

As an applied science, ethics inquires into many different kinds of problems and additional kinds of principles, and specific combinations of principles, inherent in each kind of practical problem. In addition to larger classifications of kinds of ethical problems into personal and social, they may be classified more specifically as business ethics, political ethics, medical ethics, religious ethics, marital ethics, recreational ethics, educational ethics, and so forth and still more specifically as the ethics of advertising, of financing political campaigns, of abortion, of nursing home management, of voter registration.

Normally further distinction needs to be made between science, technology, and engineering. In addition to ethics as a science, both pure and applied, the need for developing techniques for acquiring ethical understanding by individuals and for applying such understanding in practice, personally and socially, should be obvious; and the development of persons skilled as teachers, counselors, and aides in the use of such techniques should be a natural result. I do not use the words *social engineer* or *ethical engineer*, but those responsible for utilizing ethical principles and techniques in dealing with particular practical problems are called managers, directors, presidents, governors, generals, deans, agents, plus many more specialized titles for those having more limited kinds of problems with which to deal. A list of the kinds of job classifications is also a list of the kinds of ethical engineers, for each has one or more functions to perform that *ought* to be performed in accordance with the principles discovered to function best relative to his particular job.

In this chapter, ethics is dealt with primarily as a pure science. Demonstration of foundational principles of ethical behavior will be needed before many people can be convinced that such principles can and should be applied in practice. Failure to achieve confidence in a science of ethics in the past, combined with a decline in the power of traditional bases for ethical appeals, has created a widespread distrust of all ethical claims. Thus recognition that problems concerning the nature of ethics and ethical principles themselves can be dealt with by scientific methods is a necessary first step.

A second step is the pursuit of inquiry into the foundational principles of ethical theory by scientific methods. I shall propose as hypotheses some conclusions that I believe a systematic scientific inquiry will reveal as reliable. I will state the tentative conclusions without constantly repeating that they are presented as hypotheses for further testing. A third step will require testing these hypotheses by others. A fourth step will require deliberate effort to apply the principles in personal, public, and private social practice in ways to be observed as experiments verifying or falsifying claims about the hypotheses. A fifth step, if and when the hypotheses have been sufficiently verified locally, is to apply them experimentally in all kinds of situations in differing cultures around the world.

My task here is to demonstrate that a set of hypotheses can be formulated in such a way that readers will recognize both that they can be tested by means of scientific experiments and that they do in fact provide reliable answers to questions about the ultimate nature of ethical behavior. The task is complex, and satisfactory completion would require several textbooks. The most that I can do here is to sketch an outline of some of the major types of principles needed for an adequate theory of ethics.

Axiology: The Science of Values

Popular conceptions of values include preferences, standards, and ideals about believing and behaving and can be stated in terms of wishes, habits, inhibitions, character traits, virtues, or customs. They refer to ideals of health, wealth, friendship, security, and adventure and often include ideas about good education, interesting occupation, sufficient income, happy marriage, responsible citizenship, friendly relations with neighbors, acquaintances, and even all mankind, and ideals of justice, minimums of welfare, and happiness for all people. They may pertain to standards of taste in dress, to minimums of generosity and fair play in cooperative situations, and to percentages of consumption in the present versus earning and saving for future consumption.

The complexities and varieties of ideas, preferences, and indoctrinated fears and feelings of duty, together with multitudes of differing explanations that adults have heard about values, have yielded much confusion about values in our society. The conflicting varieties of ideas and ideals held in our society create doubts about the possibility of a science of values and also have support from a long history of disagreements. The way out of such confusion is not immediately evident to popular discussants.

A technical distinction needed for clarity in understanding between ends and means should not be underestimated. Technical synonyms conduce to clarity. Ends are called *intrinsic values* because their value is self-contained. Means are called *instrumental values* because their function in value situations consists of serving as means to bringing about, or maintaining, intrinsic values.

Some persons have difficulty in differentiating the means and ends aspects of their experiences. Part of the reason is that the same thing, or the same feeling, may be experienced as intrinsic value at one moment and as having instrumental value at the next. And sometimes experiences of instrumental efforts, such as cooking a meal or building a table, are enjoyed so much that they are experienced also as worthwhile ends-in-themselves. However keeping this distinction clear is essential to clarity of understanding in axiology and ethics.

Problems involved in understanding instrumental values, which often are of great, even decisive, importance as factors in dealing with practical ethical problems, do not offer much difficulty to the axiologist as a pure scientist. His primary task is to locate the nature and kinds of intrinsic values that serve as the ultimate bases for moral appeals. I propose a hypothesis about the nature of intrinsic values which is based on four other historically prominent theories, three of them originating in ancient times.

According to hedonism, intrinsic good consists of enjoying pleasant feeling; intrinsic evil consists of suffering unpleasant feeling, especially obvious in pains. According to voluntarism, intrinsic good consists of enjoying a feeling of satisfaction of desire; intrinsic evil is suffering a feeling of frustration. According to romanticism, intrinsic good consists of enjoying a feeling of desirousness, exemplified in enthusiasm, zest, and gusto, and intrinsic evil of suffering feelings of apathy, or absence of desire. According to anandism, the Hindu view is that intrinsic good consists of enjoying feeling completely contented (*ananda*, bliss) and intrinsic evil of suffering any feeling of disturbance or unrest.

Proponents of each theory often claim that it alone is true and adequate to account for all intrinsic values. But all are alike in that the differing natures of intrinsic goodness and badness as described by each theory indicate differing aspects of the nature of desires. Pleasing sensations naturally arouse desire for more, either more continuance or more recurrence. Desires, when aroused, can be enjoyed both for their vigor and intensity and for their hopeful anticipation of satisfaction. Satisfaction is felt as fulfillment of desire. Contentment, after desire, is fulfillment felt as so full that both the desire and the feeling of its being satisfied are forgotten.

The four theories are alike in that all locate intrinsic values as feelings that are enjoyed or suffered. All agree that intrinsic values are intuited or apprehended directly. So conceived, the apprehension of intrinsic value is certain. One may be uncertain about how to interpret a complex experience in which feelings of enjoyment or suffering participate as ingredients. But that enjoyment and suffering of which one is intuitively aware have an end-in-itself quality inherent in them is not open to doubt. Thus axiology as a science is founded on data at least as certain as data intuited as foundational to any other science. No empirical science has any more sound bases for its inferences than have axiology and ethics.

In addition to being alike in fundamental respects, the four kinds of intrinsic value appear to be supplementary in certain ways related to our biological natures. All are needed for a complete account of our value experiences. Each of the four seems to predominate at each of four stages in life. Infants and children seem more preoccupied with sensory pleasures and pains, youth with enthusiasm and ambition not easily satisfied, maturity with interest in and feelings of accomplishment, and old age with rest from demands on declining energy. Normal sexual orgasm tends to be initiated by pleasant feelings accompanying sensory stimulation of erogenous zones, progresses through arousal of intense desire to an orgasmic climax experienced as intense satisfying of desire, and is followed by a feeling of complete contentment.

My hypothesis, called organicism, claims that intrinsic good consists of enjoying feeling, or of feeling enjoyment, of pleasure, enthusiasm, satisfaction, and contentment, either singly or mixed. It is experienced occasionally in purified forms but more often as an ingredient in or as part of complex gestalts evolving in the flux of experience. Although some experiences may be value neutral—involving neither enjoyment nor suffering in any degree—probably most involve some intrinsic value, even if attention to complications in objects and objectives desired tends to distract attention from it.

How We Know Values

Despite the intuited nature of intrinsic values, especially when they appear in awareness in their purer forms, most of our beliefs and judgments about values occur as ideas or idea complexes such as "I prefer apple to custard pie," or "My wife is beautiful," or "My car is worth more than yours." Because we experience values as objects most of the time, we need an explanation of how intrinsic values existing as feelings of enjoyment that are subjective appear as if in objects.

When we ask how we experience values as objects, we are already inquiring into the nature of knowledge. Axiology, even as a pure science, depends upon, or interdepends with, several other sciences, including theory of knowledge (epistemology). Understanding the nature of knowledge requires distinguishing between subjects and objects and between apparent and real objects. Issues regarding apparent and real self will not detain us here, although they often do become important relative to some ethical problems.

When values exist as feelings, they are clearly subjective, except when we say, "How are you feeling this morning?" intending to make feelings the object of attention. But it is not always clear what is meant by subjective. What is subjective pertains to a self; but, despite firm habits of self-conception that most people have acquired, most also have variable self-conceptions. For example, when I study anatomy, I treat my brain, heart, and stomach as objects that I, as a self and subject, am studying. But when I try on new clothes to see whether they fit me, I include my body as parts of my self. When the clothes itch or fit too tightly, I regard them as objects. But when I am dressed up for a party and say, "Look at me," then I regard my clothes as parts of my self. The point I am making is that what is experienced as subjective varies; thus problems occur regarding locating feelings as subjective. Since what appears as objective at some times appears as subjective at others, no fixed line can be drawn between what is experienced as subjective and as objective for all occasions.

Those who sharply divide subjects from objects and locate feelings in subjects have no way of explaining how values, when understood as feelings, can appear as if in objects. When objects appear to have intrinsic value, these thinkers either have to resort to some other theory of the nature of intrinsic value as existing in objects or to insist that all such values are illusory. My hypothesis holds that intrinsic values appearing as if in objects can be explained in much the same way that subjective experiences of color, shape, solidity, form, process, and complexity appear as if in objects. One's idea of a triangle is clearly one's own (subjective) idea, and yet it appears in awareness as a visual object, either as an image while one is thinking about it or as something real when drawn on a chalkboard. One's idea of the table he perceives is in his head, yet the table appears as if really outside his head. Detailed explanations about the multiplicities of conditions involved in projecting ideas in one's mind in such a way that they appear to be ideas of things existing outside of one's body and even at a great distance are required for understanding the nature of knowledge of objects.

Scientists who neglect to understand the nature of knowledge often proceed with misunderstandings about how physical objects, such as tables or molecules or energy, are known, and how their knowledge requires unconscious projection of ideas existing in their minds as if existing in the real world. Those who do understand the nature of knowledge and both the natural capacity and necessity of minds projecting ideas in this way should have no difficulty understanding how knowledge of valued objects involves projecting feelings as ingredients in idea complexes.

The term *empathy (einfuhlung)*, long employed by aestheticians, is relevant. One experiences beauty whenever felt intrinsic value appears as if present in an object. So interpreted, beauty is a very common constituent in experience. The multiplicities of ways in which persons perceive, conceive, and imagine objects serve as bases for multiplicities of kinds of objective values, both kinds of beauty and of ugliness, about which many choose to dispute. Although individual differences and multiplicities of factors causing different conditions to be different provide bases for continuing discussion and disagreement, a fuller understanding of the nature of knowledge will reveal that these multiplicities condition the physical, biological, and social sciences, as well as axiology and ethics.

The multiplicities and complexities referred to above do not eliminate the uniformities that occur in and through them. The principles discovered by physical, biological, psychological, and social scientists continue to function, and axiologists depend on them. Each principle is a complicating factor in understanding the nature of intrinsic value, but each also supplies conditions in terms of which intrinsic values can be understood. For example, a psychological principle, traditionally formulated as hedonistic paradox, states that persons normally seek and find pleasant feelings not by seeking them directly but by looking for other objects and activities that yield them as accompaniments. A person goes to a restaurant not to obtain pleasant feelings but to obtain a meal of well-prepared meat, vegetables, drink, and dessert. If the meal is well prepared, the diner experiences enjoyment.

Organicism finds axiological paradoxes present for all of its foundational theories and reformulates the hedonistic paradox as an organicistic paradox: one normally seeks his ends-in-themselves not directly but as accompaniments of activities experienced enjoyably. Thus ethics as a science cannot be expected to be something simple or as something that can be stated as unexceptional absolutes, as many people wish. But the foundational uniformities inherent in human nature provide continuing, if complex, bases for ethics as a science.

Whether discoveries in physics, chemistry, biology, physiology and, more specifically, encephalography will enable us to predict value experiences and ethical decisions from evidence presented to scientists in these fields alone,[1] axiology as a science does not await these discoveries since it has its own primary data in intuited enjoyments. But efforts to formulate principles discoverable about such intrinsic values, their knowability, their complexity, and their variability as constituents in complex experiences have not yet been sufficient to regard axiology as an established science. Evidence assembled in the field of aesthetics, the science inquiring into the nature of beauty, ugliness, and fine art, constitutes a huge storehouse of materials available to axiologists.[2] Axiology remains inadequate as long as it does not provide solid foundations for aesthetics and religion, as well as for ethics and the social sciences, including those involved in policy decisions.

Ethics: The Science of Oughtness

Ethics as a science is defined by the problems to which it is committed. My exploration is limited to one of its problems: that of oughtness. My hypothesis is that oughtness consists of the power that an apparently greater good has over an apparently lesser good in compelling our choices. A fuller statement includes the power that an apparently lesser evil has over an apparently greater evil in compelling our choices. Nothing more is needed to understand the nature of oughtness. There are as many kinds of oughtness as there are kinds of choices between apparently greater goods and apparently lesser goods—and between apparently lesser evils and apparently greater evils.

Note that both the appearances and the apparent compulsiveness of the power of their apparent differences are intuited. Intuited data constitute the foundations of ethics as a science. However, such simplicity and such certainty are complicated by the multiplicities of causes influencing the appearances of goods, evils, and their presence as greater or lesser. Many distinctions need clarification before all of many fundamental factors in ethical situations are understood.

A crucial distinction is that between actual and conditional oughts. Actual oughtness exists only when a person is actually experiencing a compulsion to choose. But much, perhaps most, of our thinking about oughtness occurs when we consider what we would, or should, do if certain circumstances did prevail. Driver training, for example, informs us about how many feet of road distance is required to stop a vehicle weighing so much and traveling at such a rate of speed on nonslippery pavement when there is no wind. Physical principles of inertia and friction (of brakes, tires, and pavement) play fundamental roles in formulating driving rules regarding keeping longer distances behind vehicles at faster speeds. If you are driv-

ing at a faster apeed, then you ought to keep more distance between
your car and the one in front. This is a conditional, not an actual,
ought. Actual oughtness of this kind does not occur until one finds
himself actually driving behind another vehicle and faced with a
decision as to what distance to keep.

Although some generalized rules for safe distances can be formulated, they remain conditional in the sense that they are not actual
until one is actually driving and also in the sense that their application can and should vary with the presence of still other kinds of conditions concerning which other principles can be formulated. Visibility, reduced by darkness, fog, blinding headlights, or poor vision,
is another factor in distance safety; so are relative fatigue, reduced
sensitivity under alcoholic influence, disturbances within one's car
(such as young children playing), probabilities regarding lane
changes, curvature and other conditions known to make certain locations hazardous, and unfamiliarity with road conditions. Conditional principles stated about each can serve as the basis for one or
more conditional oughts. When one's windshield has become covered with ice, the driver ought to stop until visibility is restored.
Complexes of such principles can often be found to operate in many,
perhaps most, ethical situations, so many conditional oughts are
very complex.

Every principle discoverable in every science may function as a
basis for conditional oughts. Consequently every textbook and
every work stating reliable conclusions in every science should be
considered as textbooks serving as foundational for conditional
oughts. The more we learn about the nature of things in each science,
the more principles we can and perhaps should take into consideration in judging the kinds of factors functioning in ethical situations.
Ethics as a science, as far as conditional oughts are concerned, is already supported by all other sciences in providing information
about principles functioning as factors in ethical choices. Ethics as a
science has a vested interest in having all other sciences learn as much
more as possible about the nature of things in their fields. In this
sense, every advance in science is an advance in ethics.[3]

Although actual oughts do not involve principles of which one is
unaware, when one does become aware of principles, including the
fact that there are more principles than one has been aware of, that

will help him to understand the situations in which he expects to face choices, that awareness itself constitutes a kind of obligation to learn more about such principles. The more one learns about the complexities of living, the more he becomes obligated, conditionally at least, to learn still more. Factual learning is not enough, however, for actual occasions often occur with such rapidity and strain that only a few of the conditionally relevant principles can be recalled for aid.

Repeated experiences with kinds of choices and deliberate practice in problem solving tend to generate skills in dealing with them and reusable techniques for resolving them. Habits of dealing successfully with problems in choosing may be developed to enable people to deal with their actual oughts more efficiently. People who master skills in efficient acting upon their actual oughts are said to have developed a good character. An older word used to denote capacity for efficient handling of actual oughts is virtue, meaning strength. The strength or capacity needed to deal with choices of megalopolitan complexity is somewhat different from that sufficing for nomadic or agricultural societies. The importance of mastering knowledge from many sciences, technologies, industries, and travel in providing the needed strength is misunderstood by many who still retain ideals of ethics originating in simpler societies.

PERSONAL ETHICS

Principles for Choosing

In addition to the principles contributed by other sciences to understanding ethical situations, ethics has its own general principles that should be stated as hypotheses held tentatively at least until evidence supporting them seems overwhelming. Consider some examples: "One ought always choose good in preference to bad, other things being equal," and "One ought always choose a greater good in preference to a lesser good, other things being equal."[4] These appear to me to be self-evident, but if anyone objects that they are not so, ethics as a science should pursue experimental research until the issue is settled to common satisfaction in one way or another. Since the most troublesome choices tend to be those involving degrees, ethics as a science is challenged to deal with the problem of possible quantification of values. The problem is less difficult where instrumental values seem closely associated with instrumental units that are measurable. A person may enjoy two chocolates twice as much as he enjoys one. But since the ultimate locus of the problem is enjoyment or suffering of feeling, the ultimate locus of the problem of precision in choosing is in the nature of such feelings.

Some scientists have confidence that biological bases for feelings are measurable and thus that, sooner or later, our increasing ability to measure brain functions will provide needed measurment for value experiences. Psychobiologist R. W. Sperry claims that consciousness "is an integral part of the brain process itself and an essential constituent of the action," that "conscious phenomena interact with and causally determine the brain process," and that "a reciprocal causal interaction exists between values and related technological, economic and social conditions."[5] As techniques for measuring brain processes become available, they will make possible the measurement of values as conscious feelings.

I do not wish to dispute these claims or to discourage hopes for improved measurement of brain processes and demonstration of at least closer correlations of subjective feelings with these measurements. However, the ultimate value locus of ethics is the feelings of enjoyment and suffering themselves, no matter what physical and biological conditions are essential to their existence and nature and how closely correlations can be demonstrated. The more and less in the better and worse feelings intuited appears as it does to a particular person at a particular time, and these appearances are the ultimate value bases for choosing.

Fortunately, the hedonistic calculus of pleasures and pains can be adapted as a calculus of enjoyments and sufferings to include the intrinsic values experienced as feelings of pleasantness and unpleasantness, enthusiasm and apathy, satisfaction and frustration, contentment and disturbance, and their mixing and blending in countless ways. It is not a measuring device. It is an intellectual chart useful in exploring some complications resulting from the multiplicities of characteristics that participate in value experiences. The calculus explores four main kinds of more and less: quantity, duration, intensity, and quality. It yields various principles. One ought always to choose a larger quantity of intrinsic value in preference to a smaller quantity, other things being equal. One ought always to choose more enduring enjoyments in preference to less enduring enjoyments, other things being equal. One ought always to choose a more intense preference to a less intense enjoyment, other things being equal. One ought always to choose a higher-quality in preference to a lower-quality enjoyment, other things being equal.

Additional problems arise when one has to choose between enjoyment or suffering that is more enduring versus one that is more intense. Speculating about what would happen if we could adopt fixed units of quantity, duration, intensity, and quality that equal each other, we can propose that one ought always to choose two units of duration of suffering in preference to three units of intensity of suffering, other things being equal. And, assuming further that suffering and enjoyment also come in equal units so that one unit of intrinsic bad and one unit of intrinsic good cancel each other perfectly, we can propose that one ought always choose a combination of three units of enjoyment and one unit of suffering in preference to a single unit of enjoyment. If, however, one believes that quantity, duration, intensity, and quality differ from each other so much that common or equivalent units cannot be assumed, this part of the calculus will be abandoned. The problem of evaluating units of quality proves especially difficult since so many different cultural and individual variations exist.

When feelings of enthusiasm and apathy, satisfaction and frustration, contentment and disturbance, and their relative purities, mixtures, and blends are added to feelings of pleasantness and unpleasantness calculated by hedonists, one faces still more problems of choosing between a unit of satisfaction and a unit of enthusiasm, for example, and between a unit in which pleasantness, enthusiasm, and satisfaction blend and a unit of pure pleasantness. Qualitative complexities resulting from ideas, with their own qualitative differences (ranging from a birthday cake to a moon expedition), discourage most intellectual experimenters from further serious efforts to quantify intrinsic values.

Nevertheless a lack of precision in judging feelings and a lack of a clearly reliable calculus do not eliminate the need for choosing, both conditionally and actually, between apparent values appearing to differ by degrees. When faced with an actual ought, each person chooses as best he can. When faced with an opportunity to learn more about how things work, or what principles operate, in any field (including any science) where he is likely to encounter choices in the future, he tries to learn as much as he can. When feelings appear to correlate somewhat with recognizable instrumental values, one tends to utilize those instruments to improve his feelings as far as possible. Then degrees of more and less of instrumental goods tend to occupy attention and choosing. The science of economics, which is an important branch of ethics as a science, seeks reliable principles on the basis of which one ought to choose the apparent good in preference to bad, apparent greater good in preference to lesser good, and apparent lesser evil in preference to greater evil.

Further research regarding principles for choosing is needed. In addition to more general technical ethical principles for choosing, we need specialized studies of how the value aspects of principles in all of the sciences modify those principles and how those principles function in ethical situations as complex value aspects. The more each scientist and technologist becomes aware that the principles he discovers function also as ethical principles—that is, as principles occurring as factors needing consideration in occasions where persons are compelled to choose—the more his own formulation of those principles is likely to contain phrases conducive to wiser choice. Each principle is, in its own way, a principle for choosing.

The Nature of Self

"Acts are right because they are intended to produce the best results for one's self in the long run."[6] Proposing this definition of rightness as basic to the needed world ethics calls for some explanations. "Best results" includes all relevant instrumental values and ultimately the intrinsic values one experiences during a lifetime. "In the long run" may be regarded as a redundant phrase, except that many of our right and wrong choices and acts do pertain to trivia and to short-run problems. One who neglects to concern himself with the values of his life as a whole, insofar as he can, surely does not act rightly when opportunities present themselves for such concern. "Intended" refers to willing as well as willful choice, presumed to be free even though caused by all the causes and conditions presenting choice situations as they appear at the time of choosing.[7] "One's self" refers to a central and perpetual problem to be explored in what follows.

Although what a person means by "self" is often quite clear and obvious, at other times doubt and uncertainty about it prevails. Indeed, it is one of the most controversial problems that has ever faced mankind. One's self is so omnipresent in one's experience that it functions relative to all of one's intentional activities and so has to be interpreted by all of the psychological and sociological sciences, at least, by the different ways in which it functions. Since a person intuits the ways in which his self appears to his self, the science of ethics has another sound starting point. On the other hand, since persons develop self-conceptions as a consequence of their participation in activities, private and public, and have such conceptions shaped by observations about how one's self and its actions are received by others, all mature conceptions of self have been shaped by multiplicities of inferences, many of which may be quite unrealistic and some of which may be actually false. Seen in this light, self-conceptions may be a very poor starting point for a scientific investigation unless the investigator is already highly critical and sensitive both to the multiplicities of variations in self-functions and to the varieties of self-deceptions.

Controversies still rage over whether self is to be identified with a detachable soul, destined to rebirth in a body countless numbers of times or only once in heaven or is purified only when freed completely from bodily association, over whether self is essentially static, even eternal in nature, or is dynamic and variably evolving, or is merely a momentary illusion, and over whether self is essentially simple or complex and, if complex, in how many different ways, such as rational, emotional, willful, biological, social, economic, political, and physical.

How a self conceives itself makes a great difference in whether and how much happiness it enjoys. How a culture conceives and idealizes self makes a great difference in how it survives, prospers, and suffers and whether it is progressive or conservative, active or passive, gregarious or lonely, evolving or static, militant or peaceful, and rich or poor in varieties of personality types. How self is conceived generally in the emerging world culture can determine whether mankind can survive its crises and act in ways that justify hopes for a more lasting future.

The best way of conceiving self generally is in terms of pairs of opposites. Each self is both simple and complex, both a whole and many different kinds of parts, both stable or substantial from birth to death at least and variable in its functions and nature (some changes terminate parts of self and some changes alternate emphases on different functions of self), both active and passive, both a subject of knowing, willing, and acting and an object of the knowing, willing, and actings of others, and both actual in many ways and having potentialities of many kinds.[8] Perhaps most important, a self is both individual and social. Although an adequate ethics will enable persons to deal rightly with problems having only private consequences, self is essentially social in many ways, and a fuller understanding of such ways seems necessary for an adequate world ethics.

Three of the ways in which each self is essentially social include: self-conceptions are social in origin; association with others is the source of most of one's desires; and many, perhaps most, desires can be satisfied better through associating with others.

George Herbert Mead first effectively called attention to the fact that at least some our self-ideas originate socially. Distinguishing between "I" and "me," self-as-subject and self-as-object, he points out that an infant's awareness lacks self-concepts and discovers self-as-subject ideas by being treated as an object by others. When tickled by another, an infant responds by withdrawing, giggling, and wanting more. He thereby discovers his own nature as subject as withdrawing, giggling, and wanting more when tickled. Thus the ways in which an infant is treated by others determine in a large measure his original conceptions of his own nature.[9]

Desires have many causes. Some of them are biological and physiological. Desires for food, drink, exercise, and rest, for example, may all occur without association. But the kinds of food, drink, and exercise we can have, are judged safe, preferred, and idealized are influenced by our associations. Most of our fears, and thus our idea of what is needed for security, are caused by others. We enjoy games taught us by others, and desire to repeat them. We find ourselves esteemed or despised, and desire more esteem or freedom from being despised. Our conceptions of what is possible in the way of clothes, houses, automobiles, travel, occupations, and professional accomplishments are not innate. They are acquired from others. Too few people realize how much their own desires have resulted from social sources.

Satisfactions of desires depend partly on the desires. Desire for what cannot be obtained ends in frustration. Most of our desires having social causes can be satisfied only by social means. My desire to play games, marry, own a home, become employed, own a car and tools, travel, and keep healthy all depend on others for their satisfaction. Even the desire of the hermit and recluse for privacy originates in antipathies developed in association and can be satisfied only if others are willing to leave him alone. Increasing populations, faster transportation, and other factors shrinking our globe increase the prospects of social factors' having some part in the satisfaction of all of our desires.

Self-conceptions are of many kinds. Each time a person finds himself in a new situation requiring him to behave in a new way in order to adapt appropriately, he thereby creates-discovers a new aspect of himself. Some self-conceptions change from the ways of behaving in infancy, childhood, youth, and maturity to retirement and old age. Some persons retain, at least in memory, earlier conceptions with approval; others reject and forget their earlier ones. As a person joins each new group—play group, neighborhood group, village, city, state, nation, and mankind; whether small or large group, observer or participant group, or aggressive or defensive group—another aspect of self develops.[10]

Self-conceptions develop by identifying one's self with something else, such as one's body, one's clothes, one's family, one's community, one's occupation, race, or religion. "The generalized capacity of identification is the soil in which are rooted all possibilities of morality."[11] Possibilities range from feeling identified with one's bodily organs, cells, molecules, atoms, and subatomic particles in one direction and with one's family, community, state, nation, and mankind in the other. Some feel identified not only with all sentient beings (including animals and insects) but also with all existence ("Atman is Brahman"). Thus not only are there levels of self-conceptions but also conceptions of a self as inclusive of levels. Presumably each of these functions, aspects, and levels of self involves values. If so, then a self is a multivalued being, and this fact and the varieties of values and particular values constitute part of the bases of personal ethics.

Self-conceptions tend to grow by trial and error. If one's action or reaction brings him suffering, he is less likely to try it again. Thus both internal abilities and disabilities and external proddings and opportunities and absence of proddings and opportunities combine both to initiate trials and to determine success or error regarding a self's actual nature. The pragmatic theory that a thing is what a thing does helps us to understand the nature of self. A self's conception of itself is a result of many ventures, some in response to being treated as an object by others and some as a result of initiating acting and observing how others respond.

A fuller understanding of self-conception development will involve familiarity with dialectic—how a person provokes another, is provoked by the other, responds to that provocation by more or less provocation, and observes how the other responds to his response. Dialectical processes, especially those in larger families, become quite complicated and cause varieties of subtleties in ways of responding, especially in members inclined toward gregariousness. Some persons develop very rigid self-concepts, and others evolve numerous varieties of flexibility.

Persons who become aware that self-conceptions can evolve through identifying self with more functions, especially responsible group functions, thereby develop an obligation to understand further, explore, and achieve those functions when possible. Societies that become aware of better conceptions of self thereby develop moral obligations to induce such conceptions in their developing members. The moral importance of the role of educational institutions in providing such self-conceptions is often overlooked. Occupational or professional competence, responsible citizenship, reliable parenthood, as well as stable habits of maintaining health all function in terms of self-conceptions. Self-conceptions are central to the nature of rightness and wrongness because the best results sought are sought for a self in terms of its self-conceptions.

Implications of our quantum-leap conceptions for self-conceptions include expectations that a self will grow from a largely un-socialized, and thus unhumanized, infant at birth through many stages of increasing capacities relative to many social ways of func-tioning until it acquires the capacity to acquire additional capacities at will. By becoming multifunctional in many ways with many kinds of cultural traits, each self organizes its functions and capacities into a unique system. The greater the numbers and kinds of cultural traits—among them linguistic, scientific, technological, economic, and political—each person appropriates as constituents of his own personality, the richer each becomes relative to such traits. Com-pared with earlier times and more rural conditions, contemporary megalopolitan selves can hardly avoid achieving considerable luxur-iance of personality unless they happen to be artificially restricted in some way. I believe that luxuriant individualism is an ideal implied by the emerging quantum-leap system. It entails multiplicities of complexes, intricate interdependencies, varieties of functions, flex-ibility relative to the numbers and kinds and preoccupations per-taining to each function, as well as limits to its growths and varia-tions. The more complexly acculturated a person becomes, the more unique does his organicistic combination of available uniformities become.

Self-Interest

Each self is naturally self-interested. All of a person's interests, no matter how caused, are his own. A person naturally wants what he believes to be best for himself. If rightness consists of intending to produce the best results for one's self in the long run, and if a person naturally wants to do what is best for himself, he naturally wants to act rightly. If oughtness consists of the power that an apparently greater good has over an apparently lesser good in compelling our choices, then each person always wants to choose as he ought.

I propose a self-interest theory of ethics as best for mankind and as inherent in our quantum-leap gestalt. I do not propose a selfish theory of ethics. Those who fail to distinguish between self-interest (wanting what is best for oneself) and selfishness (wanting what is best for oneself without regard for what is best for others) do not have a clear understanding of either the nature of self and its best interests or of ethics as man's quest for the best. The problem of becoming wisely self-interested has many aspects. Two will be treated: values of unselfishness and evils of overabundance.

VALUES OF UNSELFISHNESS

The values of unselfishness can be demonstrated by each person for himself. A principle of reciprocity tends to operate in human nature. It works both negatively and positively. Slap me, and I will want to slap you. Despise me, and I will despise you, at least for despising me. Admire me, and I will admire you, at least for admiring me. Help me, and I will want to help you, at least to help you help me more. Granted that the principle does not work with mathematical precision. Nevertheless, those who deliberately seek to be generous in their dealings with others find their generosity repaid, sometimes in surprising ways.

Anyone who has not already learned from his own experiences that selfishness results in antipathies toward himself is unlikely to try an experiment carried on by students in my ethics classes for several years. At the beginning of the semester, I asked each to select one person whom he liked and who liked him, one whom he disliked and who disliked him, one whom he liked and who disliked him, and one whom he disliked and who liked him. Each student approached his selectee, complementing him about one or more traits of his character or circumstances. Records were kept of attitudes expressed before, during, and after each of several approaches. At semester's end, each student reported on any changes in his own attitudes as well as in those of his selectees. Results varied considerably, but no student failed to be impressed by the effects of his own efforts.

There are ten principles regarding wise self-interest that anyone can test for himself.

1. In whatever way a person is actually social, his own interests involve the interests of others.

2. To satisfy one's own interests in such circumstances, one must act in ways that will either not harm the interests of others or will promote the interests of others or both.

3. One naturally likes to have his interests satisfied, so when he finds his own interests satisfied by cooperating with others in ways satisfying the interests of others, he naturally wants more such satisfaction.

4. Desire for more satisfaction of one's interests through cooperation

with others tends to increase more than one's interests can be satisfied through such cooperation with others.

5. Desire for more satisfaction than one receives tends to beget unfortunate consequences. When one expresses dissatisfaction with what he receives from cooperation with others, others, if they believe that they have fulfilled reciprocal obligations, find their contributions depreciated. Their desires for satisfaction relative to filling their obligations become frustrated. When their desires are frustrated, they tend to reciprocate in ways that result in further dissatisfaction for the one who desires more satisfaction than he has coming from such cooperation.

6. A principle of reciprocity apparently inherent in human nature resulting from socialization operates both negatively and positively. Those who refuse to help others satisfy their interests are refused help by others. Those who help others more tend to receive more help from others in satisfying their own interests.

7. Initiative in cooperative efforts to pursue interests in often possible. Negatively, one can so act as to assure others that he is not hindering them from pursuing their interests. Positively, one can act so as to help others pursue their interests. The more you desire to satisfy your interests where cooperation is required, the more unselfish you should be in helping others pursue their interests.

8. The principle of reciprocity usually reflects sincerity and insincerity. If one merely pretends to help others, the most that he can expect from others is a pretense to help.

9. Reciprocation is seldom equal. The interests of different persons differ somewhat, so even when persons try to reciprocate equally, these differences function in such reciprocation. Delay should be expected in receiving some rewards. When received later, sometimes they appear as surprises. If your efforts to help others pursue their interests were genuine, you did not always expect immediate returns. So when returns arrive later unexpectedly, they may appear as more than deserved. Of course, others often forget to reciprocate even as we forget. But those who deliberately (or even habitually) act unselfishly testify that they come out ahead in the long run.

10. To the extent that the principle does work, each person has within his own power a means for increasing satisfaction of his own interests.[12]

A world ethics needs to provide greater confidence in the principle of reciprocity than prevails in demoralizing megalopolis today. Our quantum-leap gestalt should not only encourage such confidence but also demonstrate clearly how and why it can and should be exploited in the interests of more luxuriant individualism. A complex self has a complex of self-interests. An intricately interdependent self has interests in his interdependencies, their intricacies, and how each contributes something of value to it. A multileveled self has many levels of self-interest. A multifunctional self functions self-interestedly in many different ways.

Wise self-interestedness manages to retain vital organic wholeness throughout any conflicts of interests among one's complex of self-interests. The nature and purpose of ethics is to serve as the arena for decision making. Only when conflicts among one's self-interests appear to require an act of choosing does obligation occur. The more interests one has, the more likely conflicts are to appear, unless he has succeeded in surmounting them with facility; thus the more obligated, or ethical, he becomes. Our quantum-leap system should promote both increased luxury of self-interests, greater facility for reducing or removing conflicts between them, and greater sensitivity to the need for becoming both more ethical (in the sense of seeking more cultural riches to choose between) and less ethical (in the sense of seeking to reduce the need for agonizing choices between limited alternatives). The importance of accepting the values of impersonality and of intimate personality in developing habits of reciprocation at many levels, through many functions, in many degrees, and with many variations should become evident as one becomes more at home in the new gestalt. Luxuriant wise self-interestedness is a natural ingredient in our quantum-leap conceptions. Developing it may be essential to human survival.

EVILS OF OVERABUNDANCE

The evils of overabundance—of both desires and means for satisfying desires serving as stimulants to desires—tend to be overlooked in Western society. Wise self-interestedness, intending to avoid feelings of frustration as intrinsic values, will assent to the principle of Gotama, the Buddha: "Desire for what will not be attained ends in frustration. Therefore, to avoid frustration, avoid desiring what will not be attained."[13] The principle is sound whether one is poor or rich and whether one lives in a poor culture or with the riches of many cultures.

In a world where billions of people suffer from shortages of food and other necessities of life, references to overabundances of anything, except population, may appear insensitive. But in the emerging world culture, which is both megalopolitan and global in complexity and richness, problems of overabundance have already become aggravated and promise to become more so if mankind survives. The issue at stake here has to do with developing personalities having too many and too complex interests, so that pursuit of self-interest automatically results in too much frustration. The problem is related to the rising expectations of many persons trained to achieve abilities for which no suitable opportunities exist. The problem is partly one of human resources and partly one of ill-organized personalities.

Varieties of individualistic ideals have been advocated in the past. The rugged individualism of the pioneer, the competitive individualism of bartering capitalism, the antirational individualism of romanticism, the drugged individualism of many hippies, and the irresponsible individualism of existentialism all eulogize individualism in one way or another. I am advocating for mankind a luxuriant individualism born and nurtured in multicultural riches. In developed countries, opportunities and many unconscious and conscious pressures tend to promote the development of personalities with interests resulting from studying many sciences, many technologies, many cultures, and sometimes through many languages. The rich varieties of interests each person acquires have already been described as luxuriant. But each person also has his own limits of growth in varieties of personality enrichment. Overabundance beyond these limits becomes an evil.

Hence the world ethics being proposed here is designed to put forth efforts to master the doubly complex problem of expanding self-conceptions to include concerns for the interests of many others so as to reduce conflicts with others and of withdrawing from too many interests, which become superabundant when they cannot be integrated within a self because conflicts among them constitute debilitating frustrations. Wise self-interest includes sufficient altruism to assure needed assistance by others and exploiting available varieties of cultural riches up to that point where adding new varieties becomes self-defeating. Simpler societies provided simpler personality patterns as examples to follow. But the complexities of the emerging world culture too often offer multiplicities of patterns without providing an additional pattern for organizing these patterns.

Our quantum-leap system gestalt should provide such a pattern or principles for shaping needed varieties of patterns. The more fully each person feels identified with the natures, substances, functions, and processes of others, the more such feelings of interexistence contribute to concern for the welfare of others with whom he interexists. Each person can and should acquire conceptions of limits to which his welfare and that of others are identical. Respect for the uniqueness of each person requires that others recognize their nonidentity with him also and, although one may promote the welfare of others by noninterference, recognize limits to interexistence.

SOCIAL ETHICS

Although social ethics is essentially an extension of personal ethics, groups do exist, have general and specific natures, function as stable entities, and behave as beings with interests, sometimes selfishly and sometimes wisely, in ways that can be studied and understood scientifically. Not only is each person essentially social, but also every society is essentially personal in the sense that groups and institutions exist in persons and nowhere else. Persons and groups interdepend. There are no groups apart from persons. No biological homo sapiens infant becomes human until he has been socialized.

Mistaken neglect of social ethics and failure to use scientific methods in dealing with its problems, theoretical and practical, are part of the cause of contemporary crises. Social ethics is foundational to all the other social sciences, including jurisprudence and the public and private administrative policy sciences. I would be mistaken in saying that the teaching of sociology in the United States universities, colleges, and secondary schools resembles a cauldron of conflicting ideologies more than a science with demonstrated principles upon which teachers, students, and policy deciders can rely. But I would be only partly mistaken. The combined ignorance, biases, and license characterizing much teaching warrant severe castigation.

The fault is not with the nature of the subject matter. The nature of groups and of culture, including institutions, is as open to scientific investigation as any other subject matter, and much more so when compared with what some physical scientists are trying to do. As a society, we lack the will to take the social sciences seriously enough to invest the billions needed for research and to demand from researchers the rigor needed for convincing demonstrations. Today the science of ethics, and specifically social ethics, is caught in this heap of neglect. Our quantum-leap system gestalt will require rigorization, realistic systematization, rapid development, and sufficient financial support for sociology as a basic science. The intimate interdependence of social ethics with all other problems and solutions in the social sciences will require that social ethics shares in such rigorization, systematization, development, and support.

Groups

Groups differ; they range all the way from two persons casually interacting for only a moment to the whole of mankind. Yet all groups are alike in consisting of persons as members associating with some minimal degree of conscious participation. The persons in each group differ from each other often in many respects; yet all are alike in some way as a result of sharing membership in the group. The numbers of kinds of groups are so many that adequate classification cannot be presented easily. Convenience dictates mentioning two main types—general or multifunctional groups and specialized or special-purpose groups—but these often overlap and intermingle.

GENERAL PURPOSE GROUPS

General or multipurpose groups are those concerned with the general welfare of each member. They tend to be identified with geographical locations, small or large. Traditionally, and today, most persons live in family groups. Although families differ in intimacy, size, and function, families have tended to embody concern for the common and individual welfare of their members. They often share a home, a common location. Extended families, tribes, clans, and races often function as general welfare and multifunctional groups. Some of these share a homeland, a common location. Villages, cities, states and nations tend to be multifunctional groups, although when multifunctional groups become hierarchically arranged, so that neighborhoods consist of families, villages or neighborhoods, cities or counties of villages or precincts, states of cities and counties, nations of states, some functions tend to be performed more effectively at some levels than at others. Thus even general purpose groups tend to lose or gain special functions when these are transferred, partly or wholly, to other general purpose groups (and sometimes to specialized groups).

Although persons may function more fully as members of family, village, state, and national groups than of county, city, regional, international, or world groups today, the tendency in history of civilizations has been for persons to become organized into larger and larger groups. Population pressures and awareness of resource limitations, together with increasingly complex and more frequent interactions, are forcing us to become more fully aware of our existence as members of mankind as a whole. The current prevalence of nationalism as a philosophy of political organization locates authority for general welfare primarily in national groups, although these vary greatly in their abilities and willingness to provide for such welfare. The incapacity of nations to meet and solve our world crises is evidence of the need for some kind of world organization that does have the needed capacity. Thus the relative importance of that group consisting in mankind as a whole continues to increase. What effects organizing such a group and a suitable world government will have on other groups remains to be seen. But the problems of relocating or allocating different portions of responsibility for general welfare at different group levels will continue to plague policy deciders guided by our new system gestalt until some optimum division of labor has been established.

If competent and efficient systems for assuring general welfare can be embodied in a world government, the need for duplicating such services and assurances at lower levels will diminish. Although I cannot predict the future course of group developments, I do not expect that all welfare functions can be allotted to a world government, at least for a long time to come. Not only do lower-level groups now bear most of the responsibility but entrenched habits and vested interests in present systems are not likely to change rapidly unless crises prevent them from functioning adequately. Nevertheless changes are increasing in rapidity, and many new needs have become so complex and costly that they can be met efficiently only by higher-level groups. As we approach the limits of complexity that persons and groups can organically unify, the need for eliminating some general-purpose groups will increase. Counties have become obsolete in some places. Even urban boundaries have become detrimental factors in megalopolitan developments. Difficulties in maintaining small nations motivate efforts toward regional international developments. Research into the most desirable ways of distributing general welfare functions at different group levels is something in which those guided by our quantum-leap conceptions will naturally engage in.

Changes in the importance of present family groups can be expected. But how much, in what ways, and how soon, I cannot predict. Experiments with communes in the United States and China have not yet warranted promise that they will replace families. But decreasing percentages of time each person spends in family groups in comparison with all other groups is already having significant effects on the nature and role of family living. One serious product of megalopolitan growth is a decline in percentages of times persons spend in primary-group association. (In primary groups, people interact face to face in ways such that the care each has for the personal welfare of the others is obvious and continuous.) Neighborhoods and children's play groups have supplemented family groups in which each person's sense of recognition of the intrinsic value of other persons intuitively inspires loyalty to policies and practices aimed at assuring their welfare. Without primary group association, a biological infant cannot become humanized enough to respect the values, and consequently the rights, of others. Diminution of primary group participation in contemporary life is partly responsible for growing demoralization, rising crime rates, and loss of confidence in many institutions.

This humanizing function must be increased both quantitatively and qualitatively if persons are to achieve sufficient feelings of loyalty to policy principles relative to multiplicities of kinds and levels of groups. Thus any diminution of primary group humanization resulting from decline in family group participation will need to be replaced by some more effective group effort if human society is to survive. Although we do have ways of increasing the numbers of persons with whom each person can feel identified and personally loyal to, nevertheless there are limits to the number of persons with which each person can become genuinely intimate. But assured provision that each infant will be appreciated and become able to appreciate others as worthy ends-in-themselves is necessary to group living. How to ensure such provisions, especially when changes in the relative importance of the general welfare functions of groups at different levels continue, constitutes a central problem for social ethics, even if we do not succeed in making the new system gestalt operational pervasively.

Each person needs at least one other "contact person," someone with whom he can share intimate feelings, beliefs, and problems. Confidence in and conscientious participation in our increasingly complex system will be facilitated if each person can make primary-group-type contacts with persons at each level and in each specialty. Successful personnel departments provide an atmosphere of friendliness. Some religious groups, especially those emphasizing total participation and providing general welfare functions for members, enable members to "love everybody." However achieved, it seems obvious that our quantum-leap system gestalt will naturally accept as a primary social obligation the assurance of sufficient participation by each person in primary-group types of existence and development and recurrent (preferably constant) refreshment needed to maintain morale for personal and social living. Ideals motivating luxuriant individuals tend to turn into selfish, highly destructive, antisocial tendencies without such assurance and refreshment.

SPECIAL PURPOSE GROUPS

Specialized groups also are of many kinds, ranging from those consisting of two persons, such as a pair playing cards for recreational purposes, to a worldwide television audience. Specialization and division of labor occurs, sometimes necessarily, within groups, including all general welfare groups, and when two or more persons join in performing any one kind of specialized service, they thereby constitute a specialized group. Although most specialized groups probably originate within and function in more general groups, some develop considerable autonomy and in many countries become incorporated as companies with limited liability as well as limited functionability. Some such companies and some occupational and professional societies operate within one level of general groups, that is, within a city, a state, or a nation. Others function at many levels, including international or multinational levels.

Each kind of function may be dealt with by a specialized group. As functions multiply, more such specialized groups develop. As functions become more complex, they tend to become subdivided again and again, each serving as a basis for another kind of group. Each such subdivision functions also as another subdivision in each person served by the resulting groups. Each person's self-interest thereby becomes more complex, and problems of wise self-interestedness recur. The values of specialization, often very great, may be balanced somewhat by the evils of specialization.[14] Each kind of specialist, especially when recognizing his service as essential, tends to overestimate the relative worth of his services. When he does, he may expect more and demand more than is warranted. Tyrannies by specialists aggravate megalopolitan problems.

Our quantum-leap conceptions should encourage a greater appreciation of the necessities for increasing specialization, greater understanding of the limitations and evils as well as values of specialization, and greater awareness of the problems of unwise self-interestness on the part of persons utilizing the services of specialists and on the part of specialists misjudging the values and evils of their services. They should promote effective concern for filling gaps in specialized needs. These now include specialists in comprehensiveness, in axiological and ethical understanding and education, in medical research and services, in geriatrics, and in many varieties of interdisciplinary research facilitation. Contemporary evils resulting from misunderstanding the nature of groups is compounded by misunderstanding of the nature of institutions. I believe that familiarity with our quantum-leap gestalt will require removal of these misunderstandings.

Institutions

Institutions are established ways of behaving. They are social habits. Institutions exist as behavior patterns in the lives of persons. They have no existence elsewhere, although groups often allocate certain buildings to serve as the location for performing or participating in specialized institutional services. When persons meet institutional officers and buildings under inimical circumstances, they become antipathetic. The obsolescence of some institutions, combined with the drafting and deaths of thousands in the misdirected Vietnam war, angered trapped youths enough to prepare them for accepting anti-establishment attitudes encouraged by nihilistic existentialism. Current demoralization processes, although less violent than in recent years, may be expected to continue steadily until institutions, both revitalized and understood, warrant confidence in them.

One of the most useful insights in understanding institutions is embodied in Charles Horton Cooley's cycle of institutional development, depicted in figure 2.[15] Institutions usually originate to serve an unmet need. An evil or deficiency exists that needs to be overcome. When response to a need achieves sufficient consensus in a group so that members agree to participate in the needed behavior

FIGURE 2.
THE CYCLE OF INSTITUTIONAL DEVELOPMENT

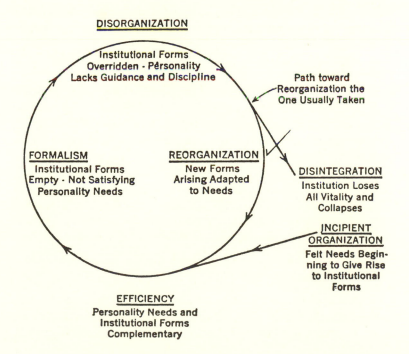

DISORGANIZATION

Institutional Forms Overridden - Personality Lacks Guidance and Discipline

Path toward Reorganization the One Usually Taken

FORMALISM

Institutional Forms Empty - Not Satisfying Personality Needs

REORGANIZATION

New Forms Arising Adapted to Needs

DISINTEGRATION

Institution Loses All Vitality and Collapses

INCIPIENT ORGANIZATION

Felt Needs Beginning to Give Rise to Institutional Forms

EFFICIENCY

Personality Needs and Institutional Forms Complementary

pattern, the stage may be called *incipient organization*. When participants feel that the institutional forms serve the needs as well as possible, the stage may be called one of *efficiency*. Here the values of the institution to participants are obvious, so conformity occurs willingly. Members not only approve but embody feelings of loyalty to beneficial institutions. Then new needs arise, and older ones decline or disappear. When established habits compel conformity to institutions that no longer serve needs adequately, the stage is called *formalism*. Persons feel compelled to conform without feeling benefited by the conformity. Some refuse to conform. New members cannot understand reasons for conforming. When some do and some do not conform, the stage is called *disorganization*. Persons torn between feeling immoral when not conforming and foolish when conforming resent institutional persistence. Persons making their first contacts with institutions in their formalistic or disorganized stages rightly reject them.

But it is not the purpose of institutions to exist at these stages; the purpose is to serve needs. The stage of disorganization normally is followed either by disintegration, when none feel compelled to conform, or by reorganization, if the original need persists in modified form. When an institution is complex, often only some part of it is replaced. But when many interdepending social functions have come to be served by intricately interlocking institutions, replacement of parts becomes more difficult. When replacement and reorganization difficulties increase, cultural lag accumulates. When cultural lag becomes great enough, institutional complexes become more and more formalistic. When drastic revision is called for but guidance in instituting more intelligent forms is lacking, crisis occurs. Our contemporary national and global crises call for drastic revision. But intelligent guidance is lacking. The urgency of interdisciplinary research efforts in producing understanding of the needed quantum-leap conceptions is great. It should have first priority.

Social Science Research

Social science research reconceived in terms of the quantum-leap system gestalt is challenged by much more intricate and dynamic kinds of problems than most social scientists envisage at present.

Acceptance of ethics as a science, or collection of sciences, contributing insights essential for understanding the nature of groups and culture both complicates research problems and facilitates their solution because the value ingredients become more obviously inherent in their nature. In addition, recognition of the impossibility of achieving exact kinds of distributive and retributive justice when persons of different ages, capacities, needs, and contributions, constructive and destructive, participate differentially and variably in multileveled, multifunctional, multidimensional kinds of groups will require the formulation, testing, and adoption of workable guidelines (codes or laws) for acceptable behavior and obligation fulfillment.

Since participation in groups with large numbers of people necessitates highly impersonal kinds of participation, persons will come to expect much treatment that is impersonal and to accept the necessity of conscientious fulfillment of obligations required by such impersonal conditions. An important part of social science research will pertain to developing principles relative to comparatively equitable settlement of issues about justice where conflicts of interests, within persons, between persons, between persons and their groups, and between groups exist in ways involving many impersonal, partly indefinite, multifunctional, and variably dynamic factors.

Our quantum-leap system gestalt will require not only better understanding of the nature of, and need for, varieties and values of groups for individuals but also continuing consciousness of such nature, needs, kinds, and values of groups by individuals. It will require understanding of and persisting awareness of the demonstrated principles of personal-social interdependence, interexistence, and ways for mutual improvement through creative interactivity. Its shaping self-conceptions and ideals of luxuriant self-development through dialogic participation in multigroup and multicultural processes induce intricately organized complexes of self-interest in each person and in many groups. Such self-interest naturally expresses itself through awareness of and acceptance of self-interested obligations to optimize luxuriant self-development through responsible participation in and utilization of at least the easily available groups and cultures. Self-interested acceptance of obligations to support such groups and cultures as needed for mutual survival and improvement should be facilitated by feelings of familiarity with and confidence in the truthfulness and adequacy of the new system gestalt.

The importance of sensitivity to obsolescence in institutions increases as social interactions become more complex and dynamic. Societies cannot afford the luxury—or evil—of obsolete, formalized, and disorganized institutions. Delays in reorganization become extremely costly when cultural lag in one institution affects the functioning of, and thus infects the nature of, other institutions and of all dependent on it. Current neglect of axiology and ethics as sciences and philosophy's comprehensive functioning constitutes vicious lag and urgently needs elimination. Since some of our most ancient and obsolete institutions are to be found as sectarian religious institutions, social science research aiming to provide insights needed in our quantum-leap conceptions should focus sharp attention on them. The central role that sectarian religions are playing in causing and failing to cure present world crises warrants devoting a separate chapter to it. Social ethics includes, or interdepends with, religious ethics, and religious ethics includes, or interdepends with, social ethics. The Philosopher's World Model calls for quantum-leap conceptions that enable persons to feel at home in the vast multi-leveled universe, in their dynamic variegated societies, and in their dialectically developing luxuriant selves.

WORLD RELIGION?
WHY NOT?

Religion is concern for ultimate values, which are ends-in-themselves and pertain to life as a whole. Each person is naturally interested in what is best for his life as a whole, so each person is naturally religious.

Religion is a branch of ethics that is concerned with life as a whole in contrast to business ethics, medical ethics, educational ethics, or political ethics, for example, which pertain to different parts of life. And to the extent that one's life as a whole includes all of its parts, religion is the most inclusive ethics.

Although a distinction between religious and nonreligious ethics can and should be made, the same problem may at first be nonreligious and then become religious, or vice versa. For example, a skin infection is normally regarded as nonreligious. One faces ethical choices as to what is best to do regarding seeking a physician, obtaining medicines, and whether and when to use the medicines prescribed. But if the infection endangers one's life, the problem takes on a religious significance. The more the infection endangers life as a whole, the more it becomes of religious concern.

Those times in life tending to have crucial significance for a life as a whole tend to be recognized by appropriate ceremonies. Birth, death, marriage, births of children, puberty, achievement of mature community citizenship, and often serious illnesses tend to be ceremonialized in each culture. The welfare of each vital society as a whole also usually is regarded as having religious significance. Societies celebrate spring (planting) and fall (harvesting) festivals, the death and installation of at least the chief officer, victory over enemies. Founding dates of vital societies and birth dates of founding fathers rate religious significance. Those who believe their welfare depends on deities must act religiously in appropriate ways. Dates and places of origins, revelations, foundings of institutions, births or deaths or achievements of founders who often become deified, and of councils' confirming or modifying doctrines or documents relevant to the welfare of society (or of mankind) as a whole tend to receive religious recognition. In days when reliable knowledge about life as a whole was scarce, writings regarded as reliable had religious significance.

Today the knowledge of life as a whole for mankind facing doomsday crises should be easier to achieve. But since so many persons, including political leaders, have been indoctrinated with solutions relevant to situations long past in ways preventing them from taking the fresh look needed, that knowledge seems to be missing. Most of the world's religions have long-standing institutions that are impotent to deal effectively with our crises; they thus represent a stage of formalism and, progressively, disorganization. Despite keen awareness of and sympathetic concern for human sufferings and global dangers, too many of the leaders of today's traditional religions are crippled by their inability to rise above their traditional doctrines in ways needed to achieve the kind of world religion that can and will be effective in uniting mankind and solving its crises.

Religion unites; religions divide. Today we have too many religions and not enough religion. The multiplicity of religions in the world today has an antireligious effect. Religions are the chief enemy of religion. Survival of mankind may depend on getting this message to leaders of religions in convincing ways. Political and military leaders can safely ignore religious leaders as long as their own divisiveness cripples their effectiveness and demonstrates their lack of genuinely relevant and reliable religious knowledge. As long as their doctrines contradict each other, they cannot all be true. As long as their doctrines do not recognize and accept the latest scientific knowledge demonstrated as reliable and as long as they do not revise their views and their advice accordingly, they cannot be adequate.

As long as they do not trust each other, they cannot expect political and military leaders to trust them.

Part of the reason for the crippling of our religions is some misconceptions about the nature of religion itself. Generalizations about the nature of religion based on too few examples result in truncated definitions. Massive populations encultured by Judaic, Christian, and Islamic ideas of ethical monotheism, with a god who is designer, creator, preserver, or savior and culminator of the world, normally conclude that religion is belief in God. Efforts to accommodate polytheistic cultures and primitive cultures result in expanding this definition to belief in God or gods. Centuries of criticism about the personality and/or impersonality of cosmic powers and invisible forces and exposure to Asian views has resulted in a belief in God or gods, or some supernatural or superhuman powers. Such beliefs involve appropriate acts of worship and conduct.

I was raised to hold such a belief, but I had to learn that it is false. As a long-time teacher of comparative religions and philosophy of religion, I became acquainted with more and more religions. I spent two sabbatical leaves in Burma and India. Burmese Buddhists believe in the law of Karma and reincarnation and they worship those who become full-time saffron-robed monks, vowing poverty, chastity, and obedience, losing most citizen rights and duties, begging for their food, and devoting much time to yogic practices. They also hold two doctrines as true: *anicca*, no permanence, and *anatta*, no soul. Since nothing is permanent, God cannot be conceived as permanent. Furthermore since Burmese Buddhism, like most other Asian religions, is a self-help religion, any willingness to appeal to or to receive help from a diety builds up bad karmas, belief in God is bad, and appeal to God for help is worse. Burmese Buddhists explicitly argue against belief in God for religious reasons.[1]

In India, Jains, who claim to hold doctrines originating earlier than the earliest Hindu scriptures, believe that souls are eternal, that eventual escape from the otherwise endless rounds of rebirth is possible for some, and that bad karmas can be shed and good karmas accumulated by different kinds of austerities, including vegetarianism, and strict adherence to *ahimsa* (nonviolence). Jainism too is a self-help religion, and, although it does not object to recognizing some souls as deities, appeal to them for help builds up one's stock of bad karmas. No creator is needed, since both all souls and the natural world are eternal. Although Jains appear to me to be much less well organized than the Burmese Buddhists, their naked ascetics practice austerities religiously, and probably more rigorously than adherents of any other religion.[2]

Hindu polytheism, developing from the worship of nature powers, evolved a pantheon, a trinity, a trimurti, and finally *Nirguna Brahman*. As conceived by Advaita Vedanta, the ultimate reality, *Nirguna Brahman*, alone is. All else—things, persons, deities, and the highest deity—have no being different from *Nirguna Brahman*, which, itself, has no qualities. It is *sat-chit-ananda*, pure being-awareness-bliss, and nothing more. All apparent things, persons, and deities, are *maya* (illusion). Western monotheists who try to preserve their belief-in-God definition of religion by stretching it to include Hindu polytheism fail to recognize that, among those most learned and most religiously devout Hindus, all depictions of ultimate reality as in any sense a person is illusory.[3] China's ancient Taoism and Confucianism do not fit belief-in-God definitions, although mistaken well-wishers have made many attempts.[4]

If belief in God is not essential to religion, then what is? The way to find out, I propose, is to use the methods employed in inductive science. Because a definition based on only a few of the world's religions is false, one should study all of the world's religions first, if possible, before drawing conclusions. Many kinds of factors may be observed and may suggest themselves as candidates for a definition. The problem of sorting out those actually common to all religions, and eliminating those occurring in only some, is complicated and difficult.

Every religion has both beliefs and practices. Each has some beliefs about the origin, nature, and future of self, society, and the universe and about different kinds of values, good and bad, and kinds of behavior needed. Each religion has some practices designed to accomplish the goals of life as conceived in its doctrines. I have found no particular belief and no particular kind of behavior essential to religion. But I observe that all religions have one thing in common: concern for ultimate values. Thus I propose that all who are concerned with a world religion have at least this much to agree upon for a beginning. Concern for ultimate values should have a central place in our quantum-leap system gestalt.

THE FAILURE OF RELIGIONS

The world's religions are not doing the job that is needed. Our crises are becoming more serious. The divisiveness of religions, their persistent adherence to obsolete doctrines, and their unwillingness to utilize scientific methods for problems that threaten to challenge or refute orthodox presuppositions not only prevent them from being able to provide insightful contributions, reliable evaluations, and confident support for united world community action but also cause them to be major contributors to crisis conditions. The world's major religions (and I suspect the same is true of most minor ones also) are causally responsible for our global crises and for our inability to deal with them effectively. They are not the only causes; our crises have many causes. But the causal contributions of religions need to be recognized and proclaimed in ways that will challenge them to reexamine themselves in light of the charge.

Those who disagree will insist that their religion has not been given a fair trial. Other religions prevent its universal acceptance, and even its own members fail to give it loyal support. If everyone would believe and act in accordance with its principles and practices, world peace would prevail, together with prosperity, health, and happiness, if not in this world, then in the next. But the facts remain that the other religions do exist, that participation in each tends to decline as members become more broadly educated, that orthodox adherents resist surrender of doctrines demonstrated to be false in light of scientific discoveries, and that members and leaders tend not to seek to revise presuppositions in light of the latest scientific findings. The vested interests of persons who have devoted so much of their lives to acquiring and living in accordance with some doctrines, and of clergy and other supporting laity whose income, retirement benefits, specialized skills, and achievements, to say nothing of reputations, are additional factors in maintaining the status quo. Systems of income, usually difficult to establish in the first place, would be jeopardized by doctrinal revisions, so that many incumbents who have revised their own views cannot afford to relinquish their perquisites.

There are many reasons why traditional religions have become indisposed to change. But these reasons do not excuse them from their responsibility for causing, and preventing us from overcoming, our crises. These reasons become reasons why these religions should become extinct. "The most spectacular fossils in the twentieth century's museum of dead faiths are those of the traditional religions, such as Christianity, Islam, and Buddhism."[5]

In order to serve the need for an effective world religion for mankind facing global crises threatening human extinction, either the traditional religions (at least some of them) must immediately take steps to reform their doctrines enough to enable them to join in providing needed leadership, or those responsible for funding research regarding the fundamental sciences that provide knowledge for policy decisions should commission interdisciplinary research institutes to discover or design the religion needed. Either reform traditional religions immediately and sufficiently or discover and/or design a new religion suited to present needs.

CAN THEY REFORM ENOUGH?

There is some truth in every religion. Each is good or has some good for some people. A religion could not survive if it did not provide some good and some truth to some people. I cannot agree with those who would destroy all existing religions first and then try to build something better. People need religion, and almost any of the traditional religions (I include Marxism here) is better than none at all. Those responsible for religious reform should provide a better religion first and demonstrate its superiority over others. Then conversion will be easier. People rightly resist replacing something with nothing. But they also rightly seek what is better in preference to what is less good.

How can religions reform? Beginning with Christianity, we may recall ecumenical efforts. Some Protestant denominations that were previously split have been able to reunite partially.[6] Methodists, Congregationalists, and Presbyterians joined to form the United Church of Canada, for example. Many Protestant denominations have joined the Federal Council of Churches of Christ in America, founded in 1908. Now called the National Council of Churches, it cooperates with the World Council of Churches, which met first in 1948.

The fifth meeting of the World Council in Nairobi, Kenya, in November 1975 chose as its theme, "Christ Unites."[7] But with "nearly 270 churches in 90 countries . . . , you will see how difficult it is to work with a single perspective in what is obviously a pluralistic situation. . . . We cannot expect too much too soon," wrote council director S. J. Samartha from his Geneva office.[8] I challenged him to put a question to the Nairobi conference: "Is not interreligious ecumenism more urgent than merely Christian ecumenism?" His reply came in the report of the conference: "We are all opposed to any form of syncretism, incipient, nascent or developed, if we mean by syncretism conscious or unconscious human attempts to create a new religion composed of elements taken from different religions."

Roman Catholicism, disturbed by disagreements about changing the language of liturgy from Latin to the vernacular and under attack for its stand on birth control, has responded to ecumenical efforts by establishing three secretariates to deal with three problems: one with Christian unity, one with non-Christian religions, and one with non-believers. My efforts to obtain authoritative statements from officers of these secretariates resulted in a letter from Theodore M. Hesburgh, a staunch believer who has achieved a world reputation for helping to deal with the problems of mankind, including poverty, food shortages and injustice. He has expressed a "vision of our interdependent world" and has recommended that "we might all begin by a Declaration of the Interdependence of Mankind." He has faith that "the new millennium will see a union of mankind in a growing active ecumenism," for "ecumenism is bringing the Christian and Non-Christian religions together in understanding at last."[9] But he also believes that Roman Catholicism is "a true world Church that will survive and that will not change fundamentally in doing so."[10] If this belief continues to prevail, I believe that Roman Catholicism is incompetent to contribute constructively to the needed world religion and that the exclusiveness of its orthodoxy makes it one of the most divisive religions today.

American Jews are split into orthodox, conservative, and reform

groups. Many reform Jews seem sufficiently humanistic to give support to the needed world religion. But orthodox Jews, especially
those regarding themselves as Zionists, are committed to the reestab-
lishment of Israel as a religious state where all Jews can begin to exercise effective political and military leadership in a world where they
believe they have been chosen by God to show the way to others.
With few exceptions, one must be born a Jew to participate fully in
orthodox Judaism. Thus the exclusivism of Jewish orthodoxy prevents it from becoming a constructive contributor to the needed
world religion. The billions of dollars poured into military preparedness for Mideast wars serve as evidence that supporters of Israel are
interested in Jews first and the rest of humanity only next. When
Jews and Arabs, similar in so many semitic racial, linguistic, and
monotheistic religious ways, cannot achieve peace (at times it seems
each wants to annihilate the others), they provide no hope for the
agreement needed for an effective world religion.

Islam, divided into Sunnite, Shiite, and Sufi sects, and spread ex-
tensively from Arab to non-Arab countries, including Turkey, Iran,
India, China, Malaysia, Indonesia, the Philippines, Egypt and much
of Africa, has been vigorously propagated. When the British sur-
rendered India, Moslems demanded and established Pakistan as a
separate Moslem state. Bangladesh, split from West Pakistan partly
for racial reasons, remains a Moslem state. With some notable exceptions, persons for whom I have only admiration, most Moslems I
have met were intensely aggressive, self-assured, and rigorously
dogmatic. The spirit of Islam is utterly exclusivistic. A copy of the
February 1976 *Journal of the Muslim World League* arrived as I
wrote this book. Devoted to "The First International Conference on
Islamic Economics," including what to do with petrodollar affluence, the journal quotes guidance from the *Holy Qur'an*, including
"the reminder: My righteous slaves will inherit the earth." It quotes
the Prophet: "If anyone fights to cause the world of Allah (Islam) to
be superior then this type of battle is in Allah's cause." What contribution can be expected toward the needed world religion? In
"Islam Today," Sayyid Abdul A'la Maududi says: "Recent developments in the world of Islam have proved it beyond a shadow of
doubt that Muslims can be aroused and inspired to make sacrifices
only in the name of Islam; no other call can appeal to them."[11]

Indian religions are many. Yet in contrast to the three ethical monotheisms just reviewed, which are explicitly exclusivistic, the spirit of Indian religion is captured in the oft-repeated phrase, "All religions are one." Here is all the unity needed for a world religion and even more. Hope arises until one realizes that "that one is Vedant." Vedantism, at least in its most unified version, *Advaita*, nondualism, is a view claiming that all plurality is illusory. If so, then one can deduce that all differences, including all differences among religions, are illusory.

I do not wish to minimize any unifying contributions to a world religion that Indian religions may make, but a most obvious characteristic needed by a new world philosophy is complexity. If "all religions are one" presupposes that reality is ultimately simple or, worse, pure undifferentiated being, then it is based on presuppositions not fitted to deal with contemporary crises. Adoption of Advaita Vedanta as a world philosophy-religion needed to deal with today's dynamically interdependent complexities would be utterly unrealistic.

It would be a mistake to suggest that persons motivated by the Indian spirit of inclusiveness, in contrast to the exclusivistic spirit of the three ethical monotheisms, will make no contributions to the needed world religion. Yet the spirit of orthodoxy in India does not yield much hope. During January 1976, I participated in the International Seminars on Buddhism and Jainism conducted by the Institute for Oriental and Orissan Studies in Cuttack. After mentioning world crises and doomsday prophecies and inquiring what Jainism and Buddhism have to offer, I received two replies: "Overpopulation? That is a trivial problem." "Doomsday? Let it come. Reincarnation will bring us all back to face still more predictions of extinction." Belief in reincarnation effectively cripples any serious interest in grappling with overpopulation, exhaustion of resources, pollution, poverty, disease, ignorance, injustice, and war as crucial problems. If Indians succeed, in spite of debilitating religious conditions, in overcoming these problems in their own country, they may well discover practical principles that can contribute constructively to a practical world religion.

Buddhism, divided into Hinayana and Mahayana traditions, each with its own varieties of interpretation, has adapted to different cultures in different ways. It almost died out in India. Hinayana Buddhism became the prominent religion in Ceylon, Burma, Thailand,

and Cambodia. U Nu, the Burmese premier during my year of study in Rangoon University from 1955 to 1956, persuaded legislators to declare Buddhism the official religion of Burma. Imported into China, Buddhism eventually became one of China's "three truths," and converted emperors burned books of Confucians and Taoists. In turn, later Confucian emperors burned some Buddhist books.

In Japan, Zen flourished and Shin, the "pure land" salvationist sect, arose and spread, furnishing the United States with at least eighty thousand Buddhist citizens. None of these varieties promises to contribute much to the needed world religion. When I asked my Rangoon University teacher, the famous monk, U Thittila, how the Theravada doctrine he was expounding compared with views held by another sect, his response was silence. In effect, he did not recognize its existence. Neither its doctrine of momentariness nor that of Zen promises anything of significance toward the faith in endurance needed to substantiate hopes for world peace. Neither the Yogacara Universal Consciousness nor the Madhyamika *Sunya*, sometimes interpreted as "absolute nothingness," provides insights useful in dealing with today's intricacies.

The ancient Taoism of Lao Tzu provided a healthy naturalism that might serve as an example today except for the fact that it is much too simple. Its logic, the *I Ching*, consists of sixty-four hexigrams. Although it involves some principles that contemporary logicians seem not to have mastered, today's complexities require computer logic usable in predicting seemingly endless complexities instantaneously. Most of the principles of ethics of the ancient Confucius remain unsurpassed, and a world philosophy-religion-ethics failing to incorporate them would be deficient. But the simplicity of their formulation fails to take into account the multiplicities of impersonalized organizations upon which life depends and how to achieve certainty and confidence relative to problems so complex that even computer-equipped research institutes cannot come up with satisfactory solutions. Formalized teaching of Confucian principles has antagonized many Chinese, and their misuse for so long has made Confucius a favorite whipping boy of Maoists and other revolutionaries.

Marxism, included here as a religion, claims much but promises little. Adapted to political and economic problems prevailing in European industrial cities more than a century ago, Marxism rightly endeavored to improve the income and welfare of exploited workers. Some improvement has resulted. But times and problems have changed. Even a good Marxist ought to recognize this. According to Marx, "As every true philosophy is the quintessence of its age, the time must come about when philosophy will get in touch with the real world of its time."[12] Today we face overpopulation, overconsumption of resources, pollution, overkill preparedness for nuclear war, rising expectations, stagflation, and deficit spending. These were not Marx's problems. Today labor has become highly organized and yields what is at times dictatorial power, even in capitalist countries. Labor unions are potent political forces; their strikes can cripple a country. In Marx's time, owners usually managed their businesses. Today, after the managerial revolution, owners, as stockholders, depend on a professional managerial class unknown to Marx. The growth of special-interest groups, whether minorities, professions, occupational specialties, age groups, sex groups, sectarians, manufacturing associations, and increasing numbers of bureaucats, including those in the military is a significant fact of life today. Marx's solution, no matter how relevant to the problems of his time, is much too simplistic for today.

Orthodox Marxism suffers from formalization of preconceptions and proposed solutions adapted to conditions existing more than a century in the past. Followers who accept Marx as the ultimate authority are forced to repeat mistakes and to defend and rationalize away contradictions that have been pointed out again and again. Dialectical materialism presupposes the ultimacy of dialectical logic, but Russian technicians put men on the moon using a symbolic logic presupposing the impossibility of dialectic. Theoreticians struggling with this contradiction have come up with differing answers, none of them completely satisfactory. Marxist conceptions of religion, frozen in terms of Christian monotheism prevalent in Marx's culture, make it impossible for orthodox Marxists to understand the genuine nature of religion and the need for it in the world today. The fact that Marxist doctrines are propagated and backed by the second strongest military force in the world today makes it one of the chief obstacles to achieving the religion needed. Continued political and military enforcement of its uncompromising doctrines persists as a major source of prospects for the extinction of mankind.

Prospects for sufficient reform of the world's major religions are very dim, although the presence of some reformers in every religion leaves room for a little hope. Christianity has produced Unitarianism. Judaism has its reform sect. Islam has its liberals. Jamil Hanifi says: "Islamic society, when faced with grave dislocations consequent to Western contact, or internal pressures, must make major alterations in its institutional structure if it is to survive. . . . . Only a new religious-reformist initiative, only a movement which claims religious ultimacy for itself, can successfully challenge the inhibiting nature of the old value system and its Islamic base."[13]

Indian adaptationism is represented by Sri Aurobindo whose expansive writings and experiment in globalized city planning, architecture, and social relations have come to fruition in Auroville in Pondicherry). Even if his vision signifies more an absorbing of all Western civilization into the all-encompassing unity proposed by Vedantism, the seriousness and extent of his efforts in studying and approving many Western ideas show how synthetic efforts are possible. Banaras Hindu University philosophy professor N. K. Devaraja asserts that "there is no reason why [Hinduism] should not fashion new philosophical views and outlooks answering the needs of the modern age."[14]

Some reform movements have dedicated followers. But my wish for a more rapid development of a neo-Christianity, a neo-Judaism, a neo-Islam, a neo-Hinduism, a neo-Buddhism, a neo-Marxism, that will evolve smoothly toward a new world religion now seems quite unrealistic.[15] Changes causing current crises are occurring too fast. The reform rate in the traditional religions is increasing somewhat but far from enough. Even with ideal conditions for reform, with dominant leaders in each aware of our need and willing to cooperate and compromise, the process would take too long. If other efforts enable postponement of doomsday, then one might more ably wish for sufficient reform. Faced with present evidence, one who seeks to be realistic will at least examine the other alternative.

HOW TO DISCOVER THE RELIGION NEEDED

The world needs a world religion. Mankind cannot survive contemporary crises without it. "We shall not reach, nor can we sustain, an organic world civilization without the help of a new living religious faith."[16] Religion as concern for ultimate values involves both beliefs about those values as intrinsic and as comprehensive and practices intended to achieve and maintain values so conceived. The world religion needed involves the world philosophy needed. I have proposed that such philosophy will be humanitarian, humanistic, scientific, comprehensive, adequate, and quantum leaping. Here I emphasize the need for a widespread feeling of human community without which the other needs (such as world government and world economy) depending on and interdepending with it cannot be achieved.

All of the previous reasons for needing a world religion persist. The failure of religions to function successfully as the needed world religion does not eliminate the basic need inherent in human nature for religion that extends the ultimate values with which it is concerned to all mankind. Generally each wisely self-interested person, in seeking what is best for himself in the long run, tends to serve his own needs better by conceiving himself and his values in ways that include some, many, and eventually all others. Persons who identify themselves in ways that include interests in ultimate values for all mankind normally report more satisfaction with their ideals than those ignoring or excluding others. Each has more to live for, more to hope for, more to value. Each society in need of reducing conflict with other societies needs the services of feelings of a world community to reduce fears and antagonisms both among its own members and among members of other groups.

New reasons for a world religion spring from the urgency of present crises and threats of total disaster inherent in their unimpeded accumulation. An absence of feelings of larger unity is fertile soil for the growth of narrower loyalties with antagonisms to other groups intrinsic to them. The more intricate our economic and political interdependencies become, the more easily expressions of narrow antagonism can trigger explosive forces believing their welfare depends on getting a bigger slice of the pie by taking it away from someone else. A soundly based religious faith in the worthwhileness of mankind as a whole is necessary to counteract appeals to narrower loyalties.[17] The growing overkill capacity of nuclear military establishments provides increasing access to the means for activating nuclear weapons by narrowly selfish suicidal individuals who, expecting only evil for themselves, are willing to have all mankind share the same immediate fate. A religious fanatic believing all persons so sinful that they deserve extinction or that inevitable reincarnation will provide all with a better chance may feel divinely obligated to eliminate mankind now. The sooner a reasonable and demonstrable belief in the humanistic doctrine that every person is intrinsically good and that a feeling of community enhances that belief and actions supporting it, the sooner divisive forces now threatening mankind can be thwarted.

A deliberate systematic use of scientific methods applied to the problem promises the most reliable way to discover the religion needed. The problem is interdisciplinary because religion has concern for and depends upon all of the particular values contributing to life as a whole, including the life of mankind as a whole. Each of many general sciences has a contribution to make to understanding it, formulating it, testing it, and promoting it. Sound scientific methods will include examining the truths and benefits of existing and past religions, as well as new possibilities only now being suggested. They will find important clues in present needs, and they will leave open possibilities for still newer needs and additional formulations in the future.

Scientific discovery itself intermingles with scientific invention, just as each act of observation receives data from external sources and interprets them in terms meaningful to the person who brings some of the conditions of meaningfulness with him to the observation. I believe that enough evidence can be found inherent in human nature of a need for a world religion, and of many traits needed by such a religion, so that such a world religion can be discovered. But if some evidence remains inconclusive and if it can be demonstrated further by scientific methods that the presence and propagation of a world religion with certain traits will be most beneficial for mankind, then scientists should demonstrate further that the remaining needs for a world religion should be designed accordingly. Scientific method itself includes both elements of discovery and invention, for every hypothesis, no matter how completely drawn from the aspects of the problem it is designed to solve, has an element of invention in it.

This proposal to discover the world religion needed presupposes that understanding our crises will produce a willingness to do what is necessary to formulate the needed philosophy and consequent practices and to do what it takes to propagate it. As a philosopher, I can propose this model. But how to produce the willingness and willfulness to do what is needed to formulate, test, and propagate it is a task for decision makers who have responsibilities regarding allocation of funds for public purposes.

If the scientific research is successful, it will reveal both the general nature of religion as something growing out of and ministering to some needs inherent in human nature, and thus common to all persons and peoples at all times, and the particular kind of religion required to solve the newer problems and to serve the urgent needs peculiar to our own times. The more persons, peoples, places, and times included within the range covered by a general definition of religion, the more general the definition will be. (One of the urgent needs is for a general definition of religion because inadequate and reductionistic conceptions of religion are part of the cause of our present crises.) The broader the range covered, the greater the number of particular forms that religious practices may take provided that they embody tendencies to fulfill the general nature and aims of religion.

Persons and peoples in ancient and contemporary times are partly the same and partly different. Insofar as they are the same, their religious needs will be the same. Insofar as they are different, these needs will be different. Two types of mistakes should be avoided. One is that ancient and present people are entirely the same. It concludes that a religion adequately serving needs then is adequate to serve needs now (or vice versa). The other is that ancient and present people are entirely different. It concludes that all that is ancient is irrelevant and that today's religion must be entirely new. The truth is that some ancient views, ideals, and practices can be useful today, and some ancient views, ideals, and practices, no matter how firmly entrenched in persisting traditions, are not only useless but very harmful today. The task of research is to discover both what is good and true in ancient and all other religions and what is bad and false in them. The task of research is also to discover what new truths and goods are necessary to fulfill religious needs today. The task of research is to discover a religion that has all of the virtues of all other religions and none of their deficiencies.

One characteristic common to religions pertains to feelings of confidence, assurance, trust, and loyalty in the doctrines and methods involved. Whereas in earlier times persons lacking available proof technologies were more easily captured by credulity, today's feelings of confidence are beset by so many devastating kinds of doubt that regaining the confidence in a world religion needed for personal and human survival doubtless will require obviously reliable demonstrations. Tests as rigorous as those demanded by physicists, chemists, and astronomers must be used and passed. The knowingly multidisciplinary and interdisciplinary characteristics of present crucial problems will tax the abilities of masters of the theory and practice of science to provide such demonstrations. Those who would deny that science is capable of discovering and demonstrating principles pertaining to the nature of religion may well be among the chief enemies of mankind. If their efforts prevent or retard the efforts of others to promote and conduct a costly program in this area, their efforts may result in human extinction. The world religion will embody the needed world philosophy. As a minimum, it must be humanitarian, humanistic, scientific, comprehensive, adequate, and quantum-leaping.

One problem having special urgency today is the need for feeling the presence of, and for participating in, a world community. Many different ways and means are available to bring about such feeling. Many different kinds of conceptions are available for picturing how the world community should be. Warren Wager depicts it thus: "The world religion will offer, as it were, a unified field theory of energy and spirit, a way of attuning each order of being into the others, and also of perfecting its internal unity. It will address the world as the mother and sustainer of mankind. It will address mankind as a form and reservoir of our common life. It will address the self as the highest and tenderest manifestation of eternal being. It will seek the psychic integration of personality with mankind and the universe; the social integration of mankind with its persons and its cosmic ground; and human understanding of the solidarity of the cosmos with its creatures."[18]

My own proposals aim to be a bit more cautious about how much unity and community are needed and how much is best. Today diversifying and divisive forces seem much stronger than unifying forces. Thus the primary need is for greater unity and much stronger feelings of world community. Yet too much unity can be as evil as too much diversity. The urgent need for unity tends to project a demand for complete unity. But complete unity, if it were achieved, might be more dangerous than present divisiveness. The world religion "cannot be a religion of identity."[19] Our urgency calls for optimum, not maximum, unity. It calls for enough, not perfect, unity. It calls for feelings of participation in world community enough to enable us and to urge us to act as self-interested participants in promoting the welfare, and thus survival, of such community.

The optimum amount of unity and diversity will vary as conditions change. The more complex and dynamic our interdependencies become, the greater the flexibility needed for incorporating new (and different) kinds of levels of evolving humanity into a somewhat newer unity. Such newer unity will have to be more unity in the sense that it incorporates more difference within it. But it will have to be less unity in the sense that the unity previously prevailing must become enough more diverse to include what is new and different. Thus I prefer to speak of organic unity rather than integration or solidarity, since unity is organic when it both integrates that which is diverse and also maintains enough diversity so that the diversity integrated remains both diverse as well as integrated.

Thus my proposal, stated in terms of organic unity (of organization rather than integration), involves the following: an ideal of some minimum unity-community probably needed at all times, an ideal of some probable norm of unity-community varying flexibly between minimum and maximum limits, and an ideal of essential unity (all humans are alike in being human) that can inspire the world community awareness needed to arouse cooperative action that seems necessary to prevent human extinction. Organic unity and organic community are more complex conditions of existence than integrated unity or perfect community, if such could ever exist. When the nature of organic unity has been understood, research into the most beneficial amount of world community feelings and the most efficient ways for achieving them can proceed more intelligently.

How should the minimum, the norm or the needed maximum of feelings of participation in world community be conceived? Since all human beings are alike in being human, such likeness or commonness exists as a genuine basis for feelings of community. Why and how human beings are alike have been explained differently. Some speak of the brotherhood of all men, a view sometimes explained in terms of the "fatherhood of God." Some say "Atman is Brahman," and all persons are alike in being divine, even if they differ in their awareness of and live in accordance with their real divinity. Some see all persons as indistinct from *Sunya,* absolute voidness of distinctions, which is also indistinct from "suchness," the particulars constituting each person's experience. Some see each person as a tao participating in Tao and giving particular existence to Tao. Some see persons as products of biological evolution and thus as embodying genes and genetic traits common to the human species.

Feelings of world community can be supported by awareness of common origins, awareness of common fate or common future, awareness of common needs (such as pollution, overpopulation, and extinction in nuclear war) and awareness of common nature (not merely biological but also social). One does not become fully human until he has been socialized. Despite the diversity of groups and cultures, all involve some common traits, Clark Wissler, for example, claimed that all cultures include language, material traits, art, myths, knowledge, religious practices, family and other social systems, property, government, and war. [20] All groups embody typical processes (adaptation, accommodation,), encounter typical problems (injustices, distributive and retributive), conflicts (personal and cultural), and functions (economic, political, educational, recreational, burial). Each of our sciences describes some universal principles functioning in ways conditioning every person and every group. The increasingly intricate interdependencies in megalopolitan and global living operate in ways that affect all of us more and more. Growing awareness of the human predicament depicted by doomsdayers should itself increase feelings of community. Reliable resources for promoting feelings of world community abound.

Another problem that researchers must face pertains to how like and how different from present religions the world religion needs to be. Not only should a definition of religion be based on a study of all religions, but expounders of the world religion should be able to show how it is better relative to ways in which it is both like and different from other religions. The project is enormous.

Traits of religions that seem to me to be excellent candidates for consideration include three principles: Jesus's ideas about love, exemplified when he said, "Love casteth out fear" (First Epistle to John, 14:18); Gotama's insight that "desire for more than will be attained ends in frustration"[21]; and Confucius's formulation of reciprocity: "Do not do to others what you would not have them do to you if you were in their shoes." An adequate world religion will recognize both the obviousness and the demonstrability of these fundamental psychological principles.

Traits of religions that seem to me to be good candidates for consideration include Taoist, Indian, and Jain ideals: Lao Tzu's faith in the naturalness of opposites and of their coming and going (initiation, yang, and completion, yin) and in the goodness of each. It is good to be born, good to be young, good to be mature, good to be old, and good to die. Hastening or retarding natural processes is bad. Indian ideas of "self-help" versus "other-help" (undeserved grace) doctrines seem more just and encourage responsible action. Jain *syadvada*, the doctrine that we can say about each existing thing that; (1) It is x (any truly descriptive term). (2) It is not x (some other truly descriptive term from all of those actually describing it). (3) It is both x and not-x (embodies oppositeness). (4) It is indescribable (there is more to it than can be described by any one or all of its true descriptions).[22]

I expect that researchers will conclude that confident and joyful participation in a world religion will be aided by an acceptable song, poem, sculptured symbol, and perhaps a dance. Each of the arts may be called on to express the nature and significance of such a world religion. Celebrations, festivals, holidays, ceremonies, and possibly even pageants will be considered, and whether these should occur annually, monthly, weekly, or daily should be subject to research recommendations. The religious importance of puberty rights, marriage, childbirth, and death should not be overlooked, even though greater flexibility in significance may be expected. But some ceremonial recognition of achieving mature citizenship in the world community seems a desirable world religious function. The problem of too many as well as too few holidays, for example, will be faced.

WORLD ECONOMY?
IS IT ALREADY HERE?

"People in most countries know by instinct about their international interdependencies, because they are so obviously dependent. . . . Until recently, it was quite different for Americans."[1] But now attention is being called more often to the increasingly complex and intricate kinds of interdependence of economic processes both within and between nations.

THE INCREASINGLY INTERDEPENDENT ECONOMY

Some specialization of functioning, inherent in our biological heritage, has been a fact of human life since the beginning of civilization. Division of labor as a condition for survival was present in primitive families. The existence of larger families, tribes, and clans became possible only with more varieties of divisions of functions, and the survival of some types of groups depended on developing experts in some specialties (such as hunting, preserving foods, protection from the weather, and child care).

The history of civilization has been a story of progressively more complex kinds of economic interdependence. Each of the so-called revolutions (agricultural, commercial, industrial, and managerial) interdepended with the emergence of new kinds of specialized skills. Each particular development—mastery of horses, domestication of animals, planting, cultivating, and harvesting each new kind of plant, use of fire, melting metals, invention of the wheel, of language, of grammar, of printing, of gun powder, of sailing vessels, of numbers and accounting, of the steam engine, of the cotton gin—introduced new complexities into economic life. Recent scientific discoveries and technological inventions—such as radio and television, supersonic airplanes, moon and Mars landings, electronic computers, instant copying, data processing and retrieval systems—exemplify explosively complex factors in economic life. Although research and development funding and initiatives seem to have slowed down in recent years, the accelerating rates of new inventions and their spreading effects in industry, business, government, education, and daily lives of people continue to be amazing.

The social sciences—sociology, anthropology, human geography, economics, political science, and jurisprudence—originated partly in response to needs for recognizing the kinds of interdependence inherent in the growing varieties of groups, group functions, and variations in culture, including languages, mores, institutions, and conflicting legal systems complicating economic life. Peculiarities of the American Revolution and the American frontier favored idealizing independence, individualism, and emphases on individual liberties and rights. Western science has been dominated by analytical ideals in searching for ultimate particles existing independently of each other. Western mathematics and logic have idealized wholes as equal to, and thus involving nothing more than, the sums of their parts. Consequently inexperience with and distrust of ideas of interdependence, bolstered by fears of communism and socialism since World War II, has left a vacuum of interest in the capacity of dealing with problems of interdependence.

Despite the widespread prevalence of interdependence as a fact of physical, biological, psychological, and social life and rapidly increasing kinds of interdependencies in economic and political life both in the United States and throughout the world, inherited conditions have prevented us from becoming fully aware of such interdependence. The implications of this lack of awareness are far-reaching. They infect our ideas of economic processes, our views of political possibilities and responsibilities, our ideals about ethical duties and military obligations, our religious expectations, and even our conceptions of self, society, and the universe.

Lack of awareness of actual interdependencies constitutes ignorance and incapacity to adapt to reality. To live in the midst of interdependencies and to believe that one is still completely independent is to live illusorily. Failure to recognize and understand the facts of interdependence in personal, social, political, and economic life is to lack capacity to deal effectively with problems in personal, social, political, and economic life. When our problems increase in complexity and difficulty and our capacity to deal with them fails to increase appropriately, we will not solve our problems.

But accumulating crises finally have forced recognition of existing states of affairs. Probably few people read or even noticed Nelson Rockefeller's *The Future of Federalism*[2], presented as "a declaration of interdependence." After the recent oil shortages dramatically demonstrating how United States citizens depend on Arab oil, Rockefeller's protégé, United States Secretary of State Henry Kissinger, repeatedly called on his readers to recognize the facts of economic life. News stories, feature articles, syndicated columns, and editorials abound with evidence of and comments on what they call our *new* interdependencies.

Responding to Assistant Secretary of State John Richardson's suggestion, the Aspen Institute's Robert O. Anderson assembled the National Commission on Coping with Interdependence in December 1974. Its report urged us to "focus on American interdependence in some of our year-around local activities." It asks: "Is it too ambitious to suppose that leadership institutions involving millions of Americans can modify their ways of thinking to take interdependence into account in their year-to-year and day-to-day decisions? Of course it isn't." The urgency of needed awareness of interdependence is symbolized by the *New York Times* editorial on the bicentennial Fourth of July, "Interdependence Day," commending both our acting on our need for independence from Britain two centuries ago and for recognizing our interdependent state of being and acting accordingly now.[3]

INCREASINGLY DANGEROUS OBSOLESCENCE

The urgency with which our leaders now call attention to interdependence results from the seriousness of our economic crises. While the threat of nuclear war is held in abeyance, and while population and pollution threats have not yet overwhelmed First World countries, shortages of petroleum and mineral supplies make Americans aware of some of their dependencies. The typical response of American nationalists is to make America self-sufficient in oil supplies. Expensive, hasty, and probably wasteful efforts to build an Alaskan oil pipeline have been completed. Superpatriots suggest a military takeover of Arab oil lands. But the more closely scientists, politicians, and others observe the complexities of the situation, the more obvious becomes the conclusion that we should try to live together peacefully, negotiate as gracefully as we can for the present, and recognize that some quantum-leap kind of international economic and political organization is required to do justice to all of the increasingly multifarious factors in our intricate predicament.

Recent oil shortages did not occur as isolated events. They are related to growing rates of energy consumption and the continuing arms race. They interdepend with money shortages, resulting from deficit spending; an inability to achieve a stable international currency, resulting from imbalances of payments; mounting costs of ecological protection; and now stagflation, all having international consequences. The sudden accumulation of Arab petrodollars jarred the system, but their prudent reinvestment in First World enterprises saved it from more serious jolts.

Dramatic and personally inconvenient evidences of economic interdependence do not reveal the complete picture. Not only do many of our different kinds of economic interdependencies interact with and interdepend with each other, but they interact with many kinds of political interdependencies and also with educational, recreational, moral, and religious trends and processes. Just one example of religious influence in current economic practice is the Islamic prohibition of usury, which has caused the establishment of an interest-free bank. [4]

Economic crises result from the failure to recognize interdependence because people try to solve new problems by methods used successfully in the past. As long as conditions remain the same, this policy is safe. But when conditions change rapidly, new techniques are required. Current crises involving new complexities apparently not only surpass the capacities of economists and business experts but do so partly because these complexities interdepend with recently emerged complexities causing crises in many other fields. [5]

Our crises result only partly from incapacities to deal with growing complexities within each field; they also arise from incapacities to deal with the growing interdependencies between these fields.

They result partly from practice guided by obsolete economics. But obsolescence in economic philosophy interdepends with obsolescence in political, educational, ethical, and religious philosophies and practices as well. The economics based on and guiding laissez-faire independence, whether of persons, corporations, or nations, is quite different from the economics based on and guiding increasingly intricate kinds of interdependence. Economists must first recognize interdependence as a universal characteristic of economic existence. But now that is not enough. They must also recognize interdependence of economic processes with at least many, if not all, of the other kinds of processes, each tending toward its own limits of complexity.

We would understand our crises better and be better able to search for workable solutions if we saw them as interdependence crises. By this I do not mean merely an interdependence of crises but also crises resulting partly from our neglect of, and inability to understand, the nature and significance of interdependence itself. If we do not understand the nature and significance of interdependence when it exists as a universal characteristic both within and between the things, processes, and problems with which we deal, then we cannot expect to come up with satisfactory solutions. Our old habits, and our old philosophies (which are old habits of thinking), may continue to work up to a point, since interdependence involves both some independence of each thing as well as some mutual dependence between things. But when the complexities of mutual dependence become sufficiently predominant, the old philosophies cease to be adequate, so we should expect that guiding our practices by them will lead to disaster. The longer we delay in removing obsolescent economic theories and practices, the more dangerous we can expect our crises to become.

OVERCOMING ECONOMIC CRISES

To the extent that our crises result from our failure to recognize and understand interdependence and interdependencies, we can expect to overcome them only if we understand them. Implications of some of the characteristics of the proposed world philosophy can be deduced from economic philosophy. But first let us recall what economics is before exploring the economics of interdependence and considering the needs for more planning.

What Economics Is

Economics is intended to be a scientific inquiry into the nature of goods and services. Since goods and bads occur together in experience, life, society, and economy, economics is intended to be a scientific inquiry into the nature of ills and deprivations or damages. Economics so conceived is a value science. It inquires into the nature of certain kinds of goods and evils: utilities and disutilities. Thus economics intimately interrelates with axiology, the general science of values.

When I studied Richard R. Ely's *Outlines of Economics*, I learned that economics is the science of wealth and income (and of illth and outgo). Ely regarded economics as "the science which treats of those social phenomena that are due to the wealth-getting and wealth-using activities of man." Then it was "particularly impossible to divorce economics completely from ethics and politics."[6]

Nevertheless conceptual difficulties resulting from inadequate grounding in value theory and pressures from materialistic and logical positivistic philosophies of science to deny the existence of intrinsic values or the ability of science to deal with them, motivated some economists to define economics in ways that either omitted or reduced the significance of the value aspects of their value science.[7] Although dealing with wants and want-satisfying instruments called utilities, some economists tried to reduce economic value to exchange value and exchange value (involving utility, exchangeability, and scarcity) to scarcity. They were able to measure various kinds of factors contributing to scarcity without indulging in axiological language. Others, carrying the same tendencies further, defined economics as "the science of price."[8] Price is even more easily calculable, and statistical studies of pricing policies, encountering ever more artificial factors in pricing processes, are thus, some think, even further from the incalculable feelings of want with which other economists begin.

Although economists differ greatly in personal views about

values, the dominating tendency to isolate economic theory as far from theories of intrinsic values as possible contributed both to a more quantitative use of mathematics and toward confidence that economics is a science with a subject matter of its own. This tendency found expression in the view that "the economist is not concerned with ends as such" because "economics is entirely neutral between ends."[9] Even though economists seem more intimately involved with interdependencies, ideals about independence of sciences from each other and of science as incapable of dealing with values have contributed to a diminution of interest in the axiological foundations of economics. A major task of the needed economics is to deflate those ideals and to replace them with ideas demonstrating the continuing, if fragile, intrinsic value bases for economic values.

Economics has been concerned with four main processes: "the production, consumption, exchange, and distribution of wealth."[10] Although each can be examined separately, each interdepends with the others. A major task that economists have set for themselves is to formulate laws not only about interactions among the numerous factors and tendencies within each of the four processes but also about interactions of such factors in each with those of the other three.

The Economics of Interdependence

The first characteristic of the economics of interdependence is complexity. Next is interdependence, specifically an awareness of many more kinds of increasingly intricate kinds of interdependencies (including increasing interexistences). Third is multidimensional dynamicity—an awareness that many kinds of functions and changes, both those studied by economists and those requiring interdisciplinary study, must be understood before any one function and change can be understood completely. Multilevel causality—an awareness that interlevel causation sometimes is economically much more significant than intralevel causation—is the fourth characteristic. It is followed by an awareness that world economic interdependence already exists and that wealth and illth, income and expenditures, of all in the world increasingly affect each person in the world. Sixth is an awareness of limits, or a growing recognition that many additional kinds of limits (scarcity) exist, which function as economic determinants. Finally come quantum-leap conceptions; we must comprehend the working together of intricate multidimensional, multilevel dynamic interexistences in new conceptual gestalts.

COMPLEXITY

Economic complexities were present in primitive cultures. They were recognized by our first economists, who have been as conscious as any other social scientists of the presence and growth of complexities. Yet in spite of such increasing awareness, the organic nature of existing complexities is still not well understood, and efforts to deal with such increasing kinds of complexity as commonplace conditions of existing and knowing remain in their infancy.

The invention and availability of electronic computers have multiplied our capacities for dealing with quantities and with some kinds of complexity. Unfortunately the miraculous speeds with which calculations occur in digital computers have inspired enthusiasts to make unwarranted claims about problem-solving capacities.

The factors of production (such as consumption and exchange) have become more complex in two ways. Each factor has become more complex in itself, and the number of factors has increased tremendously.

Consider the number of factors first. Early economists distinguished three main factors of production and the kinds of income they produced: land (rent), labor (wages), and capital (interest). The capitalist was also an entrepreneur who managed his business and took risks, so he was entitled to any income (profits)[11] produced thereby. The role of government has become increasingly important as a factor in production in the United States and in socialist countries.[12] The need for subsidizing infant industries, for restricting excesses of wealthy entrepreneurs, for guaranteeing subsistence welfare and bank deposits, for providing a social security system, and for furnishing military needs in wartime, for example, have increased the economic roles of government tremendously.

As corporations and their functions became more complex, the need arose for specialized managers when owners become stockholders. The growing role of technology has forced a recognition of technical innovation and excellence as a continuing factor. Since most current technology depends on science, scientific research, pure and applied, has become a standard factor in the economics of production. Scientists and technicians must be educated, so the role of education as a factor in production has been accepted. Education depends on publishers of books and editors of newspapers and periodicals, among others, and has evolved into secondary schools, colleges, graduate schools, professional schools, and multiversities.

Health workers, technicians, managers, and consumers function as ever more significant factors in production. Environmental factors, largely ignored in the past, recently have been thrust into economics forcefully through ecological studies demonstrating the costs of pollution of air, water, and land. Although the roles of theft and bribery have been recognized by economists for a long time, growing quantities, types, costliness, and comparative invisibility of crimes have catapulted in significance recently. Rising crime rates, even of those crimes not directed at economic factors, symbolize increasing demoralization. The role of morality, the costs resulting from demoralization, and the costs required for remoralization have been largely neglected by economists. The role of morality, and now the costs of both demoralization and remoralization necessary for social, political, and economic stability, must be recognized as essential factors of production.

Economics has become more complex because the main essential factors of production have increased in numbers and complexity. [13] An introduction to economics now includes learning about quasi-rents, labor disutility, aggregate supply curve, productivity coefficient, rising concentration ratios, equimarginal rule, nonprice rationing, oligopolitic indeterminacy, downward multiplier, demand management, deposit creation, fractional reserves, shifting liquidity preferences, and zero sum game.

Consider next the complexities within each factor, including the new ones. I select only one, management, but intend it to illustrate the multiplicities of unique kinds of complexities increasing in each. The entrepreneur has largely vanished from economically developed countries, except for diminishing numbers of small businesses. The managerial revolution, under the influence of more and more complicated kinds of specialized technology through many divisions and levels of corporate organization, has continued to compel much decentralization in management. The complexity of processes at most levels requires workers with some managerial skills. Future growth in complexity can be expected, together with further distribution of managerial responsibilities.

This distribution of responsibilities has not lessened problems confronting top-level policy deciders, normally a board of directors, but has reduced the capacity of these people to act independently of decisions made at other managerial levels. Incompetence at any more narrowly specialized level or branch endangers the entire enterprise.

Additional factors of production, here treated as tasks of management, include growing complexities in advertising; insurance of many kinds; sale and recording; stock market regulations and speculations; disposal of wastes (solid, liquid, gaseous); attention to increasing obsolescence rates; inflation rates; regulatory legislation; mutiplicities of taxes (corporate, income, national and state, excise, property, sales, social security, unemployment insurance taxes and surtaxes); negotiations with union leaders, arbitrators, and court officials; fluctuation in foreign exchange rates; damage suits by workers, suppliers, and customers; energy supply shortages, computer breakdowns, and unfair competition. Whether these should be regarded as subfactors within the major areas or as major factors added to them becomes less significant as the whole process becomes more complex, because failure, deficiency, or scarcity relative to any one of them can become crucial.

Thus economics has become much more complex in several ways. In addition to increases in the number of main factors of production and increases in complexities within each of the main factors, including the new ones, it needs to recognize growing complexities of interrelations of economic factors with factors dealt with in other disciplines. For example, psychology involves a whole galaxy of specialized sciences, each of which has relevance to every factor of production. More importantly, even if still unrecognized, the role of the economy functioning as a progressing whole has complex interrelations with each of the factors and its constituent parts. The economist needs to see how all of these factors function together synthetically. Philosophy as a comprehensive science, with its own host of complexities to understand, has essential contributions to make to economic theory. Until an economist understands how philosophy in its comprehensive function constitutes a factor (or several complex factors) in production, his achievements remain inadequate.

INTERDEPENDENCE

An awareness of increasing interdependence is a more significant characteristic than complexity distinguishing past and future economics. The persisting Western preference for plurality can accommodate growth in quantitative complexity. But when we fully understand the nature of interdependence, something very important, to which Western habits of thinking may adjust only with difficulty, has been added.

Interdependence has been present in human affairs from the beginnings of economic life, but it has not been obvious, partly because earlier economies were much simpler and partly because some of the major factors of production tended to dominate economic policies for long periods.

Land dominated agricultural economies. Nomadic economy, measuring wealth by ownership of flocks, was characterized by moving the animals from place to place; thus ownership of land used only temporarily was not so important. But when grain was planted, retention of land ownership became important. Owners of such land came to be called lords.

Capital, first in the form of movable goods that could be exchanged, increased when merchants gained from shipping such goods to places where scarcity commanded higher prices. Savings, made possible by coinage and mercantile banks, increased as commerce prospered. Loans yielding interest increased such capital. The industrial revolution required factories, so capital was invested in manufacturing processes for the purpose of producing profits, or more capital. Early manufacturers, like early merchants, were entrepreneurs; they invested capital and regarded profits as justified reward for risk and wise management.

Labor, required for manufacturing, at first was plentiful and was exploited by being paid only subsistence wages. But prosperous manufacturers gradually exhausted local labor supplies, and humanitarians protested exploitation. A long fight resulted in organized labor unions—both craft unions and company unions and then federations of unions. Marxist theoreticians contributed to the Russian revolution, ousting both landed lords and the factory capitalists and establishing a dictatorship of the proletariat. The rise of labor unions increased the importance of labor as a factor in production costs but did not dominate the economics of most developing nations.

Government provided social stability, protection from foreign invaders and foreign competition, and subsidies for desirable industries; it thus required taxes for its services. The Great Depression following the 1929 stock market crash left the world economy in shambles. Government control and assistance—assuring bank deposits, establishing a social security program, providing welfare assistance to the needy and tax incentives to corporate ventures—became a major factor in controlling production. In Marxist countries, proletarian governments supposedly united labor and government in dominating their economies.

Management, growing in importance as corporations enlarged their more complex functions, became specialized and separated from capital ownership, which existed increasingly in the form of stocks and bonds. The managerial revolution shifted control away from capital owners. Decisions required the participation of many specialists representing different branches constituent in corporations. Labor then dealt not with capitalists or owners of capital but with managers.

Technology, growing in importance as life becomes more complex, is forcing a continuation of the managerial revolution except that decisions made by more specialists contribute to the decisions reached finally by the top board of policy deciders. Thus the technological revolution is producing an age of increasing specialization, growing power, authority, and responsibility of greater varieties of specialists. The struggle by specialists to increase their importance as factors in production continues. Highly trained specialists have resisted temptations to unionize. However, the American Medical Association has increased physicians' salaries by promoting a shortage of medical school graduates, and public school teachers, perpetually struggling for higher salaries and labor benefits, have joined the American Federation of Teachers.

Whether any other factors may yet dominate Western economies,

I do not predict. But in the economics of interdependence, inter-dependence, like complexity, is a dominating characteristic. It is not something, like land, that can be owned. Yet it can be owned in a sense; when one identifies with the complexities in which he partici-pates, he does own them. It is not something that produces a dis-tinguishable kind of value, as land produces rent, labor wages, and capital interest or dividends. Yet its presence as a necessary condi-tion of our complex economies does contribute to the complex pro-duct. Its absense prevents those kinds of production resulting from the cooperating efforts of both somewhat independent and some-what mutually dependent agencies. Products of the more intricately interdependent kinds of cooperative processes are values resulting from such interdependence as a factor in production. It takes a more luxuriant kind of individual to appreciate this kind of product fully. Whether it will ever become viewed by economists as the dominant factor in production, I do not predict. But that it is an essential factor in the production of increasing amounts and kinds of economic goods is a primary claim of the economics of interdependence.

MULTIDIMENSIONAL DYNAMICS

The rapidity of changes in economic institutions that must also re-tain stability if we are to rely on them is well known. But the number and intricacies of the dimensions of such institutions and processes assume greater importance in the economics of interdependence. Each of the kinds of factors of production (such as consumption and exchange) recognized by economists is such a dimension, as is each of the kinds of factors studied by all other disciplines. The impor-tance of their interactions, and differential rates of change in each kind of factor and their reactions with other factors, grows as we more fully comprehend social dynamics. Research needed to locate principles of complexity, interdependence, distance, and imper-sonality can be successful only when guided by minds capable of comprehending multidimensional processes.

The economics of interdependence thus calls not merely for multi-disciplinary and interdisciplinary research but also for directors who comprehend both the significance of each dimension and the signifi-cances of their interrelations with each other and with the whole glo-bal process. Efforts to formulate laws interlinking the laws func-tioning between each discipline become of paramount importance.

Principles functioning relative to changing conceptions of self and self-interest entailed in multicomplexities of psychological, biological, and social processes include principles relative to flexible sensitivities for distinguishing variations in values in each of the multicomplexities and in obligations relative to variations in values and value conflicts in them. The problems and principles become more subtle and involved as selves become accustomed to think in terms of interexistence (of each self and other selves, each dimension—of self and other things—and other dimensions). The more we seek to understand multidimensional dynamics, the more we recognize the necessity for quantum-leap conceptions and habitual global thinking.

MULTILEVEL CAUSALITY

Understanding the omnipresence of whole-part causation seems essential to the economics of interdependence. As multileveled organization becomes more intricately complex, each change, deficiency, disease, or destruction in any part tends to become more serious as it endangers other parts and wholes.

Improvements in larger wholes (involving multilevels), also become more difficult. The more intricate local, state, national, and regional governments become, the more difficult it will become to design and establish a beneficial world government. Yet at the same time, the longer lower-level governments suffer from conceiving their self-interests more narrowly in ways that promote conflicts between nations, for example, and fail to cooperate in whatever minimum of world government is needed to prevent devastating conflicts, the more dangerous becomes the failure to make needed improvements in larger wholes.

We are already fearfully aware that nuclear war would devastate societies, including their economies, at all levels. We have observed the example of how the discovery of swine flu, a low biological organism, in three soldiers transformed our country and many agencies in it—including medical laboratories, pharmaceutical manufacturers, physicians, hospitals, refrigerated transportation, hypodermic needle production, mass inoculation programs, mass media communications, controversial debates by scientists, columnists, and politicians, and even influences on senatorial and presidential

elections that could produce differences in foreign policy and consequences for global economic and political tragedies.

The invention of tinier transistors, physical, and electronic instruments, which make possible higher-speed computers with larger-
scale memories, enables other scientists to put men on the moon and
to guide multiple-warhead missiles with greater target accuracy.
Multilevel causal processes are becoming increasingly observable.
Any failure of economists to recognize and account for such processes as multilevel factors of production brands their economics as
inadequate and obsolete. The economics of interdependence must
include an economics of multilevel causation.

GLOBALITY

A global economy already exists. Global economics also exists.
But the absence of an effective world government, emphases of national governments on their own economic welfare as well as political sovereignty, and divisions of cooperative emphases into First,
Second, and Third World economics have discouraged efforts toward the kind of global economics needed for sound global economic planning. Nevertheless many pressures have developed to demand
such economics.

Studies of the causes of the 1929 stock market crash and the Great
Depression revealed more clearly worldwide causes as well as effects. For example, recognizing that planning for recovery should be
joined with efforts to prevent recurrence, the United States Department of Agriculture under the guidance of Henry A. Wallace conducted schools of philosophy for agricultural county agents in
various parts of the country to enlighten agents and farmers about
national and international factors to consider in deciding what crops
to plant. When I participated in one of these schools in Amarillo,
Texas, in 1940, I was told that incomes received by both west Texas
cotton farmers and Egyptian fellaheen are determined in part by
world market prices. Available evidence demonstrated that a west
Texas bumper crop dumped at reduced prices on the world market
resulted in malnutrition deaths of numerous fellaheen. During the
past four decades, examples of this sort have multiplied profusely
until the widely dramatized recent gasoline shortages produced
awareness of interdependencies, popularly, professionally, and
politically.

The importance of world economic problems and processes was recognized in establishing the United Nations Social and Economic Council, the United Nations Conference on Trade and Development, the United Nations Development Programme, the United Nations Food and Agricultural Organization, the International Bank for Reconstruction, the International Monetary Fund, the International Finance Corporation, the General Agreement on Tariffs and Trade, the International Labor Organization, and the United Nations Institute for Training and Research.

Reporting on a recent conference on the New International Order and UNCTAD (United Nations Conference on Trade and Development) IV, S. Sideri stated that in "the present drive to restructure the international economic order . . . , development cannot take place without a massive redistribution of wealth and economic activities. But this redistribution is not likely to occur without the evolution of new institutions and new rules, which in turn requires a radical change in attitudes. . . . The danger of not moving fast enough in reorganizing the international economic system and establishing the necessary mechanisms for redistribution may result in further polarization, with economic and political consequences for all, and this may well be more devastating than anything we have experienced in the present crisis."[14]

If present world economic crises cannot be overcome without adequate understanding and if understanding will remain inadequate until the economics of interdependence is formulated, developed, taught, and practiced by those responsible for deciding world economic policies, then nothing seems more urgent than formulating, developing, and teaching such economics. The economics of interdependence involves intricate understandings of both microeconomics and macroeconomics and of the interactive processes between those factors, conditions, and processes dealt with in microeconomics and macroeconomics. Additional emphasis needs to be given to thinking in terms of a world perspective, to what some will call a macromacroeconomics. This means that we need to understand the most general principles of world economic processes in relation to the principles of economic processes at several levels (regional, national, state, municipal, village) and dimensions (in relation to all the factors of production and all other disciplines). Nations, universities, and foundations have not yet invested sufficiently to make rapid development of the economics of interdependence possible.

The economics of interdependence is partly a product of a spreading recognition that economic growth eventually meets limitations and of the need for adjusting realistically to what cannot be changed and discovering new levels of economic development that grow in terms of other limits to growth. Realistic adjustment is aided by developing habits of thinking in terms of limits especially when limits function as economic determinants.

Economists have always been aware of limits, since scarcity has been an essential characteristic for a good to be considered economic. Yet efforts to overcome some kinds of scarcity have been so successful that many economists have subscribed to an economics of growth. Recent studies demonstrating some actual limits of growth have caused some economists to advocate a no-growth economy. And managers now favor a slow-growth economy. The economics of interdependence requires further attention to limits, not merely those recognized thus far but several others, as standard procedure in formulating principles for policy decisions.

In addition to recognized limits, such as those of population growth, use of irreplaceable resources, and the ability to produce replaceable resources, we need to recognize limits to permissible wastefulness, limits to pollution, limits to affordable obsolescence (in racist, religious, political, economic, educational, and linguistic institutions), limits to minimums and maximums of individual rights and duties, freedoms, and responsibilities, and limits to democratic participation in government. Still other limits, to which economists have remained inattentive, are coming to have significance and may turn out to be greater than those just mentioned.

Limits to Complexity

Although each thing, kind, person, society, economy, and discipline is becoming more complex, each has limits to its complexity, both inner and outer. Experiments needed to demonstrate reliable principles regarding such limits may often be very costly. But studies reporting the maximums of simplicity and complexity and the range between them for each kind of thing-process, including economic things-processes, should be supported.

Limits of Interdependence

Interdependence requires both some independence and some dependence. There are limits to how much independence and how much dependence can exist before interdependence disappears. But there are also limits to interdependence. Except for the universe, which has no upper or lower or future limits to novel emergents, each thing-process has its own limits. Although each is involved in many kinds of interdependencies, doubtless there are limits to the numbers of kinds that it can participate in, or that can participate in it, effectively. A part of the task of each discipline is to discover what and how many characteristics and their interdependencies function in the things-processes that each studies and also what limits exist, not only regarding the number of characteristics and their interdependencies but also regarding each characteristic and each interdependency and how and when variations in one function as limitations relative to another or all others. Newly emergent higher-level organisms may incorporate both newer and more varieties of characteristics and interdependencies, but each of these will be found to have its limits, as will the organizing capacity of the new organism.

Limits of Multidimensional Dynamics

Each changing thing has its own kinds and rates of change. Each highly complex organism embodies many different kinds and rates of change, which interact with each other in ways essential to healthy functioning. But each organism has limits regarding the numbers and varieties of different kinds of change it can embody. It must survive by integrating its interdependencies with varieties of both internal and external kinds of change (and permanence). Beyond certain organizable limits, it begins to disintegrate. When such limits function as economic determinants, they become problems for economists and for policy deciders.

Limits to Multilevel Causality

Although there may be no limits to extensions of some causal processes upward and downward in the hierarchies of levels, other causal processes do terminate in each event functioning as an entity in the limited natures of things and processes at each level, in some conflicts where opposing forces tend to cancel each other, and through exhaustion of any originating entity through a progressive dilution of its being and nature through participations in other cause-effect events, each of which diminishes proportionately its relative role in each new event. Even if interlevel causation extends beyond our knowledge of such causation, still there are limits to our knowledge of such causation. These limits need to be taken into account in any adequate philosophy.

Neglect of multilevel causation makes increased concern about it both primary and urgent so far as increasing mastery of our present predicaments is concerned. The economics of interdependence should embrace economic problems of both financing research needed for understanding more about multilevel causal processes and about ways of profiting from such research. Nevertheless caution about overzealous enthusiasms by amateur converts to the quantum-leap system gestalt should be included if its philosophy is to be adequate.

Limits of Globality

The economics of interdependence would remain defective if it did not include a recognition that globality and needed attention to it have limits. Granted that space travel may enable us to inhabit the moon, Mars, Venus, or Jupiter, or even to construct astrocities, thereby extending the limits of economic activity beyond our globe, the economics of interdependence needs to recognize many kinds of limits to the importance of globality for each thing-process, (each person, each city, each factory, each nation). Once we are aware of the global factors that function as essential parts of our daily lives, we cannot afford to waste effort in understanding interrelations between thing-processes too distant from each other to have significant effects, such as those between chewing gum and galactic drift when deciding issues about gum-chewing policy. If our world crises can be solved only by means of dictatorial action, then forced attention to global institutions may exceed what a more ideal organic system calls for. But even a dictator will find limits to his powers and limits to the effectiveness of global influences in the lives of individuals.

Limits of Knowledge

Economists already know that limited knowledge functions as a factor in production, consumption, exchange, and so forth. The economics of interdependence urges attention to the limits of knowability, not merely by each person, each group, each nation, but by mankind as a whole. The existing universe cannot be completely reproduced in knowledge. The role of essential ignorance of the nature of things, including the nature of each thing, needs to be recognized in taking stock of our knowledge as an increasingly important factor in production. Awareness of limits to knowability enhances awareness of the value of science conceived as embodying pragmatic methods in approaching solutions to problems. We will not know how much we can or cannot know until we try to discover. Sometimes by creating things that did not exist before and operating them in the world, we can discover some knowledge that we did not have before and could not have discovered without creating and operating them. We can discover some limits of knowability only by trying to know.

Although we expect to increase our knowledge in each discipline by discovering or inventing new ones, by interdisciplinary studies, and by integrating parts of knowledge through comprehensive philosophical studies, each of these ways has its limits. Individuals, research institutes, universities, and mankind have limited abilities to understand and comprehend complexities, interdependencies, multidimensional dynamicities, multilevel causality, and globalities. The more complex, interdependent, multidimensional, multilevel, and global our problems become, the quicker we reach the limits of our capacities to know and understand. We even have limited ability to know the limits of knowability. An awareness of such limits makes us all the more aware of the need for quantum-leap conceptions that enable us to surmount some of these limits by increasing some of our capacities. If the solution of world crises requires a kind of conception to which present minds cannot leap, such solution is beyond our present capacities. If and when we do achieve the needed quantum-leap conceptions, they too will have their own limits. Thus the economics of interdependence should be ready to look for and be ready to recognize these limitations also.

QUANTUM-LEAP CONCEPTIONS

The economics of interdependence calls for, and is called for by, the philosophy of interdependence. The philosophy of interdependence depends on the economics of interdependence, the sociology of interdependence, the psychology of interdependence, the biology of interdependence, the chemistry of interdependence, the physics of interdependence, the logic of interdependence, and the metaphysics of interdependence. [15] The quantum-leap conceptions needed in economics interdepend with those in physiology, geology, astronomy, agriculture, and military science. All of these in turn interdepend with each other and with the quantum-leap conceptions in philosophy, both in its specialized fields and as a comprehensive science.

There are tendencies toward quantum-leap conceptions in economics resulting from the distinction between microeconomics and macroeconomics, with some economists emphasizing the latter. But the needed macromacroeconomics, emphasizing interdisciplinary causal principles and processes at the global level interdepending with interlevel causal principles and processes, is yet to be developed. Economics has much to contribute to shaping details of our quantum-leap gestalt. These contributions will depend partly on economists' understanding the quantum-leap gestalt, which has fundamental contributions to make their field. The economics of interdependence is in process of developing. How rapidly, fully, and effectively it will mature and contribute to human survival remains to be seen.

Need for More Planning

The economics of interdependence requires more planning. How much more is debatable.

I can see no escape from the imposition of a system of strict planning that will in effect transform the business system into a system of national, although not necessarily nationalized, enterprise. For what will be required to meet the constraints of a tightening environmental vise, both within nations and among nations, is more than a palliative application of antipollution measures and a reliance on the rationing effect of high prices. Priorities over investment, outright prohibitions with respect to certain kinds of outputs, and control over new technologies are all implicit in the environmental danger and the international redress of power.[16]

I am not sure how strict planning must be, but I do believe that planning needs to be global and regional as well as national, and that growing awareness of both the complexities and intricacies of economic as well as other kinds of interdependencies will cause more and more people to see that their own self-interest dictates a willingness to cooperate in intelligent planning at these levels.

Although the importance of planning has been recognized for a long time by corporations, private and public (socialist countries commonly announce five-year-plans), and by economists and political scientists, it had now become the subject matter of a specialized science.[17] Its importance increases as our economy becomes larger and more complex. When conceived within our quantum-leap gestalt, economic planning becomes global in size, multileveled regarding most efficient production, distribution, and consumption, interdisciplinary in its resources, ever-conscious of all kinds of limitations, and humanistic in its goals.

Planning is needed regarding restricted use of irreplaceable resources, overpopulation, pollution, distributive justice, health, and financial stability; military expenditures; distribution of voting power regarding policy decisions; and relative emphases on industrial production or humanistic services in adopting policies. More important is the need for planning a comprehensive world philosophy, including a minimal (if not yet optimal) world ethics, a minimal (if not yet optimal) world religion, and a minimal (if not optimal) world government. Even more important is planning the development and support of competent, adequate, sufficiently financed interdisciplinary research institutes commissioned to plan for such planning. Yet such research institutes can function only if someone else leads in establishing them. Interdependence between the needs for planning regarding irreplaceable resources, planning for a new world philosophy, and planning research institutes to plan for such plans is such that each dialectically influences the others. Despite the rapid pace of social change, the rate of interprodding of awareness of need for resource-use planning and of the need for interdisciplinary research institutes to plan for making such plans is still very slow.

I emphasize planning interdisciplinary research institutes because we must first plan to understand; if we do not understand, we can hardly expect to carry out our plans intelligently. I advocate more, not less, science and technology because it appears realistic to try to cope with increasing complexities. But our scientific and technological research should be directed at all of our problems, including axiological, ethical, religious and other philosophical problems, as well as economic, political, and industrial problems, and at global as well as regional, national, state, municipal, and corporate levels. Economic planning independent of political planning in a world where economic and political processes increasingly interdepend is folly.

"The fully planned economy, so far from being unpopular, is warmly regarded by those who know it best."[18] I do not advocate a fully planned economy, unless it includes plans for much unplanned economy also. We need an optimally planned economy. "Optimally" does not imply "fully."

WORLD GOVERNMENT? WHY NOT TRY INTELLIGENCE?

The Philosopher's World Model includes ideals about world government. I have not formulated a utopian ideal for two reasons. First, ideas of an optimum government projected from one problematic perspective can be expected to change when new problems arise and call for a changed perspective with its own needs and ideas about their satisfactory fulfillment. Further change is to be expected. Second, current doomsday prospects call for urgent action to establish the minimum world government necessary for human survival. The practical difficulties preventing establishing any kind or amount of an effective world government today are so great that intelligence calls for idealizing the minimum needed for survival. If we succeed in establishing some minimal world government enabling us to survive present crises, then we may have enough time and the inclination to consider what other services the government should render. Our present predicament calls for a minimum, not an optimum, world government.

THE KIND OF GOVERNMENT NEEDED

The world government should perform whatever functions are necessary for human survival that cannot, or will not, be performed by other governments. The threat of nuclear holocaust puts control of mankind-devastating armaments at the top of most lists. This

control alone, some think, will be sufficient to preserve mankind because once we stop pouring billions into armaments, we can use
these funds to solve our other crises.

But the persisting coexistence of leading military powers, seeming
equality in balance-of-terror weapons development, and a willingness to discuss minor issues diplomatically and in the United Nations
Security Council cause us to become accustomed to living under the
threat of war, which thereby comes to seem less threatening. Many
in the United States have confidence that the present stalemate can
be perpetuated into the future indefinitely. Many others feel so help-
less about doing anything to influence the course of future military
events that they have become fatalistic. In such an atmosphere, ex-
citement about overpopulation as the prime cause of human extinction has occupied attention. As long as we fear the population bomb
and nations cannot or will not act in ways to reduce population
growth, the growing need for control of total population growth
seems to require world government action. Some persons put population control as the primary purpose of the needed world government.

I am one of those who fear population growth so much that a
world government policy seems called for. Yet when Indian Ambas-
sador T. N. Kaul announced recently that fifteen million vasectomies had been performed, my picture changed; national action to
meet this crisis may yet be possible. But given India's massive population, fifteen million is only a small percentage, and the will to act
effectively evident in India's recent emergency has not extended to
Latin American, African, or all Asian countries. The problem remains critical. If Indian efforts succeed in ways obvious to others,
enough pressure may be brought to bear on delinquent nations to re-
lieve this crisis without world government intervention.

Increasing concerns about the dangers of overpopulation have
sharpened our awareness of limits to our resources. Both replaceable
and irreplaceable resources are limited, and too copious and rapid
use of both will impoverish future generations. Statistics on the
growing rates of consumption of irreplaceable resources, to say
nothing of extreme imbalances of use in First and Third World countries, promise early exhaustion of some essentials. First World coun-

tries seem unlikely to reduce their consumption rates unless forced to do so, and Third World countries, while accusing First World countries of being excessively wasteful, still seek development requiring a larger share in the consumption of such resources, even if not parity in wastefulness. Therefore many believe that as long as these tendencies prevail, only a world government powerful enough to retard consumption and to restrict, if not eliminate, waste will enable mankind to survive for several centuries more.

Pollution promises a gradual destruction of vital air, water, and agricultural resources. Although some such problems are clearly local, others are related to global winds, ocean currents, and agricultural production and thus obviously affect world welfare. The results of ecological studies have aroused citizen protests in the United States enough to require some industries to install expensive antipolluting devices, others to cease functioning, and prospective ventures to conform to legislated limits. But these efforts prevent only a small portion of total pollution, and have not been duplicated in all First World countries. How Third World countries can afford to finance similar efforts remains unclear. As long as Second World countries rate the proletarian revolution as having higher priority than resource exhaustion through pollution, little effort can be expected from them. Only an effective world government devoted to human welfare can prevent the destructive ravages of pollution sufficiently.

Some include stagflation, deficit spending, monetary instability, persisting racial and religious tensions, any one of which may trigger a destructive war, among the causes of our world crises that can be mastered only by a world government. I will limit my survey of reasons for a minimal world government to three more. Two of these, although pertaining to increasingly obvious trends, have not yet become widely regarded as serious threats to human survival. I urge their addition to the World Order Models Project list. (See chapter 2). These trends come to focus on increasing interdependence and increasing demoralization. There are limits to both kinds of increase beyond which mankind survival is threatened just as decisively as exceeding the limits of other kinds of growth.

Interdependence, a universal condition of existence, has become

more obvious as a result of ecological studies, of wider awareness of
the dangers of fallout from nuclear bombs and leakages from nuclear
power plants, and of recent oil shortages. One purpose of the Philosopher's World Model has been to call attention to increasing interdependence as a fact of existence—physical, biological, social,
economic, and political—and to promote accepting it and adapting
both to it, and through it. The more intricate our interdependence,
the more a failure in any one essential function endangers the whole.
The reluctance of some nations to participate voluntarily and sufficiently in fulfilling the responsibilities and duties inherent in interdependent living may so endanger all of us that only an effective
world government can assure relief.

Demoralization, which cripples our confidence and trust in
others, in our societies, in our mores and institutions, and in the reliability of commonly accepted behavior patterns, leaves us more narrowly self-interested and often genuinely selfish. So long as demoralization is contained within a persisting morality, it may not become
irreversibly dangerous. But when demoralizing trends both contribute to and are fostered by many other delibitating conditions hastening the decline of a civilization, their importance should not be underestimated. When national systems are caught in these trends,
nations themselves contribute, sometimes unwittingly, to hastening
their decline.

Remoralization is important. The more interdependent we become, the less safe we become from destructive self-interest. My proposed wise-self-interest theory can be expected to help eliminate
present crises only if, when, and because each person can be led to
see that his own best interests are intricately involved with the interests of mankind as a whole. Although some miraculous spread of
faith in such conviction is not impossible, I believe that the establishment of a world government endowing world citizenship and authorized to propagate ideals of increasing identity of individual and
mankind self-interests may be the only way to ensure sufficient willing identification and consequent voluntary action jointly serving
the interests of each and all.

My last reason for proposing a world government is one that
many place first: the need for guaranteeing individuals fair treat-

ment relative to their fundamental rights. Bills of rights have varied in length and in the numbers of rights held to be minimally essential. The number of rights has tended to increase as mastery of production of goods and services has increased. So to be realistic, the Philosopher's World Model must recognize that the rights, duties, privileges, and responsibilities that can and should be regarded as minimal will continue to depend on, and interdepend with, many other conditions in society.

If some minimum number of rights cannot be guaranteed worldwide without a world government, then any demand for such guarantee is automatically a demand for world government. I treat a concern for individual rights last in this list not because I regard it as of least importance but because I believe that existing national governments are less likely to regard lack of such guarantees as of sufficiently crucial seriousness to become motivated to surrender enough power to ensure them. Recurrence and publication of atrocities may change the picture. But, at present, I suspect that monetary destabilization is a crisis much more likely to cause the establishment of effective world government than concern for human rights.

Thus, although the dangers of war, overpopulation, overconsumption of resources, pollution, stagflation, deficit spending, monetary instability, persisting racial and religious tensions, rising expectations, too intricate interdependence, demoralization, and violations of human rights could be avoided or reduced by appropriate actions of an established world government, the prospect that enough nations can be induced to surrender to such a government the powers needed to accomplish such avoidance or reduction appear dim. It is possible that some new, still more urgent crisis—perhaps climatic changes drastically reducing food supplies, an epidemic of a newly emergent uncontrolled disease, or increasingly successful terrorist blackmail threatening world dictatorship—may crystallize needs for an effective world government. But until such possibilities become actualities, nations seem unlikely to act.

My proposal regarding the minimum functions of a world government does not consist in a definite list, but in research projects designed to discover both which functions are in fact necessary for human survival and which functions each of the nations is willing to

support through surrender of its own relevant powers. If the functions I have suggested vary relative to the degree of willingness with
which nations can be induced to transfer needed powers, wisdom
dictates that proposals await the outcome of such research.

HOW TO ACHIEVE IT

Overcoming the Difficulties

A major obstacle to achieving world government is the inability of
anyone, apparently, to design a system that will seem fair to all, or
even to a majority, of persons and nations. Nations and persons who
have power are unwilling to join a new system unless their share of
power as participants seems somewhat correlative to their present
share. Persons who lack power, especially those in larger and more
populous nations, believe they should have a greater share and will
remain unwilling to join in a system that perpetuates seeming injustices.

The problem is particularly embarrassing for the United States
and other First World countries that idealize, practice, and advocate
democratic policies. In spite of the declining competence of citizens
to vote intelligently on national issues and the growing distance between the citizen voter and decisions reached by Congress (after depending on congressional committee hearings from research consultants and special-interest lobbyists), Americans still uphold
representative democracy as the best system of government for
them. However, most do not believe a democratic world government is possible.[1]

Why do Americans tolerate this inconsistency, or what Marxists
call a contradiction, in their foundational political policy? With
more than two hundred nations in the world, we would have a
senate of more than four hundred members. The United States
would elect only two senators, holding one two-hundredth of the
voting power of this body. With a world population of about four
billion people, for example, electing delegates at the rate of one for
every twenty million people would yield a house of representatives
with two hundred members. The United States, which has a popula-

tion of little more than two hundred million, could elect only ten delegates. Its voting power would be ten out of two hundred, or one-twentieth of the total. It would be outvoted by the U.S.S.R., with twelve or thirteen votes, and both together would be outvoted by the People's Republic of China, with seventy-eight or seventy-nine votes. Furthermore these now-powerful nations would have only about half of the total votes.

As long as nations retain the right to settle questions of international policy by war, some consider the size of armed forces as a way to evaluate present powers. The United States and the U.S.S.R., according to one report, control 60 percent of the world's military expenditures.[2] Neither is willing to surrender any power for a combined voting power of 1 percent in the world senate and a combined voting power of 11 percent in the house. No matter how much many desire a democratic world government (delegates elected to represent one-person-one-vote proportionately), it is not a live option today.

If we are to achieve an effective world government today, even one with minimal functions, it must be on some other basis. I suggest that what is called for is a system that both ensures currently-powerful nations correlatively powerful status on a temporary basis and promises currently less-powerful nations opportunities for increasing their voting power by definitely established means. I propose the principle that the basis on which intelligent government should be established is demonstrable understanding of the issues, especially of the crisis issues. These issues have become so increasingly complex that nothing less than competent multidisciplinary and interdisciplinary research will suffice. So I propose, first, a system in which an understanding of problems arising from policy decision is achieved through interdisciplinary research and then a modification of that system designed to induce nations to surrender sufficient relevant power, on a trial basis if necessary, to deal effectively with one or more critical problems.

Designing the System

Two main principles are essential to the system. The first pertains to ensuring that policy decisions will be based on understanding

benefiting from adequate and reliable interdisciplinary research.
The second pertains to ensuring some minimum of democratic participation by some minimum number of citizens volunteering to qualify as reliable voters by achieving the necessary understanding.

DESIGN FOR ENSURING UNDERSTANDING

Presupposing the principle that an uninformed vote is not worth
casting and may be detrimental, and the principle that most global
crises are so complex that they are beyond the understanding of most
citizens and most senators, I propose eliminating voting by both citizens and legislators and then establishing voting privileges based on
a demonstrated understanding of the issues involved in each policy
problem occurring for decision. Those who qualify themselves to
understand issues regarding policy questions for decision can
demonstrate their understanding by taking a test prepared especially
for this purpose before voting. Those who pass the test have their
vote counted immediately; votes of those who fail are not counted.
The system is designed to bring expert knowledge to bear effectively
in each policy decision process.[3]

Such a system requires many functionaries. Although exactly how
necessary functions will be divided among the staff of specialists
trained to carry out the functions is a matter for research, and revisions based on experience, I do propose some ideas that may serve as
ideals for constructing the system initially. I believe that about nine
agencies will be needed to perform nine kinds of functions essential
to the legislative process.[4]

Policy problems, questions, and proposals that disturb citizens,
public officials, or staff personnel deserve initial hearings and preliminary screening by *initiators*. They must be responsible both for
giving all proposals a fair hearing and for eliminating trivial, misunderstood, and irrelevant issues. Citizens, officials, and staff
should have recourse to extraordinary techniques for forcing consideration of some issues when initiators seem to have been insuffi-
ciently considerate in evaluating their proposals.

Fixing the legislative calendar is the responsibility of *steerers*.
Once an issue has been accepted for legislative consideration, time
must be allowed for research, printing, and distributing results and
for learning by prospective voters. Holidays, working days, and

other responsibilities of researchers, distributors, and voters must be taken into consideration. Not too many complex issues should come up at the same time unless decisions will be made by different voters assisted by different researchers. More urgent issues should be given preference. Some complex issues may require several simultaneous decisions, and some may require some decisions first before further research can be undertaken for others.

The development of reliable information on all relevant aspects of issues entered in the legislative process is the responsibility of *researchers*. Their task commits them to competence in all relevant disciplines. They must have the ability to combine thoroughness, objectivity, and fairness to genuine alternatives. Much material may be already available in libraries, in memory banks, and in the minds of some scientists and technicians. Sometimes much original research will be required, though hopefully the tasks dealing with the unique complexities of each issue will, as legislative research accumulates, be kept to a minimum. In addition to a permanent staff of specialists in research and in interdisciplinary research management, experts on different aspects of many complex issues will have to be employed, either as consultants or for temporary research duties.

Preparation of research results for voters (and examiners) in a form that is clear, accurate and adequate and includes all information that is necessary for understanding each legislative issue is the responsibility of *informers*. They must sift from all the material those factors bearing significantly on the decision, being careful not to omit anything essential, not to bias the result by accidents of selection, to evaluate the relative importance of different factors when difference is evident, and, occasionally, to request researchers for clarification and/or further research. High school debaters' handbooks provide examples of ways of lining up arguments and evidence for and against each issue, together with sample statements and bibliographical references. Each issue may require its own peculiar methods for clarification and presentation, but the handbook outlines seem suggestive as models. A second function of the informers, or perhaps of an additional agency, is to distribute the information to prospective voters promptly, conveniently, and without distortion. Whether printed matter by mail or memory-banked material by computer console, receipt of information in usable form sufficiently before voting time must be assured. When information seems unclear to examiners or voters, further information may be required.

The preparation of clear, accurate, fair, brief, and rapid-scoring tests to show whether voters understand the material distributed by the informers is the responsibility of *examiners*. The tests should be prepared so that all who understand what is essential to make an intelligent decision will pass and all who do not so understand will fail. When issues are complex enough to have different parts, it may be that one person will pass part of the test and vote on one part of an issue but fail and not vote on another part. Where test results reveal ranges of degrees of understanding and the number of voters who pass is less than minimal, problems of deciding on a minimal passing score needed for sufficient genuine understanding become crucial. When examiners and other agency officials decide that not enough voters have enough understanding to decide public policy reliably, they may request further research, information, or voter learning before authorizing a decision on an issue.

Administering the tests, including scoring them and counting the ballots accurately and quickly, and ensuring any secrecy needed regarding test questions between the time of serious consideration by examiners and final tabulation of results is the responsibility of *voting supervisors*. Prompt reporting is to be expected. Job security and financial rewards, together with appropriate penalties for malpractice, should be such that none is likely to respond to temptations of offers by special interests.

Assurance that no important public issue has been neglected by the legislative process and that policies that have become obsolete will receive appropriate repeal legislation is the responsibility of *planners*. This agency is not essential to establishing the system, since initiators of the system should have settled upon major plans before its establishment. However, since many policies will not work out in practice in ways intended by legislators, an agency whose function it is to observe such deviations, especially those producing unforeseen bad results and to call to further legislative attention any need for revision, seems advisable.

Since functions are not always performed efficiently, whether unwittingly or intentionally, an agency authorized to hear claims

about violations of agency regulations, deficiencies, and responsibilities for accidents is needed. Naming these functionaries *judges*
should not confuse their functions, which are limited to claims
arising within the legislative system, with those of the judicial and
administrative branches of government, each of which may have its
own system of judges to consider rule infractions within its branch.
When violation frequency indicates a deficiency in the legislative
system, judges should be empowered to compel initiation of further
legislation about such deficiency.

The tasks of staffing, training, advancing, and dismissing personnel in all agencies and of financing salaries, purchasing equipment
and supplies, keeping accounts, and securing support for the system
are responsibilities of *administrators*. Their tasks include ensuring
continuity of the program, promoting smoothness in cooperation of
the interrelated agencies, improving the excellence of the legislative
process when possible, keeping the public informed about the services being performed, and convincing whomever is the responsible
source of financing that the services rendered are worth as much as,
or more than, the money invested.

DESIGN FOR ENSURING FEASIBLE DEMOCRACY

Presupposing the principle that the more democratic the legislative system, the better, I offer the following suggestions for making
the proposed system as democratic as possible. By democratic, I
mean the opportunity for all interested citizens to participate voluntarily in the legislative process without regard to race, creed, color,
sex, age, nationality, or any other restriction that has nothing to do
with adequacy of understanding issues coming up for policy decision.

As issues become more complex and intricate, the number of persons who can understand them decreases, and the numbers of persons able and willing to try to understand them also decreases. If
democracy means "for each person one vote," then a system requiring understanding of more complex issues becomes increasingly un-
democratic in this sense. Of course, if increasingly complex issues
continue to be dealt with by persons who vote but do not understand
what they are voting about, such a system becomes increasingly unintelligent.

A third principle presupposed here is that when problems become too complicated for understanding by voters, whether citizens or legislators, intelligence calls for preferring understanding to democracy when these two principles conflict. The system is designed not to abandon democracy as a principle under circumstances in which it may become ineffective or detrimental, but to keep it as much as possible. Sometimes emergencies require quick decisions that cannot await completion of cumbersome democratic processes. The system recognizes that, under such circumstances involving conflict between democracy and understanding, it is better to subordinate democracy to understanding.

Doubts about assuring maximum democratic opportunities should be allayed somewhat by examples of the kinds of democratic participation that may be expected in each of the nine agencies outlined here. One responsibility of the initators would be to make sure that all interested citizens can have a hearing for proposals they would initiate (unless too many introduce trivia constantly). If initiators become overwhelmed by citizen proposals, they may call for legislation designed to require those who submit proposals to give some minimal evidence of understanding the issues themselves and of their relative significance for the legislative program. Even at the level of initiation, limits of feasibility for democratic participation may be discovered and legislated about. But restrictions embodying such limits should be designed to ensure a maximum participation by responsible citizens having serious proposals for consideration.

Steerers seem unlikely to be influenced much by citizen requests, although they should hear and consider evidence about factors that may significantly affect calendar decisions, indicating a need for more urgent action or delay. Researchers should expect citizens and special-interest groups to volunteer information relative to issues. Each should be heard, unless experience teaches that more than some maximum limit of input from each person or interest becomes too costly or too likely to bias research results. Citizen surveillance of tentative results may indicate that further research is needed for issue understanding. Informers, examiners, and voting supervisors seem unlikely to receive citizen influence, unless unclarity, unfairness, and inconveniences from their work call for attention.

Planners should welcome—and encourage—citizen suggestions

about long-range needs, present inconveniences, gaps in present legislation, and obsolescent policies. However, if they are over-whelmed by too many suggestions, regulations may become neces-sary to restrict the number submitted. Judges, although their au-thority is limited to violations internal to the system, must listen to citizen complaints about violations of rights or privileges or dam-ages resulting from conduct by persons or agencies within the sys-tem. Administrators should expect advice from all sources, especial-ly that resulting from dissatisfaction with its services.

Of primary importance is the need for devising some optimum ideal of citizen participation. There are too many participants when the system becomes too costly in time, money, and effort demanded both by staff needs and in the lives of citizens, all of whom have other problems and needs for their time, money, and effort. And there are too few participants when so few pass tests and vote that the number approaches a kind of oligarchy (not a single oligarchy for the whole system but a kind of oligarchy in the sense that only a few actually participate in each particular decision).

The problem of too few becomes aggravated as issues become more complex and understanding more difficult. Is there some mini-mum number of participants regarding each issue below which the system is no longer democratic? Is there a minimum number for all issues, both simple and complex? Or do complex issues warrant con-sidering a reduced number still democratic? I expect that as experi-ence in dealing with the legislative process and new problems ac-cumulates, more reasonable suggestions regarding practical policies will emerge. Ways will be found both for increasing participation when such participation is beneficial and for practical principles re-garding when the minimum number must necessarily be decreased in order to achieve legislation at all. It may happen that, as in the United States Constitution which provides for the president to ac-quire dictatorial powers under emergency conditions, some provi-sion may have to be made for a condition in which a single expert who most fully understands the issue should be entrusted with deci-sion power. I would expect such conditions to be very exceptional.

Even though ideals of optimum citizen participation cannot be decided wisely in advance of practical experience, the system, because it is designed to keep as much democratic participation as possible as well as to maximize expertise in providing reliable under-standing, has been called *demospeciocracy*. Neither the name nor the specifics of the system design are necessary to the Philosopher's World Model. But they do exemplify an attempt to demonstrate that we can devise a more intelligent system for legislating policy deci-sions if we are willing to rise above our entrenched habits and to take a quantum leap to a new level of political organization.

Establishing the System

Five additional proposals seem desirable in establishing the sys-tem: modifications conducive to *minimalization*; principles for in-ducing nations to participate; research needed for locating readi-ness; establishment of a government for a trial period; and estab-lishment of a flexible government permanently.

MODIFICATIONS CONDUCIVE TO MINIMALIZATION

The system is designed to serve urban, state, and national, as well as world-level, needs for intelligent legislation. Further suggestions are needed for adapting it to the proposed minimal world govern-ment. If nations can be induced to surrender sufficient power to establish a world government only if its power is strictly limited, then what modifications seem reasonable in order to initiate a tenta-tive world government as a kind of working hypothesis?

The issues with which the government will deal during the trial period will be strictly limited, so the functions of the initiators will be taken care of largely before establishment. Since the number of issues can be expected to be small (unless multitudes of subordinate issues arise) and the readiness for decisions obvious to all concerned, the employment of specialized steerers seems unnecessary. Although much research will have to be completed before establishment as a means to inducing nations to join, setting up a permanent as well as consultative research institute concentrating on problems related to its limited functions seems necessary. Informers, examiners, and voting supervisors will have especially difficult problems unless the number of official languages is limited. The importance of these functionaries will depend on decisions about the number of lan-guages and spread or concentration of examining and voting locations. Possibly the planners' functions can be merged with those of other researchers during the trial period, although reliable evidence relative to whether to expand responsibilities of the world government will require researchers with planners' qualifications. Judges' functions can be merged with those of the administrators as long as the number of violations remains small.

If enough people participate and if the trial period is long enough—perhaps ten years—efforts to differentiate these functions can be expected. The more kinds of responsibility with which the government is entrusted, the more issues with which it has to deal, the greater the complexity of issues, the greater the number of voter participants, and the longer the period during which the government functions, the more useful will become differentiation of the nine staff functions. But reduction of their number to fit closer to the needs for dealing with fewer responsibilities, fewer issues, fewer voters, and shorter time seems appropriate.

MODIFICATIONS FOR INDUCING NATIONS TO PARTICIPATE

I propose a trial period, such as ten years (although the actual length should be decided after further research and consultations with nations), during which special safeguards should protect the interests of dubious nations. Three areas of interest should receive special attention: voting power, undesirable control, and costs.

Voting Power

How much expertise and how much multinational participation should be expected for dealing with initial and highly urgent issues? Although international interdisciplinary research institutes exist already, the total number of persons genuinely qualified to understand any one of the crucial complex global problems may be very small. The task of increasing needed expertise can be overcome by sufficient financing for training experts in the relevant fields and issues. The problem of increasing the democratic spread of experts qualified to vote on issues can be handled by distributing training needed to persons in different countries.

However, in order to appeal to existing nations, we must propose an initial distribution of voting power somewhat correlative to existing powers (economic, political, and military). Thus more powerful

First and Second World nations will respond to appeals only if voting power by their citizens is proportionately great. Less powerful nations will respond only if they are guaranteed means for an eventual increase in the voting power of their citizens. Once the system has been adopted, even on a trial basis, national interest should increase financial support for training specialists qualified to vote on world government issues. If significant maldistribution of such voters continues, support by the world government for such training may be distributed in corrective ways. But the initial distribution of voting power will require negotiation, and proposals for the most widely acceptable distribution should be presented for serious consideration only after sufficient research.

The initial agreement should allow for some shift in voting power by nations during the trial period and, although it is preferable to eliminate the requirements related to national origins of voters at the end of the trial period, some limitations on rates of shift for a second trial period might be required by some nations before they will consent to inducements. I believe that as more persons become acquainted with the extent and complexities of interdependencies, the decisions of adequately trained voters will tend to express more concern for the welfare of mankind and comparatively less for that of the nations they represent. In this way the national origin of qualified understanders will become less and less significant, and regulations about some minimum number of voters of any particular national origin will tend to become irrelevant and obsolete. But as long as the national interests of persons being appealed to for trial participation are very strong, sensitivity to these interests, and their strengths, is necessary in devising and negotiating regulations regarding national distribution of qualified voters during the trial period.

Undesirable Control

Government involves both controlling and being controlled. An effective world government will control the behavior of nations and persons relative to its limited responsibilities enough to achieve the goals for which it is responsible. If crises result from the inability of nations to act cooperatively voluntarily, then they can be overcome only if a world government has the ability to cause those nations to cooperate enough to overcome them. Nations not currently volunteering to cooperate may continue to regard cooperation, and any compulsion to do so, undesirable. If the world government cannot, or does not, compel cooperation, it is ineffective. If it is effective, some nations will experience somewhat undesirable control.

Nations may be induced to participate in a world government only if they can withdraw such participation when the amount of control becomes more undesirable than anticipated. As long as uncertainties remain regarding both the ability of an untried world government to remove crises and the unforeseen effects of its controlling power, some nations can be induced to participate only if their welfare is not endangered by adverse developments. So provisions for withdrawal under stated circumstances can function as safeguards providing sufficient assurance to induce some nations to join in initiating the system.

Costs

A world government cannot function effectively if it lacks adequate financing. If nations doubt the viability and effectiveness of the world government, they may be unwilling to grant it authority to tax people or nations or to engage in other money-producing enterprises. I do not offer a specific plan for dealing with this question; further research regarding the issues at stake here will be needed. Doubtless some temporary system of financing can be agreed upon for the trial period, though one can argue for the value of trial operation of a proposed permanent system so that unforeseen difficulties can be met and handled during this initial period. Satisfactory experience with a proposed permanent system will increase the likelihood that nations will be willing to commit themselves to the system.

Additional research doubtless will uncover additional kinds of reluctance and additional means for inducement. A provision for repealing the constitution and discontinuing the world government under certain conditions—for example, after it has fulfilled its responsibilities relative to present crises—may allay some fears. Or a provision requiring periodic review of the government or at least of many or all of its policy decisions (a principle already inherent in the demospeciocratic system), should comfort others. Requiring all policy conclusions to include an automatic termination clause after some definite period so that voter reapproval would be needed testifies to their continuing vitality.

Proponents of a minimal world government should not hesitate to recommend provisions for periodic constitution review. Such provisions have more significance than being initiation inducements merely. The constitutions of national, state, and municipal governments should also be reviewed. As conditions continue to change (whether because problems become more difficult or because world peace provides conditions enabling some levels of government to perform functions more efficiently than before), a shifting of functions in the interest of improved benefits should be expected as a matter of intelligent political practice.

RESEARCH FOR LOCATING READINESS

The kinds of research that will be needed even for initiating the system should include at least these efforts: to clarify the kinds of self-interest, both general for all nations and particular in each nation, to which appeal can be made; to discover other beneficial modifications; to locate persons in all nations already qualified to vote understandingly; to discover the attitudes of the deciders in each nation regarding all proposals requiring negotiation; and to evaluate attitudes regarding priorities among the kinds of readiness so that negotiators will not waste time trying to reach agreement on proposals lacking sufficient support or having to low a priority rating.

ESTABLISHMENT OF GOVERNMENT FOR A TRIAL PERIOD

The success or failure of the government will depend on many unforeseeable factors, such as new crises, natural catastrophes, or even new inventions for good or ill. Also the skills embodied in establishing it and in using it to eliminate crises seem of central importance. If present crises worsen too much, a world government will need more authority to operate effectively than is contemplated in the present plan unless provisions for rapid addition of authority in event of further crises have been included.

ESTABLISHMENT OF FLEXIBLE GOVERNMENT PERMANENTLY

My proposal does not call for requiring all national governments to participate in either the trial or permanent proposals. The issue of the values of participation by some nations will be settled partly by the success or failure of the world government to perform as desired. The more intricately interdependent we become, the more each nation will find itself both dependent on other governments and depended upon by them, and the kinds of interdependence have a tendency to increase. Willingness to participate will depend partly on the quality and quantity of information about the nature of existence, life, and society as complex varieties of interdependent systems and the values of those reciprocal interactions enhancing the stability, health, and welfare of each.

RESEARCH PROPOSALS

The urgency of world crises appears to require immediate massive cooperative efforts on the part of many nations. Since no such massive efforts appear to be underway, I fear that only some dictatorial effort will be equal to the task as crises worsen. But I still hope that intelligent cooperation may become actual, and I offer some specific suggestions that may prove helpful toward surviving these crises.

Interdisciplinary Research Development

NEED FOR EXPLOSIVE EFFORTS

If intelligent solution to world crises is to be achieved soon, the world needs a crash program of investment in much more research. Such research should be directed in ways that bring needed enlightenment about our world problems and practical proposals for dealing with them. It should be interdisciplinary in the sense that each science is seen both as contributing to and as being contributed to by an increasingly clear and useful comprehensive view of the nature of existence, society, and human values. That is, in addition to stimulating efforts in each of the present sciences—and in some of these more than others either because they have been neglected or because they have more to contribute—in addition to initiating and supporting such new sciences as are needed, and in addition to promoting interdisciplinary efforts both between closely related sciences and between those more distant, we need to seek to achieve a comprehensive understanding that can come only from combining the resources from all of the sciences. These efforts should be funded massively.

QUANTUM-LEAP SUGGESTIONS

More and more research, no matter how richly funded, will not provide the needed solutions if the funds continue to subdivide sciences into subsciences and specialties into subspecialties. I do not mean that such subdivisions will not be needed, both in the sense that new particular needs will require new particular research and that each higher level of interdisciplinary research will require additional kinds of higher-level specializations. I mean that global problems now demand global answers and that scientific generalizations needed for such global answers must include comprehensive principles that reveal the nature of our whole problem because they reveal something fundamental about the nature of our whole world.

Specifically I propose the development of a science of interdisciplinarity. Research begins by observing examples of successful and unsuccessful interdisciplinary research. Such research may include the cooperation of only two sciences or three or several. If all are alike in having been successful, we should be able to locate common elements, including elements common to their success. If some are also all alike in being unsuccessful, these too need to be studied to see whether they have any common elements, especially elements common to their failures, since we wish to learn how to avoid failures.

The kind of interdisciplinary research I intend to focus on here is that in which sciences themselves sometimes change and improve as a consequence of their interaction with other sciences. Sciences can influence each other in four ways. First, sometimes ideas in one science influence those in another in ways that improve the other science. Second, sometimes two sciences influence each other in ways that improve both. Third, sometimes new ideas arise from the mutual influence of two sciences. When these new ideas become stabilized and utilized, they may become a new science. In this example, we have some new ideas that did not exist before in either of the cooperating sciences. Finally, sometimes ideas newly emergent from two sciences in turn reinfluence either one or both of the cooperating sciences. That is, in addition to ideas borrowed more directly from the other science, each may now be influenced beneficially by the newly emergent ideas produced by their cooperation. These four ways become more complex when more than two sciences are involved. I propose distinguishing three stages in the development of interdisciplinarity as helpful in conceiving its full nature.

The first stage consists of observing many successful and many unsuccessful efforts at interdisciplinary research for each of the four or more ways in which sciences may influence each other. Generalizations about such successes and failures may then function as working hypotheses for guiding inquiry into whether and how additional knowledge may be obtained from deliberate efforts at interdisciplinary research relative to still other disciplines. If new knowledge from interdisciplinary research is worthwhile relative to some disciplines, then we ought to invest in and stimulate research relative to such other disciplines. Our first gains from interdisciplinary research have originated from within or between two or a few disciplines, without any conception of the possibilities of gains from planned stimulation of interdisciplinary research. Now the time has come for us to exploit the possibilities for additional gains by stimulating research involving still other disciplines. Funding for such stimulation and such research is now a recognized need.

The second stage consists of extending interdisciplinary efforts begun in the first stage universally. In the first stage, generalizing from some successful interdisciplinary achievements presumably enabled us to attain still other interdisciplinary achievements. Now we can systematically exploit possibilities for success by extending our interdisciplinary observations to ways that include all of the sciences. Since I regard axiology, aesthetics, ethics, epistemology, logic, philosophy of science, philosophy of language, metaphysics, and economic, political, religious, and educational philosophy as sciences, I intend that all these sciences be included in the second stage.

This second stage includes three emphases. First, it universalizes interdisciplinary research by extending it to include all of the sciences. This may call for further development in some of the sciences that have been neglected so that interdisciplinary evidence relative to them can be included also. Second, it universalizes interdisciplinary research by testing initial working hypotheses formulated from earlier observations through extending such testing to interdisciplinary circumstances involving all of the sciences. If all additional observations support an original hypothesis, then it is strengthened through such universalization. If not all additional observations support an original hypothesis, then it must be reformulated to account for the additional data. Such universalization of testing a hypothesis should result in formulating a still more adequate hypothesis.

Third, it universalizes interdisciplinary research by systematically exploring the implications of the knowledge embodied in a universalized interdisciplinary hypothesis for each of the original sciences. Each person in each science should be able to achieve some expanded knowledge about his own science from acquaintance with the interdisciplinary principles and their implications for his science. Such new knowledge by a particular scientist may generate new insights that suggest still other kinds of interdisciplinary studies. Dialectical interaction between such scientists and those scientists concerned with universalizing interdisciplinary principles may continue to result in additional advances for both.

The third stage is concerned with problems involved in seeing how conclusions of all of the various sciences together with the generalized conclusions from all of the interdisciplinary studies fit in a consistent whole. A comprehensive understanding of the nature of existence based on all disciplinary and interdisciplinary conclusions functions as a world hypothesis that in turn has implications for each of the sciences. Just as new ideas emerging from the cooperation of two sciences may form a new science that in turn may benefically influence each of the two sciences, so new ideas emerging from all of the sciences and interdisciplinary research to form a world hypothesis (resulting from such multiscience and interscience cooperation) may themselves constitute a new science, which in turn may beneficially influence all of the cooperating sciences. The formation of such a world view functions as a scientific hypothesis with implications for each of the sciences.

If a generalized world view has resulted from extending interdisciplinary research in this way, then its constituent hypotheses can function as principles useful in each of the sciences for testing the adequacy of its own principles insofar as they have implications for other sciences and for the world view. The same holds for the interdependence of interdisciplinary conclusions and the comprehensive conclusions. If we can assume that the existence interpreted by our sciences, our interdisciplinary generalizations, and our world view involves no inconsistencies, then we should be able to improve the probability of our conclusions when those in our sciences, those in our interdisciplinary generalizations, and those in our world view are consistent with each other. Although consistency is not a sufficient criterion of truth, at least inconsistency is a criterion of falsity. Availability of a reliable world view hypothesis therefore may prove very useful as an aid in testing conclusions in each of the sciences.

My proposed science of interdisciplinarity may develop one stage at a time, and benefits may be derived from the first stage even before the second and third develop. But once the process is started, there seems to be no reason for not developing it through all three stages (if funding and manpower are available) because benefits will be greatest when the development is fullest. Not the least of the benefits is modification resulting from interactions between the largest and the smallest parts that may be needed in either or both the world view and each of the particular sciences as a result of attempting to see what implications each has for the other. The growing need for each scientist to understand the problems in his own science better by understanding how they are related to problems constituting the other sciences involves a growing need for each to understand how his problems relate to those involved in trying to understand existence, or the universe, as a whole.

The implications of this proposed science of interdisciplinarity for dealing with practical problems of personal living, national policy, and global survival can be tremendous. When scientific research first focuses on problems about the nature of values, obligations, religion, society, and government and then produces a world view, the implications of the world view for present moral, religious, social, and political practices may require radically different conceptions and practices than now prevail. If many of our present views are false or inadequate and if scientific research extended as interdisciplinary research through the three stages proposed for the science of interdisciplinarity yields truer or more adequate views, then if our demonstrations have been sufficiently rigorous and convincing, we may become able to change our course in time to avoid doomsday.

Sufficient investment in such a science is a most urgent need that should claim top priority from our policy deciders, financial suppliers, interdisciplinary research institutes, and scientists themselves. I propose this science of interdisciplinarity as a most serious candidate as a quantum-leap conception.

RESEARCH INSTITUTES AND UNIVERSITIES

Complaints that interdisciplinary interests are thwarted in universities because opportunities for advancement and tenure are channeled through departments emphasizing single disciplines seem justified. As long as this is the case, we must look to interdisciplinary research institutes that are not hobbled by established structures and tenure systems for most progress in the research needed. Universities are primarily teaching institutions and only secondarily research institutes (although research functions of some universities have expanded considerably recently under federal support). Universities have tended to become more and more multiversities, with the *uni* in *university* pertaining primarily to a common budget and board of directors.

Any interdisciplinary research that occurs in universities tends to be between two or three disciplines, except where area studies gather resources from several disciplines to establish another one. Universities do not, as far as I know, have even a philosophy of science common to their separate science departments. My own experience as a teacher of philosophy of science revealed that different philosophies prevail in different science departments and even that radically different philosophies may be advocated in the same department. A loss of interest in philosophy as comprehensive by most teachers of philosophy leaves most universities without even a philosophy department resource for attending to interdisciplinarity comprehensively. Thus universities seem not very promising loci for promoting needed explosive efforts in interdisciplinary research.

DANGERS

In recommending interdisciplinary research so highly, I am painfully aware of many misusages of some institutes: incompetent personnel in both management and research positions, severe lack of adequate and permanent funding, lack of standards developed to deal with problems peculiar to such institutes, lack of supervision and openness to inspection of much work done, and the necessity some institutes face for producing results that funders desire or of becoming extinct. The dual difficulties—achieving sufficient independence from funders, public or private, to pursue unbiased objective research and achieving sufficient funding on a continuing basis to ensure completion of projects and security for researchers—need to be overcome on larger scales.

The task of evaluating the quality of institutes, when honest research often must report no decisive results and when some institutes emphasize expertise in grantsmanship and a highly polished reputation, calls for objective research. Research institutes recruiting staff from university departments complain of acquiring too much tunnel vision in their own staff members, and struggle with problems of increasing communication among members with specialized training. Efficiency in interdisicplinary research projects cannot be expected until experience has produced qualified managers for such institutes, programs, and projects. The task ahead for interdisciplinary research institutes is fraught with enormous difficulties.

On the one hand, we cannot expect too much from such institutes until they are adequately funded, adequately staffed, and adequately managed. But they appear just now to have the most potential for more quickly adapting to current needs and to grasping our global crises and the need for quantum-leap conceptions in designing research and seeking solutions.

Present Research Resources

The tremendous task of achieving enough competence to design, initiate, and operate successfully the needed minimal world government by means of a crash program investing in more research may discourage many. But a survey of some present research resources, most of them originating in recent decades, should reveal something of the capacities we already have for supporting organized research. Research institutionalization exists already at three levels: research institutes, associations of research institutes and world research institutes.

RESEARCH INSTITUTES

Research institutes exist both nationally and internationally, both privately and publicly, both as independent agencies and as associated with other agencies with varying degrees of dependence, both on a project-to-project basis and on a continuing basis with permanent staffs, and both as highly specialized and limited in authorized range of disciplines, problems and languages and as more broadly available for explorations over wider ranges of problems.

Within many nations, interdisciplinary research institutes exist both privately and publicly. Private institutes, sometimes called *think tanks*, range in structure and substantiality from one-man-institutes willing to employ whatever staff is needed if and when a research contract becomes available to Rand Corporation, accustomed to being entrusted with large-scale classified military experiments. Some individual private research institutes specialize in international affairs and thus seem more directly involved in problems that will be significantly affected by the development of a world government. For example, International Business-Government Counsellors, Inc., Washington, D.C., does research for about forty United States corporations involved in international business. Business International Corporation publishes *Business International*, which has editorial offices in sixteen countries.

Public research agencies exist at many levels: school district, university, municipal (not only do some cities engage in research but some have become organized internationally: Council of European Municipalities, Luxembourg; Inter-American Municipal Organization, New Orleans; International Union of Local Authorities, The Hague), county, state, regional, and national. Many state governments support continuing legislative counsels, and the United States House and Senate have many standing committees, as well as special committees, some with permanent staffs and some with huge budgets for their investigations. The Library of Congress was established partly to serve as an up-to-date information base for all kinds of research. Memorial libraries, such as those containing donations from Presidents Hoover, Kennedy, and Johnson, function as research institutes.

Each of the departments of the administrative branch of the U.S. government maintains its own research efforts. The Department of Defense, for example, has its own specialized library and research staffs. The Federal Bureau of Investigation is primarily a research institute. The Central Intelligence Agency has its own Office of Research and Development. The Department of the Treasury, with its Internal Revenue Service data banks is a huge research organization.

Research is sufficiently important that United States federal institutions have been established solely for purposes of advancing scientific research. The National Academy of Sciences, the National Research Council, the National Academy of Engineering, and the Institute of Medicine, each with many subdivisions, have been established for promoting science and its use in improving human welfare. The National Science Board, composed of prominent scientists, serves as an advisory council to administrative and legislative agencies. The National Science Foundation, the National Institutes of Health, the National Institute of Education, and the National Foundation for the Arts and the Humanities spend millions of dollars annually in research grants. The extent to which American governments already engage in research, much of it interdisciplinary, is amazing.

Unfortunately a lack of coordination in overall planning for research persists, though concern for this lack occasionally results in another specialized research program. In spite of these massive amounts of private and public research efforts throughout the world, the lack of any central coordination of research, combined with insufficient funding, leaves many major problems unattended.

International research institutes, private and public, can be divided into those primarily regional in concern and those not regionally restricted. Classification is difficult because private institutions need a home base in some nation and often depend on public support while public institutes often depend on information from private institutes. In addition, institutes with regional emphases find their problems conditioned by global factors and their conclusions having global implications; while institutes intending to be global in extension often find a regional division of labor necessary.

Private research institutes with regional emphases include the Bariloche Foundation, Buenos Aires, and the Center for the Study of Developing Countries, New Delhi. Both are located in, focus attention on, and propose solutions from the perspective of Third World countries. Private institutes aiming at global solutions include the Institute for World Order, New York, and the Club of Rome, Rome.

Public institutes, primarily international in character, include those supported by one nation, those supported by a regional group of nations, and those tending to seek support in many or all nations.

Supported primarily by one nation, the International Development Research Centre, located in Ottawa and established by the Canadian Parliament in 1970, has an international board of governors and regional offices in Senegal, Kenya, Beirut, Singapore, and Bogota. Its research focuses on problems in less developed countries and outside metropolitan areas, balancing research talent drawn from both more- and less-developed countries. During its first five years, the center approved 274 projects costing more than fifty million dollars. The East-West Center in Hawaii has an Institute of Advanced Projects, which supports research on Pacific and Asian problems.

International research institutes supported by a regional group of nations may be exemplified best, perhaps, by the twenty-year-old European Cultural Foundation with headquarters in Amsterdam. It studies problems related to the European Common Market and possibilities for a United States of Europe. NATO (North Atlantic Treaty Organization, Brussels),[5] COMITERN (Comunist International, Moscow), OAS (Organization of American States, Washington), OAFU (Organization for African Unity, Addis Ababa), ASEAN (Association of South East Asian Nations, Singapore), OCAS (Organization for Central American States, San Salvador), ADC (Asian Development Center, Manila), and OPEC (Organization of Petroleum Exporting Countries, Vienna) all have research needs and services.

International research institutes not restricted regionally number in the thousands. The 1972-1973 *Yearbook of International Organizations*, lists more than four thousand with more than twenty-four hundred nongovernmental organizations and two hundred intergovernmental organizations, and projects for more than nine thousand nongovernmental organizations and eight hundred intergovernmental organizations by the year 2000.[6] Not all of these conduct research, but all have interests in the outcomes of research. The numbers of international societies already existing with research activities and further research interests bearing on world problems and the need for effective world government are increasing. (For selected examples of such organizations, see appendix 1.)

ASSOCIATIONS OF RESEARCH INSTITUTES

International associations of research institutes exist both privately and publicly.

Probably the most substantial private association is the International Federation of Institutes for Advanced Study. Established in 1972, headquartered in Stockholm, with twenty-two member institutes in seventeen countries, it aims "to further transnational, transdisciplinary research with the aid of a network of cooperating Institutes and Laboratories distinguished in their respective fields, to serve as a focus and forum for the serious study of selected major global problems in a long-range perspective where Member Institutes share a common interest and specific cooperative efforts are required to initiate specific studies, programmes and projects of transdisciplinary and transnational character in the natural sciences, technology, social sciences and humanities." Federation officers, proceeding cautiously, are limiting membership to twenty-seven institutes during an initial period and have approved only very restricted sponsored research projects. "IFIAS has not ventured any project based on pure philosophical research." It has considered "studies aimed at defining the ethics and motivations of scientists . . ., but for various reasons we have not chosen to engage ourselves as yet in research of that kind."[7] Thus a structure has been established, but research regarding the value, necessity, and methods of establishing a minimal world government to cope with "an increasingly complex, rapidly changing, and interdependent world" has not yet appeared on its agenda, apparently.

The International Chamber of Commerce, headquartered in Paris, unites more than sixteen hundred organizations in its interest in surveying the world economy. However, it draws most of its data from studies made by other organizations. It cooperates with United Nations agencies. But no evidence of interest in developing a more effective world governments appears in its 1975 annual report.

The Union of International Associations, originating in 1907, headquartered in Brussels, has 161 members in 43 countries. It receives a thousand periodicals, computerizes much of its data, publishes *International Associations,* a monthly, the *Yearbook of International Organizations,* the *Directory of Periodicals Published by International Organizations,* and many other volumes. It has also produced (in 1975) the *Yearbook of World Problems, Integrative Disciplines and Human Development.* [8]

WORLD RESEARCH INSTITUTES

Institutes focusing primarily on the problems of mankind and human survival that have widespread private and public support are needed.

The United Nations University has been established as such a research institute. Its rector, James M. Hester, is aware of the challenge requiring its services:

The world is in the midst of its greatest metamorphosis since the cataclysm of the Second World War. A concatenation of crises . . . have contributed to the dissolution of . . . international structure and to the creation of a global condition in which new uncertainties, attitudes and possibilities abound. . . . The key question now is whether we are capable of formulating, expressing, believing and acting on a conception of world interdependence appropriate to the reality of world conditions. . . . The nation-state can no longer be the principle focus of thought and action for intelligent humans. All major national problems now interlock . . . with conditions elsewhere in the world. . . . The major problems confronting humanity are not the problems and responsibilities of single nations, . . . but of the entire interdependent world. [9]

The United Nations University is both a single multidisciplinary research institute and an association of multidisciplinary research institutes concerned with world problems. It will both incorporate institutes within itself and associate with others. Headquarters have been established in Tokyo as a result of an initial donation of funds by the Japanese government. A provisional office was opened in December 1974, when twenty-five governments had expressed intention to become associated with it. However, funds for this autonomous institute have been slow in coming. A substantial endowment will be necessary to prevent the institute from becoming dependent on politically biased donors. Success in the use of scientific methods depends on freedom from influences tending to bias research efforts and results. Failure to endow this university sufficiently can be expected to result in failure to achieve needed research results. Although authorized by the United Nations in 1972, and functioning under a rector in 1975, it will not be fully established until it has been fully funded. That may take decades, and it may never happen. Thus a major part of its establishment remains for future accomplishment.

In the Philosopher's World Model, the United Nations University (or something similar) can and should play a central role in studying, guiding, and promoting interdisciplinary research aimed at aiding the development of a world government sufficiently effective to enable mankind to survive and to evolve a world political-economic-social system most favorable to increasing human health, wealth and happiness. In practice, its capacities are very limited, and so its achievements now fall short of hopes. It may generate tremendous dissatisfaction, since too many will hope for too much from it. The first priorities—world hunger, the management and use of natural resources, and human and social development—are broad areas of research, and workable proposals can hardly be expected soon; each area is itself a complex of areas, and these three areas interdepend with each other and with all other major ones not included because of limited funds. Its task seems impossible, yet the stakes are so high that it cannot shrink from the task or hesitate to do its best. If responsible criticism should become overshadowed by irresponsible criticism, tragedy for it, for scientific research, and for mankind could result.

If mankind is capable of intelligent government, the founding of the United Nations University may be, or yet become, a major stepping-stone on the path that must be climbed with great effort and diligence in developing the system needed for survival. The multi-complexities of the problem to be faced require quantum-leap conceptions of the kinds of organizational structures and processes needed. Basic to the task is the need for a comprehensive philosophy that explains how such quantum-leap conceptions are needed, how they cohere in terms of a quantum-leap organic logic and metaphysics, and how they enable the generation of multiplicities of acceptable (workable as well as consistent) solutions as needed, and at least initial demonstrations of its superiority over competing philosophies.

The desired world research institute, or the United Nations University, requires an adequate comprehensive philosophy because its major function is to comprehend mankind's research needs in ways that will discover and fill any major gaps and adjust imbalances in information required for human survival. Its task requires an organic perspective in terms of which one can see that justice is being done in fitting all of the parts appropriately in the total picture. Its task is difficult because each of many different kinds of wholes— geographical, cultural, dimensional, disciplinary—requires its own integrative principles, which conflict with those in others when carried too far. The management of conflicts, both apparent and genuine, requires a conception of complementary opposites to replace the more popular, and culturally entrenched, tendencies to conceive conflicts in terms of contradictory opposites incapable of reconciliation. Forces opposing adoption of the needed comprehensive philosophy may well be considered the chief enemies of mankind.

Scientific and Professional Society Reforms

Although professional societies, including those of specialized scientists, are not research institutes, wise self-interested understanding of the need for improved interdisciplinary research and its significance for their professional welfare make these societies focal points for urging greater understanding of and responsibility for human welfare. Greater awareness of the nature of and needs for a science of interdisciplinarity in solving problems, including problems within each science, should benefit everybody.

Granted that scientists must specialize. Science should be conceived both narrowly and broadly because some of its tasks call for more and more specialized refinements and some for more and more comprehensive integrations. For too long too many people have conceived their specialized endeavors as too independent of each other. Departmentalization of budgets continues to perpetuate such conceptions. But a growing awareness of the interdependence of the sciences should increase the awareness of responsibility for understanding and actively participating in the growth of knowledge depending on such understanding. Excellence in the specialized sciences depends not only upon competence within each but also upon competence regarding the interdependencies of each with others both directly and through their mutual contributions to, and through their receiving contributions from, that comprehensive science which helps to give them their fullest significance.

For too long too many have assumed that each scientist—or department or corporation responsible for deciding what each scientist shall do—has an unrestricted right to study whatever he pleases in whatever way he pleases for as long as he pleases. I too favor complete freedom as one aspect of the scientific attitude and method because restrictions may bias the outcome of research. But when imbalances occur—when too many study linguistics and not enough metaphysics or too many study law and not enough medicine—then social welfare may be endangered. Someone should have a responsibility for filling the gaps. When the survival of mankind is endangered by the absence of needed scientific knowledge, someone surely has a responsibility to try to remove the danger. Some minimal intelligence in the management and direction of scientific endeavors is thus also essential to the nature of science. Gaps must be filled. When a reliable, comprehensive perspective is missing, this becomes the greatest gap of all.

At present, self-discipline by scientific and professional societies is largely missing from the American and, I believe, the world scene. The kinds of problems most of them focus upon are comparatively trivial. The reasons for this misplaced preoccupation are both internal and external to each science and profession. Perpetual inflation and social factors conditioning perpetually insufficient funding now pressure professionals to participate in unwanted unionization rather than to demonstrate to society's deciders of policy and funding how their contributions deserve appropriate rewards. Lack of scientific and professional excellence can be blamed partly upon a society that does not appreciate such accomplishments enough to provide sufficient appropriations. Locating causes of deficiencies and preoccupation with trivia does not remove them. Locating responsibility both in society generally and in scientists specifically provides a double, or multiple, locus for urging more efforts to expand interdisciplinary research intelligently and responsibly.

I am urging increasingly self-conscious efforts for self-understanding and self-improvement by those responsible for the conduct of each science and each profession by establishing and actively supporting commissions to examine needs for professional self-discipline and for accepting currently unfilled responsibility by the profession to itself, to other professions, and to society as a whole. Those not accustomed to thinking in this way doubtless will not be willing. But a fuller consideration of all factors should lead to the conclusion that anything short of such willingness and effort and some success constitutes a danger to mankind, and thus to the society in which the profession has its source, being, and welfare. The quantum-leap conceptions required by the Philosopher's World Model entail correlative quantum-leap responsibility. Interdependence of responsibilities interdepends with responsibility for interdependence.

Laissez-faire policies were possible when luxuriant conditions prevailed. But when frontiers are gone, the limits of growth have been reached, and too much freedom by some anarchistically destroys freedom of others, then intelligent management is called for. The Philosopher's World Model calls for awareness of the need for some minimums of achievement of intelligent self-control, self-management, and self-discipline by each of the sciences and each of the professions. When such management becomes necessary, self-management serving both internal and interdependent needs develops or management by something outside of the science or profession becomes necessary and develops. Research regarding standards—principles of wise self-interestedness—for scientific and professional societies could benefit all.

Self-management of sciences and professions that interdepend with each other and with economic and political processes, including those at global levels, can be adequate only to the extent that it is recognized, understood, and participated in responsibly. From the larger perspective of human survival, professional preoccupation with personal income increments and unemployed persons is trivial when it prevents necessary attention to the problems and tasks of the survival of mankind within which such increased income and employment must occur. Of course, each unemployed and underpaid scientist or professional naturally fears for his own survival. The very intricacy as well as magnitudes of interdependencies involved

in personal employment and mankind survival require both the unemployed scientist and the unscientifically guided mankind to cooperate in supporting each other. If they do not, neither can expect to
survive.

I am very conscious of the extremely pessimistic implications of
the Philosopher's World Model and the probability that some dictatorship—whether benevolent or malicious, whether rational or irrational, whether intelligent or foolish—will actually occur, perhaps
of necessity. But I would be untrue to my calling, both as a person
and as a professional philosopher, if I failed to state as best I can
what appears to me to be the most intelligent way and to advocate it.
This model calls for urging more concern for global self-interests by
not only individual scientists but also by scientists grouped in departments, institutes, colleges and universities and in societies, local,
state, regional, national, and international. The number of scientific
societies is astounding. The list of international societies of scientists has grown long. (See appendix 2.)

It remains to be seen whether scientific and professional societies
can discover and act on the wisdom of self-discipline conceived in
terms of interdependencies of the sciences and professions with the
larger problems of mankind threatened with extinction as inherent in
their wise self-interests. But they constitute an important focal point
for urging a greater assumption of responsibility that seems to flow
from the quantum-leap system gestalt depicted in the Philosopher's
World Model. The interdependence of interdisciplinary research institutes and scientific and professional societies should become more
important as such research institutes employ more scientists and develop interest in the adequacy of their training for interdisciplinary
research.

The Philosopher's World Model: You Need It; It Needs You

If mankind is threatened with extinction soon if we do not change
our producing and consuming habits, which will involve changes in
our philosophies guiding policy decisions, does not wise self-interest
call for such changes? If other world models point out only parts of
our problem, neglecting growing demoralization and declining competence for self-government, is not the more comprehensive Phi-

losopher's World Model, incorporating parts from other world models, needed to ensure that intelligence will prevail?

Increasingly intricate interdependencies of many kinds can be understood and modified only by means of increasingly complicated conceptions, philosophical and scientific. A quantum-leap system gestalt, embodying organic conceptions in metaphysics, logic, ethics, religion, economics, and government, as well as in other fields, is needed to grasp megalopolitan and global processes in ways that can reveal the organically intricate and evolving ways of deciding and acting needed to ensure a more lasting human survival.

Enlightened self-interest should reveal that each person has a stake in the welfare of mankind, as well as of nations, states, cities, professions, families, and healthy bodies. Many persons and societies concerned with world welfare already exist. (See appendix 3.) The enormous research potential is some evidence that we can master our fate. Quantities of unemployed university graduates exist as a resource waiting to be used. Ought not each person urge support of comprehensively interdisciplinary research institutes to achieve the understanding needed for human, national, and personal survival? World crises become more complex while we wait. Must we suffer the shock of devastating war, the ordeal of catastrophic holocaust, before terror and disgust cause any survivers to repeat "Never again!" willfully enough to organize a minimal world government?

The Philosopher's World Model is not utopian. It aims to help mankind postpone doomsday. If we can muster enough intelligence to survive, I hope we will also use it to increase human happiness. No person is wise until he is happy. And no person is wise unless he is alive. Let us benefit from future shock, which calls for increasingly complex kinds of adaptive comprehension and cooperative action. We cannot benefit from the shock of extinction. Many persons must contribute to the research needed, to its comprehensive organization, and to use of results by policy deciders and managers responsible for our collective fate. Will you contribute? What will be your contribution?

INTERNATIONAL SOCIETIES WITH RESEARCH INTERESTS

INSTITUTES FOCUSING ON WORLD PEACE

Canadian Peace Research Institute, Oakville.
Carnegie Endowment for International Peace, New York.
International Confederation for Disarmament and Peace, London.
International Institute for Peace, Vienna.
International Peace Research Association, Oslo.
International Union of Peace Societies, Vincennes.
Peace Research International, Philadelphia.
Professors World Peace Academy of Japan, Tokyo.
Stockholm International Peace Research Institute, Stockholm.
Pugwash Conference on Science and World Affairs, London.
Universities and the Quest for Peace, Binghamton.
World Brotherhood, Geneva.
World Council for Peace, Helsinki.
World Without War Council, New York.

INSTITUTES INTERESTED IN WORLD GOVERNMENT

Asian Parliamentary Union, Tokyo.
Association of Secretaries General of Parliaments, London.
Commonwealth Parliamentary Association, London.
European Civil Service Federation, Brussels.
International Commission for the History of Representative and Parliamentary Institutions, Ithaca.

International League for the Rights of Man, New York.
Inter-Parliamentary Union, Geneva.
Society for Comparative Legislation, Paris.
Universal League [for World Government], The Hague.
The Working Group World Union, The Hague.
World Constitution and Parliament Association, Denver.
World Council for the Peoples World Convention, Geneva.

ORGANIZATIONS INTERESTED IN IMPROVING SCIENTIFIC KNOWLEDGE

Association of International Libraries, Geneva.
Committee on Data for Science and Technology, Frankfurt am Main.
Commonwealth Scientific Committee, London.
Econometric Society, New Haven.
European Committee on Standardization, Paris.
European Scientific Association for Applied Economics, Geneva.
International Committee for Social Sciences Documentation, Paris.
International Computation Centre—International Bureau of Informatics, Rome.
International Council of Archives, Paris.
International Federation for Documentation, The Hague.
International Union for the Scientific Study of Population, Liège.
International Union of Independent Laboratories, London.
Scandinavian Council for Applied Research, Stockholm.
Scientific Committee on Oceanic Research, Warnemunde, Germany.
Society for Social Responsibility in Science, Bala Cynwyd, Pennsylvania.
Science and Expansion Society, Liège.
World Confederation of Productivity Science, London.

ORGANIZATIONS WITH MANAGEMENT AND DEVELOPMENT INTERESTS

Asian Development Center, Manila.
Asian Industrial Development Council, Bangkok.
Association for Systems Management, Cleveland.
Eastern Regional Organization for Public Administration, Manila.
European Society for Management Development, Brussels.
Institute for Management Sciences, Providence.
Inter-American Planning Society, Bogatá.
International Academy of Management, Geneva.

International Council of Practitioners of the International Plan of Accounts,
     Brussels.
International Development Association, Washington, D.C.
International Federation of Operational Research Societies, London.
International Foundation for Development Alternatives, Lyon.
International Management and Development Institute, Washington, D.C.
Society for General Systems Research, Washington, D.C.
Society for International Development, Washington, D.C.

UNITED NATIONS AGENCIES WITH RESEARCH INTERESTS

U.N. Conference on Trade and Development.
U.N. Industrial Development Organization.
Food and Agricultural Organization of the U.N.

UNITED NATIONS RESEARCH INSTITUTES:

U.N. Institute for Training and Research, New York.
U.N. Research Institute for Social Development, Geneva.
International Development Institute of the IBRD (World Bank).
International Monetary Fund Institute, Washington, D.C.
International Institute for Labor Studies, Geneva.
International Institute for Educational Planning, Paris.
African Institute for Economic Development and Planning, Dakar.
Asian Institute for Economic Development and Planning, Bangkok.
Latin American Institute for Economic and Social Planning, Santiago.
International Center for Advanced Technical and Vocational Training,
     Turin.
U.N. Social Defence Research Institute, Rome.
International Centre for Theoretical Physics, Trieste.

INTERGOVERNMENTAL AGENCIES ASSOCIATED WITH
THE UNITED NATIONS

International Atomic Energy Commission.
U.N. Educational and Scientific Organization.
World Health Organization.
International Development Association.
International Finance Corporation.
World Meteorological Organization.
General Agreement on Tariffs and Trade.
International Criminal and Police Organization.

INTERNATIONAL SOCIETIES OF SCIENTISTS

International Association of Legal Science, Brussels.
International Association of Penal Law, Rennes.
International Association of Schools for Social Work, New York.
International Astronomical Union, Utrecht.
International Committee for Historical Sciences, Paris.
International Economic Association, Paris.
International Federation of Philosophical Sciences, Berne.
International Geographical Union, Chicago.
International Institute of Administrative Sciences, Brussels.
International Mathematical Union, Djursholm.
International Political Science Association, Brussels.
International Social Science Council, Paris.
International Society of Criminology, Paris.
International Union of Anthropological and Ethnological Sciences, Waterloo.
International Union of Architects, Paris.
International Union of Biological Sciences, Bergen.
International Union of Biochemistry, Cleveland.
International Union of Geological Sciences, Haarlem.
International Union of Geodesy and Geophysics, Toronto.
International Union of Psychological Science, East Lansing.
International Union of Pure and Applied Biophysics, Boston.
International Union of Pure and Applied Chemistry, Oxford.
International Union of Pure and Applied Physics, London.
World Federation of Scientific Workers, London.

In addition to single-discipline international societies, multidisciplinary societies can be expected to organize internationally. Two of these are Asociacion Internacia, Caracas (which includes the American Association for the Advancement of Science and seven other Latin American societies) and the International Council of Scientific Unions, Paris.

SOCIETIES INTERESTED IN WORLD WELFARE

Support for programs in interdisciplinary research needed to develop the quantum-leap conceptions designed to guide mankind through solutions to current crises is needed from many sources. If the many societies already devoted to promoting peace, survival, improved justice, and quality of life for mankind can be induced to accept the need for more interdisciplinary research as a means to their ends, the Philosopher's World Model, which is intended to serve the same ends, may prove to be useful as a guide and stimulus to needed results.

Local, municipal, and state societies may be the most effective locations for personal influence. The World Affairs Council of Philadelphia, publisher of Henry Steele Commager's "A Declaration of Interdependence," serves as an example for other cities.

In the United States, several societies emphasize world welfare. Some have a limited mission and have terminated: the Aspen Institute for Humanistic Studies, which supported the National Commission on Coping with Interdependence, 1974-1975, published *From Independence to Interdependence* by Ralph L. Ketcham, *Organizing for Interdependence* by Adam Yarmolinsky, *Living with Interdependence* by Abraham M. Sirkin, *Attitudes of Americans on Coping with Interdependence* by Michael W. Moynihan, and *A New Civic Literacy, American Education and Global Interdependence* by Ward Morehouse. The Commission on Critical Choices for Americans, New York, 1973-1977, published fourteen books during 1976-1977. The Initiative Committee for National Economic Planning, White Plains, New York, promoted Senate bill 1795 on balanced growth. Common Cause,

Washington, D.C., a continuing effort to influence national legislation, has large popular support.

The Foreign Policy Association, New York, published *The Interdependence of Nations* by Lester Brown (1972) and *Interdependence and the World Economy* by James E. How (1974). The Council on Foreign Relations, New York, published *The Management of Interdependence* by Miriam Camps (1974). The American Association for the Advancement of Science, usually restrained in its political proposals other than those supporting legislation providing funds for science, recently published an article by Richard A. Cellarius and John Platt, "Councils of Urgent Studies" (*Science* 177 [August 25, 1972]: 670-676), proposing "coordinating councils that could focus and legitimize research on solutions of our major crises" and extending such coordinating functions to "International Councils for Urgent Studies." The Council for the Study of Mankind as a Whole, Santa Monica, the World Institute Council, New York, the Council for International Studies and Programs, New York, the National Council of Associations for International Studies, New York, the International Center for Integrative Studies, New York, the Conference on World Affairs, New York, the sixty-year-old Council on Religion in International Affairs, New York, the World Institute Council, New York, and World Good Will supported by the Lucis Trust, all exemplify American efforts to improve world welfare that may be urged to give fuller support to interdisciplinary research.

The World Future Society, Washington, the World Future Studies Federation, Rome, the Survival Institute of the Future, London, Ontario, and the World Association of World Future Studies, Amsterdam, should all favor more interdisciplinary research. Societies interested in business welfare (among them, Rotary International, Evanston, Kiwanis International, Chicago, Optimist International, St. Louis, and U.S. Jaycees, Tulsa), social welfare (such as the Masonic Service Association in the United States, Silver Springs, Benevolent and Protective Order of Elks, Chicago, Knights of Columbus, New Haven, Lions Clubs, Oak Brook, Independent Order of Odd Fellows, Baltimore), political welfare (League of Women Voters, Washington), and religious welfare (Unitarian-Universalist Service Committee, Boston, American Friends World Service Committee, Philadelphia, American Humanist Association, San Francisco, International Humanist and Ethical Union, Utrecht) all exemplify agencies to which and through which urgings for more comprehensive interdisciplinary research needed for human survival may pass.

NOTES

1. John Platt, "What We Must Do," *Science* 164 (1969): 115.

2. Aurelio Peccei, *The Chasm Ahead* (New York: Macmillan, 1969), p. xiv.

3. Alvin Toffler, *The Eco-Spasm Report* (New York: Bantam Books, 1975), p. 64.

4. Immanuel Velikovsky, *Worlds in Collision* (Garden City: Doubleday, 1950), pp. 384-386.

5. Immanuel Velikovsky, *Earth in Upheaval* (Garden City: Doubleday, 1955), p. 4.

6. Peccei, *The Chasm Ahead*, p. 1.

7. Robert L. Heilbroner, *An Inquiry into the Human Prospect* (New York: Norton, 1974), p. 136.

8. See Archie J. Bahm, "The American Cultural Predicament Today," *Journal of Thought* 5 (October 1970): 214-230.

9. (New York: Random House, 1970.)

10 W. Warren Wager, *Building the City of Man* (New York: Grossman, 1971), p. 4.

11. (New York: Ballantine Books, 1968, 1971.) See also Paul R. Ehrlich and Ann E. Ehrlich, *Population, Resources, Environment*, 2nd ed. (San Fransisco: W. H. Freeman, 1972).

12. See Donella H. Meadows, Dennis L. Meadows, Jorgen Randers, and William W. Behrens III, *The Limits to Growth* (Washington, D.C.: Potomac Associates, 1972).

13. See *Models of Doom: A Critique of the Limits to Growth*, ed. H. S. D. Cole, Christopher Freeman, Jarie Jahoda, and K. R. L. Pavit (New York: Universe Books, 1973).

14. Meadows et al., *Limits to Growth*, p. 29.

15. See Dennis C. Pirages and Paul R. Ehrlich, *Ark II* (New York: Viking, 1974), pp. 25-28, and Meadows et al., *Limits to Growth*, pp. 63-78.

16. See Barry Commoner, *The Closing Circle: Man, Nature and Technology* (New York: Alfred A. Knopf, 1971), chap. 6.

17. Ibid., pp. 293-294, 299.

18. Toffler, *Eco-Spasm*, cover.

19. *Monthly Statement of the Public Debt of the United States* (Washington, D.C.: U. S. Department of the Treasury, August 21, 1976), p. 1.

20. Toffler, *Eco-Spasm*, p. 51.

21. Leopold Bellak, *Overload: The New Human Condition* (New York: Human Sciences Press, 1975), p. 73.

22. Associated Press, Washington, D.C., July 4, 1975.

23. *Christian Science Monitor*, August 6, 1975.

24. *Christian Science Monitor*, August 6, 1975.

25. *Albuquerque Journal*, March 11, 1975.

26. UPI, Washington, D.C., March 21, 1975.

27. *Christian Science Monitor*, April 24, 1975.

28. *New Mexico Daily Lobo*, February 5, 1974.

29. Federal Bureau of Investigation, *Crime in the United States, 1975* (Washington, D.C.: U.S. Printing Office, 1975), p. 49.

30. Leslie T. Wilkins, "Crime and Criminal Justice at the Turn of the Century," *Annals of the American Academy of Political and Social Science* 408 (July 1973): 13.

31. January 1973, U.S. Department of Justice, Washington, D.C.

32. See Archie J. Bahm, "Is American Society Ethically Deficient?" *Journal of Social Philosophy* 5 (September, 1974): 8-9, and "American Moral Degeneration" *Journal of Thought* 11 (November 1976): 247-280.

33. See Archie J. Bahm, "The New Conservatism," *The Colorado Quarterly* 8 (August 1959): 131-141.

34. See John Platt, "Science for Human Survival," *The Science Teacher* 40 (January 1973): 11-13.

CHAPTER 2

1. See Archie J. Bahm, "Regionalism versus Globalism," *Alternatives: A Journal of World Policy* 3 (1978): 527-553.

2. Initiated in 1968, the Club of Rome's executive committee included

Aurelio Peccei, affiliated with Fiat and Olivetti, Alexander King, scientific director for the Organization for Economic Cooperation and Development with headquarters in Paris, Saburo Okita, head of the Japan Economic Research Center, Eduard Pestel of the Technical University of Hannover, Hugo Thiemann, head of the Battelle Institute in Geneva, and Caroll Wilson of the Massachusetts Institute of Technology.

3. Although I have included these models in a chapter on why other world models have failed, I do not intend to be derogative of their achievements. Many of their conclusions are incorporated (or can be) into the Philosopher's World Model. The earlier generational models prepare the way for the later models. I would have been more polite to use the heading, "Other World Models: How Much Each Succeeds." However, since deficiencies still exist from the viewpoint expressed here, and since the purpose of the Philosopher's World Model is to remedy some of these shortcomings, this purpose is best served by pointing out ways in which such models fail to be fully adequate. My chief criticism is not that they did not achieve their goals (as other critics have claimed) but that they did not set their goals high enough.

4. Including Alison A. Anderson, J. M. Anderson, Ilyas Bayer, William H. Behrens III, Farhad Hakimzed, Steffan Harbordt, Judith A. Machen, Donella H. Meadows, Peter Milling, Nirmalla S. Murthy, Roger F. Naill, Jorgen Randers, Stephen Shantis, John A. Seeger, Marilyn Williams, Erich K. O. Zahn. Meadows is author of *Dynamics of Commodity Production Cycles* (Cambridge, Mass.: Wright-Allen Press, 1970) and, with Donella H. Meadows, compiler of *Toward Global Equilibrium* (Cambridge, Mass.: Wright-Allen Press, 1973).

5. Donella H. Meadows, Dennis L. Meadows, Jorgen Randers, and William W. Behrens III, *The Limits of Growth* (Washington, D.C.: Potomac Associates, 1972).

6. (Cambridge, Mass.: Wright-Allen Press, 1971.)

7. (New York: Ballantine Books, 1968.)

8. (San Francisco: W. H. Freeman, 1970.)

9. (New York: George Braziller, 1970), p. 166.

10. (New York: Alfred A. Knopf, 1971), p. 299.

11. H. S. D. Cole, Christopher Freeman, Marie Jahoda, and K. L. R. Pavit, eds. (New York: Universe Books, 1973).

12. Dennis L. Meadows, William H. Behrens III, Donella H. Meadows, Roger F. Naill, Jorgen Randers, Erich K. O. Zhan (Cambridge, Mass.: Wright-Allen Press, 1974).

13. Dennis L. Meadows and Donella H. Meadows, comps. (Cambridge, Mass.: Wright-Allen Press, 1973).

14. Meadows, *Limits to Growth*, p. 27.

15. (New York: E. P. Dutton, 1974.)

16. Ibid., p. 9.

17. Mesarovic has explored a mathematical systems theory of organizations in his *Theory of Hierarchical, Multilevel Systems* (New York: Academic Press, 1970).

18. Mesarovic, *Mankind at the Turning Point*, p. 146.

19. Ibid., pp. 69, 144, 145.

20. Ibid., p. 203.

21. F. S. C. Northrup, *The Taming of the Nations* (New York: Macmillan, 1952), p. 286.

22. See Archie J. Bahm, "Philosophy and Interdisciplinary Research," *Spectrum: Essays Presented to Sutan Takdir Alisjahbana on His Seventieth Birthday*, ed. S. Udin (Jakarta: Dian Rakyat, 1978), pp. 39-60.

23. A third book, *Beyond the Age of Waste: New Directions in Science and Technology*, by Dennis Gabor, Umberto Colombo, Alexander King, and R. Galli, has not reached me.

24. Amilcar O. Herrera, Hugo D. Solnik, Graciela Chichilnisky, Gilberton C. Gallopin, Jorge E. Hardoy, Diana Mosovich, Enrique Oteiza, Gilda L. de Romero Brest, Carlos E. Saurez, and Luis Talavera, *Catastrophe or New Society? A Latin American World Model* (Ottawa: International Development Research Centre, 1976), pp. 7-8.

25. Ibid., pp. 9, 26.

26. Ibid., pp. 52, 107.

27. Jan Tinbergen, *Reshaping the International Order* (New York: E. P. Dutton, 1976.)

28. Ibid., pp. 4, 61, 63, 82-84, 109, 184-185.

29. Ibid., pp. 102, 105, 107, 124.

30. Ibid., p. 107.

31. Ervin Laszlo et al., *Goals for Mankind: A Report to the Club of Rome on the New Horizons of the Global Community* (New York: E. P. Dutton, 1977).

32. Saul H. Mendlovitz et al., *On the Creation of a Just World Order* (New York: The Free Press, 1974), pp. 37, 68.

33. Ibid., pp. 80, 102, 112, 145.

34. Ibid., pp. 188, 210.

35. Ibid., pp. 257, 276, 260.

36. Ibid., pp. viii, xvi.

37. (New York: The Free Press, 1974), p. xx.

38. Ibid., pp. 2, 92, 99, 119.

39. Ibid., pp. 9, 19, 104.

40. (New York: The Free Press, 1975.)

41. Ibid., p. 51.

42. Ibid., pp. 438, 485, 493, 494.

43. Ibid., p. 4.

44. Ali A. Mazrui, *A Federation of World Cultures: An African Perspective* (New York: The Free Press, 1976), pp. 399, 471, 496.

45. Ibid., pp. 2, 9, 11, 13, 453.

46. Ibid., pp. 308, 453.

47. Ibid., p. 490.

48. Ibid., 246, 308. Africans are welcome to join the Planetary Citizens now. As Planetary Citizens, persons are all equals. Joining a world society of concerned citizens can provide a feeling of community more quickly than any program requiring a series of steps, of gaining loyalty to some larger whole (such as a nation) and then some still larger whole (a region) and then some still larger whole (the Third World) and only then to the whole world. Any excess of loyalty to any one lower level that has been achieved can become an obstacle to achieving sufficient loyalty to the next higher level. Going to the top as soon as possible is the most efficient way to achieve desired parity of respect.

49. (New York: Macmillan, 1967.)

50. Ibid., p. 413.

51. Hudson Institute, *A Slightly Optimistic World Context for 1975-2000*, Research memorandum No. 8, HI-2146-P (November, 1974). The first volume of the *Prospects of Mankind* series, *The Next 200 Years: A Scenario for America and the World* (New York: William Morrow, 1976), appeared in May, 1976.

52. (New York: Random House, 1972.)

53. Ibid., p. 344.

54. Ibid., pp. 256, 349.

55. (New York: Basic Books, 1973). See also his *The Cultural Contradictions of Capitalism* (New York: Basic Books, 1967).

56. Ibid., pp. 205, 208, 297-298, 487.

57. Bell, *Cultural Contradictions of Capitalism*, pp. 278-282.

58. George Cabot Lodge, *The New American Ideology* (New York: Alfred A. Knopf, 1975), pp. 288, 302, 309, 310, 321, 324.

59. Ervin Laszlo, *A Strategy for the Future: A Systems Approach to World Order* (New York: George Braziller, 1974), pp. 183, 225. See also two books he edited, *The Systems View of the World* (New York: George Braziller, 1973) and *The World System* (New York: George Braziller, 1973), and his *Introduction to Systems Philosophy* (New York: Gordon and Breach, 1972).

60. Laszlo, *Introduction to Systems Philosophy*, pp. viii, ix.
61. Ibid., p. 194.
62. Laszlo, *World System*, pp. viii, v, 10.
63. The issues at stake here have been explored in two of my articles: "Systems Theory: Hocus Pocus or Holistic Science?" *General Systems* 14 (1969): 175-177, and "General Systems Theory as Philosophy," *General Systems Bulletin* 4 (September 1973): 4-7.
64. See my *Polarity, Dialectic, and Organicity* (Springfield, Ill.: Charles C. Thomas, 1970), and *Metaphysics: An Introduction* (New York: Harper and Row, 1974), pt. 3.
65. (New York: Grossman, 1971), pp. 4-5, 19, 23, 25, 26, 29, 46. See also his *The City of Man* (Boston: Houghton Mifflin, 1963), and a book he edited, *History and the Idea of Man* (Albuquerque: University of New Mexico Press, 1971).
66. Wager, *Building the City*, pp. 51, 52, 53, 54, 79, 140.
67. Ibid., pp. 90, 121, 132.
68. Ibid., pp. 53, 55, 125, 135, 136, 137, 168.
69. Ibid., pp. 33, 37, 38, 45, 49, 50, 79, 143.

CHAPTER 3

1. Roy Wood Sellars, *The Principles and Problems of Philosophy* (New York: Macmillan, 1926), p. 3.
2. For a fuller account of some problems constituting metaphysics, see my *Metaphysics: An Introduction* (New York: Harper and Row, 1974).
3. See John Dewey, *Philosophy and Civilization* (New York: Minton, Balch and Co., 1931).
4. For a fuller account of "What Is Philosophy?" see my *Philosophy: An Introduction* (New York: John Wiley and Sons, 1953), chap. 1.
5. See Archie J. Bahm, *The World's Living Religions* (New York: Dell Publishing Co., 1964), chap. 11.
6. See ibid., pp. 257, 276.
7. See ibid., pp. 276-286.
8. See Dewey's *How We Think* (Boston: D. C. Heath & Co., 1910), *Essays in Experimental Logic* (Chicago: University of Chicago Press, 1916), and *Logic: The Theory of Inquiry* (New York: Henry Holt & Co., 1938).
9. See Archie J. Bahm, *The Specialist* (Albuquerque: World Books, 1977).
10. See C. P. Snow, *The Two Cultures and the Scientific Revolution* (Cambridge: At the Cambridge University Press, 1959).
11. See Archie J. Bahm, "Systems Theory: Hocus Pocus or Holistic Science?" *General Systems* 14 (1969): 175-176.

12. See Archie J. Bahm, "General Systems Theory as Philosophy," *General Systems Bulletin* 4 (September 1973): 4-7.

13. See Archie J. Bahm, *Yoga: Union with the Ultimate* (New York: Frederick Ungar Publishing Co., 1961), and *Yoga for Business Executives* (New York: Citadel Press, 1965).

14. See Archie J. Bahm, *Tao Teh King by Lao Tzu* (New York: Frederick Ungar Publishing Co., 1958), pp. 123-216.

15. See Alan Watts, *The Spirit of Zen* (New York: Grove Press, 1958), *Psychotherapy East and West* (New York: Pantheon Books, 1961), and *Tao: The Watercourse Way* (New York: Pantheon Books, 1975).

16. For example, S. Radhakrishnan, ed., *History of Philosophy Eastern and Western* (London: George Allen and Unwin, 1953), and Jadunath Sinha, *History of Indian Philosophy* (Calcutta: Sinha Publishing House, 1952-73; four volumes published, two in press).

17. My own studies in Asian and Western philosophies and in comparative philosophy during a quarter of a century have led to my work, *Comparative Philosophy: Western, Indian and Chinese Philosophies Compared* (Albuquerque: World Books, 1977), so, although my observations here as always are intended as tentative, I do make them with some confidence.

18. See Archie J. Bahm, *The Bhagavad Gita: The Wisdom of Krishna* (Bombay: Somaiya Publications, 1970), pp. 5-15.

19. See Fung Yu-lan, *A History of Chinese Philosophy*, 2d ed. (Princeton: Princeton University Press, 1952-1953).

20. See Archie J. Bahm, *Tao Teh King*, and Bahm, *The Heart of Confucius (Chung Yung and Ta Hsueh)* (Tokyo: John Weatherhill, 1969).

21. André Mercier, *Rapport du Comité Directeur a L'Assemblee de la FISP in 1978*, p. 5. Xeroxed copies distributed to delegates.

22. In contrast to those who claim that philosophy always follows practice and to those who claim that practice always follows philosophy, I claim that philosophy and practice interact dialectically so that sometimes philosophy and sometimes practice is more influential. One point of my argument here is that our practical crises have resulted partly from a failure of philosophy and that we can find clues to the philosophy we need in the unmet needs to which our crises are calling attention. The needed world philosophy should be a response to practical unmet needs. If such a philosophy is formulated and accepted, then we should expect it to be influential in leading us out of our crises and into a more satisfactory global existence.

23. Daniel Bell, *The Cultural Contradictions of Capitalism* (New York: Basic Books, 1976), p. 250.

24. *Science and Technology in the World of the Future* (New York: John Wiley and Sons, 1970), p. xvi.

25. See *The Humanist* 33 (January-February 1973): for a fuller state-

ment. For two American "humanist manifestos," see ibid., pp. 13-14, and ibid. 33 (September-October 1973): 4-9.

26. See Archie J. Bahm, "Science is Not Value-Free," *Policy Sciences* 2 (1971): 391-396.

CHAPTER 4

1. Archie J. Bahm, "The Organicist Theory of Truth," *Southwestern Journal of Philosophy* 6 (Fall 1975): 200-201.

2. Archie J. Bahm, "The Generic Theory of Truth," *The Personalist* 28 (Autumn 1947): 371.

3. *The Works of Aristotle*, vol. 8: *Metaphysics*, trans. by W. D. Ross, 2d ed. (Oxford: At the Clarendon Press, 1928), p. 1011b.

4. Bahm, "Generic Theory of Truth," p. 373.

5. See Archie J. Bahm, "Science is Not Value-Free," *Policy Sciences* 2 (December 1971): 391-396.

6. Recognition of the importance of waves and cycles in all sciences has grown recently. The foundation for the Study of Cycles, Inc., 124 South Highland Avenue, Pittsburgh, Pennsylvania 15206, has gathered data and published reports on cycles in many disciplines. It publishes the *Journal of Cycle Research*. The *Journal of Interdisciplinary Cycle Research* is available from Swets and Zeitlinger, P.O. Box 517, Berwyn, Pennsylvania.

7. See Archie J. Bahm, *Polarity, Dialectic, and Organicity* (Springfield, Ill.: Charles C. Thomas, 1970), chaps. 5, 6, 7, 8-12, 15-17, 20.

8. See Ronald F. Stebbing, "High Rydberg Atoms: Newcomers to the Atomic Physics Scene," *Science* 193 (August 12, 1976): 537-542.

9. Several have been surveyed in my *Metaphysics: An Introduction* (New York: Harper and Row, 1974).

10. Efforts to grasp complexities may be found, for example, in J. N. Warfield, *An Assault on Complexity*, 1973, and M. M. Baldwin, *Portraits of Complexity* (Cleveland: Battelle Memorial Institute, 1975).

11. For a fuller exposition, see Bahm, *Polarity, Dialectic, and Organicity*, chaps. 1, 2.

12. See Archie J. Bahm, *Philosophy: An Introduction* (New York: John Wiley and Sons, 1953), chaps. 17, 18, 19, 20. For some arguments against proposing any largest whole or smallest particle, see pp. 237-239.

13. For more details, see ibid., pp. 214-218.

14. See his *Three Interpretations of the Universe* (New York: Macmillan, 1934).

15. For a fuller account of temporality, see "A Multiple-Aspect Theory of Time," *Southwestern Journal of Philosophy* 2(Spring-Summer 1971): 163-171, or my *Metaphysics*, chap. 11.

16. For other summaries of the organicist conception of causation, see Bahm, *Philosophy*, pp. 244-248, and Bahm, *Metaphysics*, chaps. 19-32, esp. chap. 26.

17. For an excellent account of this struggle, see Henri Wald, *Introduction to Dialectical Logic* (Amsterdam: B. R. Gruner, 1975).

18. For a more systematic exposition of the nature of synthetic dialectic, see Bahm, *Polarity, Dialectic, and Organicity*, chap. 15.

19. For a fuller and more systematic examination of the nature of analytic dialectic, see ibid., chap. 16. Most of the following section on organitic dialectic has been quoted directly from ibid., chap. 17.

20. See Bahm, *Philosophy*, chaps. 13-19.

21. See Roy Wood Sellars, *The Principles and Problems of Philosophy* (New York: Macmillan, 1926), chaps. 14, 15.

22. See "Vedantic Contributions to Organicism," *The Philosophical Quarterly* 34 (January 1963): 243-247.

23. For other examples utilizing the diagram of types, see my *Polarity, Dialectic, and Organicity*, chaps. 2, 3-9. See also my "Relations," in *Proceedings of the New Mexico-West Texas Philosophical Society* (April 1972): 49-57.

CHAPTER 5

1. Some advocates of ethics as a science now propose this. See R. W. Sperry, "Science and the Problem of Values," *Perspectives in Biology and Medicine* 16 (Autumn 1972): 115-130.

2. See Archie J. Bahm, "Is a Universal Science of Aesthetics Possible?" *Journal of Aesthetics and Art Criticism* 31 (Fall 1972): 3-7.

3. See Archie J. Bahm, *Ethics as a Behavioral Science* (Springfield, Ill.: Charles C Thomas, 1974), chap. 2.

4. For principles for choosing pertaining primarily to intrinsic values, primarily to instrumental values, between intrinsic and instrumental values, and between productive and consumptive values, see ibid., pp. 153-165.

5. R. W. Sperry, "A Modified Concept of Consciousness," *Psychological Review* 76 (1969): 533, "An Objective Approach to Subjective Experience, *Psychological Review* 77 (1970): 587, and "Science and the Problem of Values," *Zygon* 9 (March 1974): 9.

6. Archie J. Bahm, "Rightness Defined," *Philosophy and Philosophical Research* 13 (December 1947): 266. For a comparison of types of theories of rightness and wrongness, see Archie J. Bahm, *What Makes Acts Right?* (Boston: Christopher Publishing House, 1958).

7. For an examination of issues relative to the nature of intentions and of

freedom of will, see Archie J. Bahm, *Why Be Moral?* (New Delhi: Munshiram Manoharlal, in press), chap. 9.

8. See Archie J. Bahm, "Self as Multi-Dimensional," *Research Journal of the Social Sciences* 2 (1966): 1-8.

9. See George Herbert Mead, *Mind, Self and Society* (Chicago: University of Chicago Press, 1934).

10. See Archie J. Bahm, "What is Self? The Organicist Answer," *Darshana International* 2 (January 1962): 1-27.

11. Robert L. Heilbroner, *An Inquiry into the Human Prospect* (New York: Norton, 1974), p. 111.

12. For a fuller account of these ten principles, see Bahm, *Why Be Moral?* chap. 5.

13. Archie J. Bahm, *Philosophy of the Buddha* (New York: Harper and Row, 1958), p. 15.

14. See Archie J. Bahm, *The Specialist* (New Delhi: Macmillan Company of India, 1977), chap. 2.

15. See Charles Horton Cooley, Robert Cooley Angell, and Lowell Julliard Carr, *Introductory Sociology* (New York: Charles Scribner's Sons, 1933), chap. 25.

CHAPTER 6

1. See Archie J. Bahm, *The World's Living Religions* (New York: Dell Publishing Co., 1964), chap. 5.

2. See ibid., chap. 4.

3. See ibid., chaps. 3, 6. See also Archie J. Bahm, *Bhagavad Gita: The Wisdom of Krishna* (Bombay: Somaiya Publications, 1970).

4. See Bahm, *The World's Living Religions*, chaps. 7, 8. See also Archie J. Bahm, *Tao Teh King by Lao Tzu* (New York: Frederick Ungar Publishing Co., 1958), pp. 73-86, and Archie J. Bahm, *The Heart of Confucius* (Tokyo: John Weatherhill, 1969), pp. 18-63.

5. W. Warren Wager, *Building the City of Man* (New York: Grossman, 1971), p. 22.

6. See Bahm, *The World's Living Religions*, pp. 314-319.

7. See *Christian Century* 92 (October 1, 1975): 842-845.

8. Letter to the author, June 3, 1975.

9. Theodore M. Hesburgh, *The Humane Imperative* (New Haven: Yale University Press, 1974), pp. 21, 107, 109, 115.

10. Letter to the author, September 15, 1975.

11. *The Journal of the Muslim World League* 3 (February 1967): 2, 3, 11.

12. Karl Marx, "Religion, Free Press, and Philosophy," *Kolnische Zeitung* 179 (July 1842).

13. M. Jamil Hanifi, *Islam and the Transformation of Culture* (London: Asia Publishing House, 1976), pp. 144, 145.

14. N. K. Devaraja, *Hinduism and the Modern Age* (Bombay: Current Book House, 1975), p. 149.

15. Evidences of my efforts to understand how religions have merged and can merge are found in my "Stages in the Development of Interreligious Attitudes," *Indian Philosophy and Culture* 16 (December 1971): 260-271.

16. Wager, *Building the City of Man*, p. 55.

17. See Gerard Hirschfeld, *The People, Growth and Survival* (Chicago: Council for the Study of Mankind, 1973).

18. Wager, *Building the City of Man*, p. 89.

19. Rama Shankar Srivastava, *Comparative Religion* (New Delhi: Munshiram Manoharlal, 1974), p. 296.

20. See Clark Wissler, *Man and Culture* (New York: T. Y. Crowell, 1923), p. 74.

21. Archie J. Bahm, *Philosophy of the Buddha* (New York: Harper and Row, 1958), p. 15.

22. See Archie J. Bahm, "Buddhism and Jainism in the Emerging World Civilization," *Papers, International Seminars on Buddhism and Jainism, January 11-16, 1976* (Cuttack: Institute of Oriental and Orissan Studies, 1976), pp. 1-3.

CHAPTER 7

1. *Coping with Interdependence: Report of the National Commission on Coping with Interdependence* (Aspen: Aspen Institute for Humanistic Studies Program in International Affairs, 1976), p. 1.

2. (Cambridge: Harvard University Press, 1962.)

3. Other recent books on interdependence are: Harold Brookfield, *Interdependent Development* (Pittsburgh: University of Pittsburgh Press, 1975); Lester Brown, *The Interdependence of Nations* (New York: Foreign Policy Association, 1972); Miriam Camps, *The Management of Interdependence* (New York: Council on Foreign Relations, 1974); Walter C. Clemens, *The Super Powers and Arms Control: From Cold War to Interdependence* (Lexington, Mass.: Lexington Books, 1973); Richard N. Cooper, *The Economics of Interdependence* (New York: McGraw-Hill, 1968); James E. Howe, *Interdependence and the World Economy* (New York: Foreign Policy Association, 1974); Harry A. Overstreet, *A Declaration of Interdependence* (New York: Norton, 1937); Vincent Rock, *Toward a Strategy of Interdependence* (Washington, D. C.: U.S. Department of State Bureau of Public Affairs, July 1975); Ralph L. Ketcham, *From Independence to Interdependence* (Palo Alto: Aspen Institute for Humanistic Studies, 1976).

4. See "How to Establish Islamic Principles in Muslim Lands," *Journal of the Muslim World League* 3 (1976): 27-28.

5. See Raymond A. Bauer, *Second-Order Consequences* (Cambridge, Mass.: MIT Press, 1969).

6. Richard T. Ely, *Outlines of Economics*, 4th rev. ed. (New York: Macmillan, 1925), pp. 2, 11.

7. See Milton Friedman, *Essays on Positive Economics* (Chicago: University of Chicago Press, 1953).

8. Cited by Clarence E. Ayers, *The Theory of Economic Progress* (Chapel Hill: University of North Carolina Press, 1944).

9. Lionel Robbins, *An Essay on the Nature and Significance of Economic Science* (New York: St. Martin's Press, 1948), pp. 24, 25.

10. Ely, *Outlines*, p. 12.

11. See Frank Knight, *Risk, Uncertainty and Profit* (Boston: Houghton Mifflin, 1921).

12. For a good survey of recent developments in our economy and economic theory, see John Kenneth Galbraith, *The New Industrial State* (Boston: Houghton Mifflin, 1967), and his *Economics and the Public Purpose* (Boston: Houghton Mifflin, 1973).

13. Some of the increasing complexities of economic life and economic theory are studied in Robert L. Heilbroner and Lester C. Thurow, *The Economic Problem*, 4th ed. (Englewood Cliffs, N.J.: Prentice-Hall, 1975).

14. S. Sideri, *Final Report on the Seminar on the New International Order and UNCTAD IV* (The Hague: Institute of Social Studies, 1975), p. 3.

15. See Archie J. Bahm, ed., *Interdependence: An Interdisciplinary Study* (Albuquerque: World Books, 1977).

16. Robert L. Heilbroner, in Robert L. Heilbroner and Paul London, eds, *Corporate Social Policy* (Reading, Mass.: Addison-Wesley, 1975), p. xv.

17. See *Planning Review: A Journal for Managerial Decision-Makers*. Rudolf W. Koepfel, president of the Solvay American Corporation, hails the publication of *The Limits to Growth* as catalyzing worldwide discussion of "long range world trends . . . in a rigorous way." See "Goals for Global Society," ibid. 3 (May 1975): 1. A Fifth International Conference on Planning, concerned with the International Affiliation of Planning Societies, was held in Cleveland, July 18-21, 1976.

18. Galbraith, *The New Industrial State*, p. 31.

CHAPTER 8

1. In 1934, when I began teaching college courses in ethics and sociology, I learned that, with rare exceptions, students voted against the proposal that the American democratic form of national government be adopted as the

form for a world government, with senators representing national governments and representatives elected on the basis of population size.

2. *Arms Control Today* 2 (March 1976): 3.

3. These proposals will remind some of Plato's philosopher kings. There
is one similarity: policy decisions should be made by those who have the
best knowledge. But there are many differences: it presupposes that current
problems are too complex to be understood adequately by any one person,
that scientific knowledge is derived inductively from experience and not by
intuitive apprehension of eternal forms, that many different kinds of knowledge are essential to understanding today's problems, that some minimum
number of different people with differing interests and perspectives is
needed to ensure a range of comprehension, and that dialectical developments in the interactions of these different people and kinds of knowledge
with a philosophical wholeness of perspective as well as with each other involves both elements of human creativity and at the same time more reliable
realism regarding solutions.

Granted that the ideal interdisciplinary research institute manager is also
a philosopher, or knows enough to utilize philosophy in its comprehensive
functioning both to explore factors to their fullest extent and to test solutions
relative to human as well as to technical adequacy, the cooperative efforts
of all contributors are essential to sound results. Deficiency in a single part
may destroy the efficacy of the whole situation, so the expertise of each particular expert is as essential as the expertise of the philosopher who specializes in wholeness of comprehension and in whole-parts understanding.

4. See Archie J. Bahm, "Demo-speci-ocracy," *Policy Sciences* 3 (March
1972): 97-106. See also *The Specialist* (New Delhi: Macmillan Company of
India, 1977), pt. 3, and "Regionalism and Globalism," *Alternatives: A Journal of World Policy* 3 (May 1978): 527-53.

5. See *NATO and Science, Facts about the Activities of the Science Committee of the North Atlantic Treaty Organization, 1959-1966* (Paris: NATO
Scientific Affairs Division, 1968), and *NATO Science Committee Yearbook, 1974 & 1975* (Brussels: NATO Scientific Affairs Division, 1977).

6. (Brussels, Union of International Organizations, 1973.)

7. Per Lindblom, deputy executive secretary, to the author, January 25,
1974.

8. *Yearbook of World Problems, Integrative Disciplines and Human Development* (New York: International Publishers Services, 1975).

9. "To Illuminate Tomorrow: Higher Education in an Interdependent
World" (address to the Fifth-eighth Annual Meeting of the American Council on Education, October 9, 1975).

INDEX

About the Author

Archie J. Bahm is Professor Emeritus in the University of New Mexico, Albuquerque. His many books include *Ethics as a Behavioral Science*, *Comparative Philosophy*, and *Polarity, Dialectic, and Organicity*.